P9-AQP-079

Nietzsche's *Zarathustra*

Nietzsche's
Zarathustra

Kathleen Marie Higgins

SCCCC - LIBRARY
4601 Mid Rivers Mall Drive
St. Peters, MO 63376

Temple University Press
PHILADELPHIA

Temple University Press, Philadelphia 19122
Copyright © 1987 by Temple University. All rights reserved
Published 1987
Printed in the United States of America

The paper used in this publication meets the minimum requirements
of American National Standard for Information Sciences—Permanence
of Paper for Printed Library Materials, ANSI Z39.48-1984

Library of Congress Cataloging-in-Publication Data

Higgins, Kathleen Marie.
  Nietzsche's *Zarathustra*.

  Bibliography: p. 283
  Includes index.
  1. Nietzsche, Friedrich Wilhelm, 1844–1900. Also
sprach Zarathustra. I. Title.
B3313.A44H54 1987   193   86–30133
ISBN 0–87722–482–X (alk. paper)

Excerpts from *The Portable Nietzsche*, edited and translated by
Walter Kaufmann, are reprinted by permission of Viking
Penguin, Inc. Copyright 1954 by The Viking Press, Inc.
Copyright renewed © 1982 by Viking Penguin Inc.

Excerpts in Chapter 3 are reprinted from Friedrich Nietzsche,
Daybreak: Thoughts on the Prejudices of Morality, translated by
R. J. Hollingdale, Copyright 1982 by Cambridge University Press,
with the permission of the publisher.

Portions of Chapter 5 were previously published as an article,
"Nietzsche's View of Philosophical Style," in *International
Studies in Philosophy*, XVIII/2 (Summer 1986): 67–81.

For the friends and free spirits
who inspired me: for Janice,
for Garret, and, especially, for Bob

Contents

Preface

"WHEN I have looked into my *Zarathustra*," Friedrich Nietzsche wrote in 1888, "I walk up and down in my room for half an hour, unable to master an unbearable fit of sobbing."[1]

As Nietzsche describes its composition, *Thus Spoke Zarathustra* erupted in spurts, as an impassioned outburst. And ever since its publication a hundred years ago, there are those who read it start to finish and respond emotionally and emphatically. Thousands of adolescent students who read it annually not only enjoy it but befriend it. And on those of any age who read it in an adolescent's spirit of openness, *Zarathustra* can, as R. J. Hollingdale puts it, "make as powerful and lasting impression...as any book in world literature."[2]

The passional responses of readers to *Zarathustra*, however, are far from universally favorable. Philosopher Brand Blanshard, for instance, is vehement:

> I must confess that often, when I have tried to read the most popularly effective of German philosophical writers, Nietzsche, I have felt like throwing the book across the room. He is a boiling pot of enthusiasms and animosities, which he pours out volubly, skillfully, and eloquently. If he were content to label these outpourings "Prejudices," as Mr. Mencken so truly and candidly labels his own, one could accept them in the spirit in which they were offered.... But he obviously takes

them as philosophy instead of what they largely are pseudo-Isaian prophesyings, incoherent and unreasoned Sibylline oracles.[3]

Among those who are harshest in criticizing *Zarathustra* are many who are most familiar with and sympathetic toward Nietzsche's work. Hollingdale, although appreciative of the work's affective power, insists that Nietzsche's self-congratulations on having written *Zarathustra* are "all the more deplorable in that *Zarathustra* is not even Nietzsche's 'best book.'...When one recommends Nietzsche as a master of German prose, it is not *Zarathustra* one has in mind."[4] And Crane Brinton, acknowledging *Zarathustra's* capacity to move at least its "half-educated" readers in his 1941 book *Nietzsche,* suggests that the work virtually invited the Nazis to exploit it for propagandistic purposes:

> Zarathustra...would be lost without his "saith" and "thou" and "yet," helpless without his exclamation points. In English translation he sounds very pseudo-biblical, like the King James version gone wrong...Indeed, *Thus Spoke Zarathustra* has become, for a certain type of half-educated intellectual throughout the world, a kind of *Enchiridion*...Yet the long white robes, prophetic beard, and phosphorescent glances of Zarathustra...have unquestionably helped Nietzsche to his present prestige in...Germany...Zarathustra sounds as far-off as any Hebrew prophet, and much more unreal. All the better for Nazi use. The vagueness, the dithyrambic energy, the mantic arts, the tortured rhetoric of Nietzsche—Zarathustra seems able to move men in a way no concrete proposals at the level of mere laws or arrangements ever can move them.[5]

More recent commentators, too, have found *Zarathustra* unsavory. For instance, F. D. Luke contends that the book is a reflection of a manic-depressive temperament.[6] J. P. Stern categorizes *Zarathustra* as a manifestation of a "style of decadence" in which the component parts are not drawn into a cohesive whole[7] and with respect to the book's "prophetic" content he asks, "Can the book be read without embarrassment?"[8] And H. G. Gadamer, even while attempting to discuss the work sympathetically, notes, "The style of this text is not for everyone's taste, at any rate not for my taste or the taste of my generation."[9]

Philosophical scholarship typically underplays emotional response to the texts it interprets—and most texts, for that matter, do not invite such response. The fact that philosophical commentators often have both acknowledged *Zarathustra's* impassioned rhetoric and been emphatic in reaction is therefore doubly significant. It demonstrates that the work is, and is also considered, a work apart from the rest of the Western philosophical canon. *Zarathustra* is treated as an exception, perhaps even a philosophical embarrassment, even more distant from the mainstream of philosophical texts than Nietzsche's other outrageous works. Even Martin Heidegger, who is more sympathetic to *Zarathustra* than the other philosophers mentioned, sees *Zarathustra* as a philosophical oddity:

> What is difficult to grasp about this work is not only its "content," if it has such, but also its very character as a work. Of course, we are quick to propose a ready-made explanation: here philosophical thoughts are presented poetically. Yet what we are now to call *thinking* and *poetizing* dare not consist of the usual notions, inasmuch as the work defines both of these anew, or rather, simply announces them. And when we say that this work constitutes the center of Nietzsche's philosophy, it remains nonetheless true that the work stands outside the center, is "eccentric" to it.[10]

Categorized as a peculiarity, *Zarathustra* has been relegated to the fringes of scholarly interest, even scholarly interest in Nietzsche. Richard Schacht takes a typical strategic line when he explains his neglect of *Zarathustra* in the introduction to his monumental book *Nietzsche:*

> ...have largely passed over his literary-philosophical efforts...including not only his many epigrams, "songs," and poems, but also his most famous work, *Thus Spoke Zarathustra.* I have found it useful and illuminating at various points to refer to certain things he says and themes he develops in the latter work and consider familiarity with it to be essential to the understanding of him. It does not readily lend itself, however, to the sort of analysis undertaken here; and since there is little of a philosophical nature in it that Nietzsche does not elsewhere work out in a more straightforwardly (or prosaically) philosophical manner, I have preferred to concentrate upon his other ways of putting his points, calling Zarathustra in to give evidence only on occasion.[11]

Given Schacht's aim, which is to elucidate "The Arguments of the Philosophers" (the title of the series for which his book was written), his relative dismissal of *Zarathustra* is understandable. There are few "arguments" in *Zarathustra*—indeed, as Gadamer observes, it is not even "easy to disclose a conceptual content of this book."[12] But the tendency of Nietzsche scholarship generally to dismiss *Zarathustra* as not fundamentally important is unwarranted. The central conviction at the basis of this book—a conviction that it will indirectly defend—is that *Thus Spoke Zarathustra* deserves to be taken far more seriously than the mainstream of Nietzsche scholarship has acknowledged.

Nietzsche himself considers *Zarathustra* to be his most significant work. Why, then, does Nietzsche scholarship most often treat it as among the least important of his works? In my view there are two basic reasons. Both have to do with the interpretive strategy that is typically used to approach Nietzsche's writings. First, Nietzsche scholarship has generally approached Nietzsche's works as philosophical texts, where "philosophical" is understood in a relatively narrow sense as a term of categorization. This approach tends to focus on the arguments and propositions that can be abstracted from the text, and it tends to underplay any significance that might inhere in the work's literary form. Nietzsche's other works, which assume fictional form only on occasion and in relatively short passages, are much more amendable to this approach than *Zarathustra*. In addition, the majority of these other works are divided into short sections and aphorisms, and many of the sections involve argumentatively structured discussions.

Schacht's avoidance of *Zarathustra* is thus in keeping with common practice in philosophical interpretation of Nietzsche. On occasion one can find works that do consider the literary and/or dramatic structure of *Zarathustra*— notably Harold Alderman's *Nietzsche's Gift*[13] and Anke Bennholdt-Thomsen's *Nietzsches "Also Sprach Zarathustra" als literarisches Phaenomen*.[14] And occasionally one discovers acknowledgements that the book's dramatic sequence is important. For instance, in his recent book *Nietzsche: Life as Literature,* Alexander Nehamas, asserts that *Zarathustra* "embodies a complex narrative structure in the course of which the character Zarathustra develops radically."[15] But these works and acknowledgements are departures from the mainstream.

Far more frequently, the literary form of the book is treated as a matter of minimal interest, and the work as a whole is regarded as less sound structurally than those in which argumentative lines are clear. Arthur Danto sees both *The Birth of Tragedy,* Nietzsche's first work (published in

1872), and *Thus Spoke Zarathustra* as exhibiting an almost random argumentative sequence. Referring to them in that order, he observes:

> The former exhibits a conventional unity and develops a main thesis, while the latter acquires a certain external structure by having each segment pose as a homiletic uttered by Zarathustra. In neither book is there an ordered development, however, or a direction of argument or presentation. They may be entered at any point.[16]

The kind of structure that Danto seems to be seeking and missing in *Zarathustra* is a structure of argumentative progression—or at least an "ordered development." It is not clear whether Danto would acknowledge any type of narrative line to be an "ordered development" but it is clear that his reading strategy would undercut any possible significance that *Zarathustra's* narrative structure might have. Danto dismisses *Zarathustra's* unfolding story line as irrelevant to understanding the book—it can be "entered at any point." He is not unusual in finding no significant narrative structure in *Zarathustra.* In general, Nietzsche scholarship has dealt with the book's literary form in a cursory manner (a "series of sermons" or "pseudo-biblical prophesyings") and treated the "story" of Nietzsche's prophet as a whimsical veneer coating the work's real, propositional ideas.

The second dismissive strategy of Nietzsche scholarship grows out of the first. Because other of Nietzsche's works are taken as more significant than *Zarathustra,* philosophical scholarship tends to construct a map of Nietzsche's thought on the basis of other works, particularly those "mature" works written after *Thus Spoke Zarathustra—Beyond Good and Evil* (published in 1886), *On the Genealogy of*

Morals (published in 1887), *Twilight of the Idols* (written in 1888), and perhaps *The Antichrist* (written in 1888). Nietzsche's later thought then tends to be read into *Zarathustra*—and the unsurprising result is that little is found in *Zarathustra* that is not put more straightforwardly elsewhere. Hollingdale suggests reliance on this strategy when he observes of *Zarathustra*, "The ideas epitomized in it are often expressed so laconically that the book has acquired the reputation of being 'difficult,' which it is not to anyone who knows his other books."[17] By constructing a theory of Nietzsche's thought through his other works, it is possible, for example, to read *Zarathustra* as expressing a metaphysical theory of "will-to-power." But that term occurs only occasionally in *Zarathustra*, and in contexts that are clearly concerned with the psychological will of the human being.

The strategy of interpreting *Zarathustra* as a fictional statement of the same ideas Nietzsche sets out elsewhere ignores the fact that certain of Nietzsche's most infamous and provocative concepts are found primarily in *Zarathustra* and rarely in his other published works. Among these are the concepts of the overman and eternal recurrence, and scholars interested in these ideas are drawn to the relevant passages in *Zarathustra*. But reluctance to employ *Zarathustra* as a primary text is evident even here, particularly in connection with eternal recurrence. Nietzsche's unpublished notes that discuss eternal recurrence are taken by many who discuss that theory to be not only of equal importance to published passages, but also the key to the meaning of the eternal recurrence passages in *Thus Spoke Zarathustra*. Notes that Nietzsche never published are treated on a par with published texts (if with parenthetical apology), and the consequence is that the published text that Nietzsche deemed most important is treated as less significant.[18]

My approach to *Zarathustra* departs from both of these tendencies of scholarship. Because I believe that the book deserves to be taken seriously in its own right, I shall not approach it as a text in philosophy (or in any other discipline) and therefore a text from which one can expect certain sorts of claims and arguments. Similarly, I shall not attempt to interpret the work by adhering systematically to the generic conventions of any other scholarly convention, for example, literary criticism. One of the most impressive characteristics of *Thus Spoke Zarathustra* is its experimental quality. Nietzsche was attempting a bold invention in *writing* and the result is complex and prismatic. The common comparison of *Zarathustra* with the Bible has some justice in that both works contain diverse species of writing aimed at similarly diverse purposes. We find poems, sermons, dreams, visions, songs, stories told by a voice that varies in its intimacy with the reader, and so forth. The book thus makes a wide range of appeals to the reader. It is worthwhile to attend to these as directly as possible, without reducing the text to fit the prepackaged expectations of either established disciplines or *au courant* styles of literary interpretation.

This aim is not an abstract ideal—it has concrete consequences for the way I interpret *Zarathustra*. Most significant, I found that reading Part IV of *Zarathustra* without training my eye exclusively on philosophical argument gave me a new perspective on what Nietzsche intended in writing it. Because Part IV is far more consistently storylike than the three earlier three parts, the received scholarly view of Part IV has been one of singular disapproval. At best it is seen as an unnecessary rehash of ideas presented earlier; at worst it is seen as an embarrassing mistake that seriously mars the book.

I propose to defend the importance of Part IV and its integrity with the larger work by addressing it outside the context of narrow philosophical and literary-critical expectations. My understanding of Part IV began to unfold when I noticed that Nietzsche was making a number of intriguing allusions to Apuleius' *Golden Ass,* a work that richly satirizes pretense at wisdom. These could not, I was sure, be casual or innocent. Nietzsche was for ten years a professor of classical philology. More probing comparison of Part IV and *The Golden Ass* convinced me that the former was modeled on the latter—and that what Nietzsche was constructing in Part IV was a self-ironical satire after the fashion of a particular antique genre.

The Golden Ass, however, depicts its hero as bamboozled and led astray by his own quest for knowledge, particularly knowledge that transcends the here and now. If Nietzsche is casting Zarathustra as a kind of counterpart to Apuleius' character in Part IV, then Part IV is making a strong statement about the limitations of Zarathustra's own quest. While indicators of the limitations of Zarathustra's insights are implicit throughout the book, the straightforward thematic insistence on Zarathustra's own folly and pretentiousness in Part IV is dramatically, and also philosophically, as significant as Socrates' employment of self-effacing irony in the Platonic dialogues. In terms of *Zarathustra,* Part IV thus casts a new and important light on the material in the preceding parts. It brings to completion in unmistakable clarity Nietzsche's effort to modify Zarathustra's doctrinal message with reflections of its limited nature.

The interdisciplinary approach that I take to *Zarathustra* is one characteristic that differentiates my analysis from most scholarly perspectives on the book. A second is that instead of retrospectively analyzing *Zarathustra* as it might fit into the schema of Nietzsche's mature thought, I locate it in the context of thought experiments that Nietzsche had conducted previously. In my view, two currents of thought that were developed in earlier works are sufficiently evident in *Zarathustra* that they are crucial to understanding it. One of these is Nietzsche's thought on the problem of the fundamental value of life in a world in which tragic suffering is unavoidable. This problem was thematically central in *The Birth of Tragedy*, and for that reason I consider Nietzsche's thinking there as one of the sources from which *Zarathustra* developed.

The second current of Nietzsche's earlier thought that is centrally significant in *Zarathustra* is Nietzsche's critique of Christian morality. *Daybreak*, written two years prior to the early parts of *Zarathustra*, is a clear expression of the harsh opinions toward Christian morality that Nietzsche entertained at the time. Interpretations of *Zarathustra* as "biblical," as an alternative gospel of absolutely true doctrines, are hardly plausible in light of these opinions, and this is important for understanding the book. At the same time, lines of Nietzsche's critique of Christian morality are recurrently evident in the later work. For this reason I discuss *Daybreak* as background and as a kind of prolegomena to *Zarathustra*. It indicates firm lines of Nietzsche's antagonism toward the Christian moral worldview that were securely in place before his *Zarathustra* project was begun.

Thus Spoke Zarathustra is a long book. What I have attempted here is an analysis, not a commentary. One of *Zarathustra's* great merits is that it is open-ended and extremely provocative, and it is that provocation that needs to be addressed and not dismissed. As an invitation rather than a set of pronouncements, *Zarathustra* can never be the object of a definitive commentary. Indeed, the project of writing such a commentary would be misguided. Valuable and suggestive commentaries address sections of *Zarathustra* in considerably more detail than this book, and I indicate some of these in the notes. But my aim has not been to illuminate every section of *Zarathustra;* rather, my aim is to illuminate the book's central points and purposes. My book is more of a tour guide to *Zarathustra* than a catalog.

Many people have influenced the way I read Nietzsche in general and *Zarathustra* in particular. The person who has had the strongest impact on my approach to both is Karsten Harries, whose insights on Nietzsche were always compelling and continuously challenged me to reconsider my own ideas. Other teachers to whom I am indebted are Louis Dupré, Charles Feidelson, John Swanay, and Hans Uffelmann, each of whom made new aspects of Nietzsche alive to me.

My ideas about Nietzsche were often revised or transformed in conversation. Frequently, too, I discovered that conversations, which had a marked impact on these ideas were not primarily conversations about Nietzsche. My conversational indebtedness is therefore broad, probably broader than I can recollect. Among those whom I want to thank especially (in addition to those mentioned here in other connections) are Harold Alderman, Eileen Bennet, Frithjoff Bergmann, Eric Blondel, Mary Bodine, Judith Butler, Dana Chasin, Maudemarie Clark, Daniel Conway, Arthur C. Danto, James P. Davis, Dionisio Escobedo, Paula Fulks-Vonder Haar, Mark C. Fowler, Roger Gathmann, Robert Gooding-Williams, Charles Harvey, Timothy Higgins, David Hoy, Bernd Jager, Peter Jelavich, Kristine Keyt, Roger Lundin, Richard C. McKim, Diane Michelfelder, Christopher Middleton, Alistair Moles, Joseph Molitorisz, Patricia Muoio, Malcolm Munson, Alexander Nehamas, Richard Palmer, Michael Platt, Richard Schacht, Alan Schrift, Daniel Shaw, Linda Singer, Garret Sokoloff, Ivan Soll, Mark Toles, Jorge Valadez, Lawrence Vogel, the participants of the "Reading Nietzsche" conference held at the University of Texas at Austin in February 1985, and several audiences in attendance at recent meetings of the North American Nietzsche Society, especially those of April 1984 and March 1985. I owe special thanks to Roger Gathmann, who not only assisted me in research for this book but suggested many original insights that improved my perspective on *Zarathustra*. I also especially wish to thank Paula Fulks-Vonder Haar, whose patience in listening to my ideas about Nietzsche over many years has been matched only by her willingness to read and comment on my written efforts to express them.

My analysis of the relationship between *Zarathustra* and Apuleius' *Golden Ass*, in particular, was developed in consultation with many advisers. Among these are David Konstan, Mazzino Montinari, Stephen Phillips, Wilkins Poe, and the participants in the National Endowment for the Humanities' Summer Seminar for College Teachers on Nietzsche directed by Bernd Magnus at the University of California at Riverside in the summer of 1985. I am also indebted to the members of the audience of the Nietzsche Society meeting at Chicago's Loyola University at which I presented my analysis in October, 1985.

In addition to stimulating my thoughts about Nietzsche, many of the people mentioned above helped to provide the climate of supportiveness in which this book was written. In this regard, I am especially grateful to my parents, Eugene and Kathryn Higgins. I also want to thank Jenene Allison and Peter Czipott, Nicholas and Sheila Asher, Henry Frankel, Janice Frey, Louis Mackey, John McDermott, Hope Phillips, Rita Vonn, and my grandmother Margaret Higgins. For support of a different nature, I want to thank the University Research Institute of the University of Texas at Austin for a research grant awarded in the summer of 1985.

The pragmatic details of assembling a manuscript for publication were essentially unknown to me before I became involved with this project. In connection with these,

Preface

I want to thank my editor, Jane Cullen, for her continued advice and encouragement. I also feel an unexpressible amount of gratitude toward my longtime friend Douglas Buhrer and his word-processing firm, WordMaster. His attentiveness, skill, and sound judgment made the practical side of producing my manuscript virtually painless for me during a time that was for him very trying. In addition, his extreme patience and encouragement, from the time I first thought of writing about Nietzsche, were strongly instrumental to the book's ever having been written.

Two other people have made contributions that are difficult to acknowledge because they are so comprehensive. One of these is Bernd Magnus, whom I wish to thank here for the advice, encouragement, conversation, and friendship that so largely contributed to my writing this book with some modicum of serenity. The other is Robert C. Solomon, whose wide-ranging assistance and expressions of caring are too diverse for me to summarize. Instead, I simply express here my affectionate appreciation.

1 An *ad Hominem* Introduction to Nietzsche

Of all that is written, I love only what a man has written with his blood.[1]

OF WELL-KNOWN Western philosophers, Friedrich Nietzsche is singular in inviting *ad hominem* attack. A philosopher's writings, he tells us, are "the personal confession of its author and a kind of involuntary and unconscious memoir."[2] Although he disguises his views as universally valid truths, every opinion a philosopher promotes is "at bottom . . . an assumption, a hunch, indeed a kind of 'inspiration'—most often a desire of the heart that has been filtered and made abstract—that they defend with reasons they have sought after the fact." They are "advocates who resent that name,"[3] in whom "there is nothing whatever that is impersonal."[4]

Nietzsche's target in these remarks is the usual view of philosophical scholarship, which treats the philosophy of an individual as a definite, enduring configuration of ideas. While acknowledging that the individual's thought developed over time, scholarship depicts the philosopher as essentially the material through which the philosophy emerged. Nietzsche reverses this perspective. By his account, the philosophy is the medium through which the philosopher articulates who he is.[5] A person, and not a system of thought, addresses us in philosophical writing, and many of the specific thoughts that compose the person's philosophy are as transient as that person's spiritual states.[6]

1

But in asking us to approach a philosopher's writing as a disguised revelation of himself, Nietzsche urges us to turn this approach toward his own works. "He's told us what he thinks he's doing," we might say. "Okay, then, who is Nietzsche?"

If we turn to Nietzsche's biography, we see an uninviting advertisement for his thought. The author of *The Birth of Tragedy* turns out to be a sickly young man who is overwhelmed by Wagner's music. Although the author of *The Gay Science* claims to be full of great health, the author of *Thus Spoke Zarathustra* seems to be doing a questionable job of convalescing from a disastrous case of unrequited love. Nietzsche's retirement from writing, we discover, directly followed his production of his autobiography, but this retirement was forced upon him by a mental breakdown. Insane at the age of forty-four, Nietzsche lived only twelve more years, and in that time he never regained lucidity. One can hardly see Nietzsche's life as enviable, even before his madness. He was sick much of the time; he had very few friends, most of whom gave up on him; and his love life was so notoriously dreadful that scholars have seriously pondered how he could have contracted syphilis, the disease usually cited as the cause of his madness.

One might conclude that Nietzsche was supremely ill-advised to turn his reader's attention to the man behind his works. What reaction is more natural than to dismiss the works as products of a life of total failure? Nietzsche recognized that his life presented a poor defense of his ideas. He gave the chapters of his autobiography, *Ecce Homo*, self-ironic titles, for example, "Why I Am so Wise," "Why I Am so Clever." These are sarcastic allusions to one of Nietzsche's favorite philosophical targets, Socrates, who habitually and rhetorically denied that he possessed wisdom. But they also reveal Nietzsche's recognition that his writing might be dismissed by those who observe the personal situation of its author. His preface to the second edition of *The Gay Science* makes this recognition even more obvious. There, concluding a lengthy description of the spiritual malaise that ended with the writing of the book, he bluntly articulated the unsympathetic question we probably have somewhere in mind. 'But let us leave Herr Nietzsche: what is it to us that Herr Nietzsche has become well again?'[7]

Nietzsche's answer is consistent with his remarks on philosophers in *Beyond Good and Evil*, but it also provides a rebuttal to those who would dismiss his views in reaction to the troubled terrain of his life story. Philosophical writing is not a projection of one's external autobiography. The work of philosophy is to transpose *inner* states—such as one's state of convalescence—into spiritual form:"A philosopher who has traversed many kinds of health, and keeps traversing them, has passed through an equal number of philosophies; he simply *cannot* keep from transposing his states every time into the most spiritual form and distance: this art of transfiguration *is* philosophy."[8] Why we seek a spiritualized transliteration of a philosopher's inner states is a problem of human psychology. But, in Nietzsche's view, the communication of such states is essential to the philosopher's work.

Seen in this light, Nietzsche's efforts to make us attend to the man behind his writings do not incite us to read his biography. When he baits us to ponder "Who is Nietzsche?" he is not so much encouraging us to consider what kind of man would have led the life that he led externally as he is asking us to attend to *him*, a unique burst of human being in the world, a burst expressed in an original voice. Although the term "soul" suggests an interpretive context that Nietzsche adamantly rejects, he himself uses it in self-description. In the preface to the second edition of *The Birth of Tragedy*, he says, "What spoke here...was something like a mystical, almost maenadic soul that stammered with difficulty, a feat of the will, as in a strange tongue, almost undecided whether it should communicate or conceal itself. It should have *sung*, this 'new soul'—and not spoken!"[9] Serious philosophical work, according to Nietzsche's conception, involves the self-expression of a "new soul" of the sort he mentions here. He makes this point a few months before writing the first part of *Thus Spoke Zarathustra* in a letter to Lou Salomé:

> Your idea of reducing philosophical systems to the status of personal records of their authors is a veritable "twin brain" idea. In Basel I was teaching the history of ancient philosophy in just this sense, and liked to tell my students: "This system has been disproved and it is dead; but you cannot disprove the person behind it— the person cannot be killed." Plato, for example.[10]

It is significant that such an individual "soul" makes a contribution to other individuals that derives mainly from its novelty, not from its similarity to them.

PHILOSOPHY AS INTERDISCIPLINARY

Nietzsche's aim in writing is to express himself as a unique impulse in the world. The implications is that efforts to locate his thought on the map of traditional theoretical disciplines would strike him as misguided. This is not to say that he never uses terms of self-description drawn from such analytical terrain. Besides indicating in such passages as those already cited that he views himself as a philosopher, he calls himself "a psychologist without equal"[11] and "an old philologist,"[12] and he suggests that his talent may have deserved the epithet "poet."[13] But he also characterizes himself in other ways that are not easily accommodated by conventional disciplinary labels: an "immor-

4

alist,"[14] "a disciple of the philosopher Dionysus,"[15] a "free spirit,"[16] a "good European,"[17] and "the Antichrist."[18]

A basic premise of this book is that the thought of *Zarathustra's* author cannot be summarized by any term that also names a traditional scholarly discipline. The corollary is that the question "What is Nietzsche doing?" should not be summarily answered with "Philosophy," "Psychology," "Literature," or "Religion." This is not to deny that perspectives from a number of traditional disciplines can help us gain some grip on Nietzsche's essential project in *Zarathustra*. But my objective is to preserve a balance among these perspectives, giving occasional prominence to one or the other as it appears useful.

Instead of laying out an overarching theoretical groundwork at the outset, I shall take Nietzsche's own suggestion and return to the question of the man who is trying to express himself. The remainder of this chapter will consider the question "What were the concerns of the man who wrote this unusual book?" The focus will be on four preoccupations that give us insight into *Zarathustra's* author: his self-doubt and worry about the status of his personal relationships; his desire to order his life aesthetically, in such a way that it would resemble a play; his general concern for human suffering; and his fascination with beautiful and striking images. Nietzsche's correspondence during the time he wrote *Zarathustra* will serve as evidence of these general preoccupations.

THE CONCERNS OF *ZARATHUSTRA'S* AUTHOR

Personal Relationships

Nietzsche's correspondence during the period of *Zarathustra's* composition reveals a man not merely concerned with but entirely traumatized by the status of most of his interpersonal relationships. At the time he began *Zara-thustra* in January 1883, Nietzsche was reeling from the rejection of Lou Salomé. Although from her standpoint the relationship had never been romantic, Nietzsche had sufficient feeling of that sort to have proposed marriage to her the previous May, when they had been visiting Tribschen together. His enthusiasm for the relationship was not daunted by her refusal. He met her later during the summer in Tautenberg, after she had met and thoroughly alienated Nietzsche's sister. The latter retaliated by interfering as much as possible in Lou's relationship with her brother. Plans for a platonic ménage-à-trois made by Nietzsche, Lou, and their mutual friend Paul Rée remained intact after the Tautenberg sojourn. But these were disbanded in October, when Nietzsche alienated both the other members of this triumvirate when they all met in Leipzig. By December 1883, Nietzsche had severed his friendship with both of them and had broken off communication with his sister and mother.[19] Nietzsche was also aware that the saga of his relationship with Lou was occasioning ridicule from his circle of acquaintances associated with Richard Wagner.[20] It is hardly surprising that he responded as he reports to Franz Overbeck on Christmas of 1882: "My lack of confidence is now immense—everything I hear makes me feel that people despise me."[21]

The sense that his relationships with other people were almost universally calamitous was intensified when Richard Wagner, his estranged friend and former hero, died on February 13, 1883. "This winter was the worst in my life," Nietzsche wrote to Peter Gast.[22] At the time Nietzsche was thirty-eight years old, and the onset of middle age seems to have reinforced his feeling of virtual friendlessness. To Erwin Rohde, another friend who had grown increasingly distant over the years, Nietzsche (by this time thirty-nine) wrote, "Ah, friend, what a crazy, silent life I live! So alone,

alone! So 'child'-less."[23] And to Overbeck he wrote, "It is at root *very* wonderful that we have not been estranged from one another during these last years, and not even, it seems, by *Zarathustra*. That I would be *alone* by the time I was about 40—about this, I have never had any illusions."[24]

Nietzsche's feeling at mid-life that he was destined to unalterable isolation was fortified indelibly when his sister, with whom relations had resumed, married Bernd Förster, an anti-Semite whose views Nietzsche abhorred. Nietzsche refused to attend the wedding. In his letter of explanation, he conveyed in heartrending fashion his failure to communicate with other human beings:

> Almost all my human relationships have resulted from attacks of a feeling of isolation. . . . I have not been so profoundly ill for nothing, and am ill on the average now still—that is, depressed—as I say, simply because I was lacking the right milieu and I always had to playact somewhat instead of refreshing myself in people. I do not for that reason consider myself in the least a secret or furtive or mistrustful person; quite the reverse! *If I was that, I would not suffer so much!* But one cannot just simply communicate, however much one wants to; one has to find the person to whom communication can be made. The feeling that there is about me something very remote and alien, that my words have other colors than the same words from other people, that with me there is much multicolored foreground, which is deceptive—precisely this feeling, of which testimony has lately been reaching me from various sides, is nevertheless the subtlest degree of "understanding" that I have till now found.[25]

His Own Life

Nietzsche's letters of the *Zarathustra* era testify that his disturbance over failed relationships had almost become an obsession. But while his reaction to the condition of his relationship to others reflects some of the self-doubt that would be unavoidable to most people in such circumstances,[26] this is not the only evident factor in his portrayal of himself. In his letters Nietzche describe himself at times not so much as a self-doubting failure as a passive victim of forces beyond his control. To Overbeck he wrote of his unavailing efforts to master "a tension between opposing passions which I cannot cope with."[27] And to Gast he commented, "I regard myself as the victim of a disturbance in *nature*" (italics in the original).[28]

The extremity of the latter statement indicates the exaggerated manner in which Nietzsche interpreted the events of his life. This manner is in full force whether Nietzsche was emphasizing his misfortune or his importance. The turmoil of his social life is continuous with the flow of the fundamental forces of nature, but so is the magnificent life's task which is his destiny. Nietzsche viewed his destiny, in fact, as almost a force of nature in itself. In a letter to Heinrich von Stein, written in December 1882, he alluded to "what I have never yet revealed to anyone—the task which confronts me, my life's task. No," he concluded, "we may not speak of this."[29]

Such remarks reveal an attitude of self-importance that we may find revolting, but some of Nietzsche's remarks about his destiny indicate a facet of his perspective on his life that is more interesting for its relative rarity. They reveal a tendency to understand his life as consisting of phases that are cast as a "part" of the larger, continuing story. Nietzsche's life, as he describes it, does not flow meanderingly from one episode to another. Instead, it is comprised of segments with sharply defined boundaries, and these segments are arranged in such a dramatically sound sequence that one almost senses that he sees an aesthetic planner, or at least a plan, behind it. Such, for instance, is the impression one gets of Nietzsche's sense of his destiny when he writes to Overbeck, "If you have read the 'Sanctus Januarius' you will have remarked that I have crossed a tropic. Everything that lies before me is new, and it will not be long before I catch sight also of the *terrifying* face of my more distant life task."[30] Nietzsche's construal of his life as involving segments indicated a second concern that dominated his thought at the time of writing *Zarathustra:* he was concerned with the development of his life as a dramatic work, and he judged the components of his life by an aesthetic measure.

Cruelty and Human Suffering

The oddness of Nietzsche's perspective on the events of his life becomes more apparent when one observes how modest were his expectations of the results of his most relentless "cruelty" against the ideals of others. He concluded, for instance, in one of his *harsher* rhetorical moments, that he was far too soft toward Rée on matters in which the latter's "impoverished manner of thinking and living have disgusted me!" His sympathy was a betrayal of his own ideal of humanity; had he imposed this ideal on Rée, he might have had the impact on him. But the expression he uses to describe this impact has no force: he might have had "a creative influence."[31]

One could interpret this comment, which is hardly a product of self-irony, as a euphemism. After all, a harsh stance toward inferiors highlights Nietzsche's reputation in many quarters. This reputation is worth mentioning here, because it might well inform one's interpretation of *Zarathustra*, which includes a wide range of harsh and derogatory comments about other human beings. In the section entitled "On the Rabble," for instance, Zarathustra waxes eloquent: "The bite on which I gagged the most is not the knowledge that life requires hostility and death and torture-crosses—but once I asked, and I was almost choked by my question: What? does life require even the rabble? Are poisoned wells required, and stinking fires and soiled dreams and maggots in the bread of life?"[32]

Nietzsche's letters, however, reveal a vastly different "Nietzschean cruelty." For one thing, Nietzsche's modesty in assessing his own effect on others does not appear to be a rhetorical device in all cases. To Gast, who had written him a grandiloquent letter of praise for *Zarathustra*, Part I, he wrote: "As I read your letter, a shudder ran through me. If you are right, then my life would not be a mistake? And least of all precisely now, when I was thinking it most?"[33] Far from assuming, with Gast, that his book will circulate and have an impact comparable to that of the Bible, Nietzsche, it appears, would have been gratified if only the influence of his book would be sufficient to make his life seem something other than an error. To observe that Nietzsche had this attitude is not to refute the claim that Nietzsche is an elitist, or even the claim that he felt violent hostility toward the many that he viewed as inferiors. But it does indicate that Nietzsche's attitude toward himself was more humble than the popular image of the cruel Nietzsche suggests.

A more important revelation of Nietzsche's letters is his expressed attitude toward suffering and the mechanisms of human cruelty. He was profoundly disturbed by both. To von Stein (and implicitly to himself as well) he wrote almost chidingly:

> One gets to love something, and one has hardly begun
> to love it profoundly when the tyrant in us (which we
> are all too ready to call our "higher self") says, "Sacri-
> fice precisely *that* to me." And we surrender it too—but
> that is cruelty to animals and being roasted over a slow
> fire. What you are dealing with are problems of cruelty,

nothing more or less—does this give you gratification? I
tell you frankly that I have in myself too much of this
"tragic" complexion to be able not to curse it; my experiences, great and small, always take the same course.
What I desire most, then, is a high point from which I
can see the tragic problem lying *beneath* me. I would
like to take away from human existence some of its
heartbreaking and cruel character.[34]

The implications of this comment in connection with
Nietzsche's view of his own work are wide-ranging, for
Nietzsche links his concerns with tragedy and with cruelty
together. This suggests that such varied works as *The Birth
of Tragedy* and *On The Genealogy of Morals* are in his own
mind aspects of a common concern; and his comment relates this concern to his desire to eliminate suffering. His
biographical responses to suffering—which extend from a
precocious interest in the problem of evil to his act of embracing madness by embracing a horse being beaten—are
further evidence that horror over suffering was central to
his orientation.

The comment to von Stein indicates that suffering was
one of Nietzsche's prominent concerns, at least at the time
he wrote *Zarathustra*. It also suggests that Nietzsche's image as a champion of cruelty is faulty, for while he admits
that he has *felt* cruel impulses, at least in spiritualized form,
his comment indicates that he is appalled by them and that
cruelty is something he neither admires nor encourages.

The fact that Nietzsche's attention was riveted on problems of suffering and cruelty perhaps explains the weight-
iness of his tone both in correspondence and in *Zarathustra*.
It has often been observed that for all its preaching of laughter, *Zarathustra* is a ponderous book. Its tone is neither
lighthearted, nor black-humored. Perhaps Nietzsche re-
strained the bite of his wit, for it is clear that he recoiled

at his talent as an ironist. In this case again, he was stunned by his own capacity for cruelty. He analyzed his gift of ironic perspective as a mode of cruelty in a letter to Overbeck:

> My whole life has crumbled under my gaze: this whole eerie, deliberately secluded secret life, which takes a step every six years and actually wants nothing but the taking of this step, while everything else, all my human relationships, have to do with a mask of me and I must perpetually be the victim of living a completely hidden life. I have always been exposed to the cruelest coincidences—or, rather, it is I who have always turned all coincidence into cruelty.[35]

Zarathustra, often ironic in its context, as I shall show, nonetheless reflects in its tone the almost deadly seriousness with which Nietzsche approached questions of suffering and the nature of human life. While the book's content provides a continual attack on and mockery of Christianity, its tone and preoccupations reveal religious seriousness.[36] One might call it a religious book, following Tillich's sense that religion deals with matters of ultimate concern.[37] Among these matters are the problems of human suffering and cruelty. And as many of the cited comments about Nietzsche's own life reveal, the ultimate significance of a human being's life is another of these matters that absorb Nietzsche's attention during the period under discussion. It will become clear in Chapter 2 that these concerns are all a part of the same problem from Nietzsche's perspective. For now I simply observe that they are among Nietzsche's fundamental preoccupations.

Images of Beauty and Power

The concerns of *Zarathustra*'s author—his interpersonal relationships, the value of his life from an aesthetic standpoint, and the problem of suffering and its implications regarding the ultimate meaning of being human—sound like an agenda for the spirit of gravity. In a sense this is fitting for the author of the letters of the *Zarathustra* period is a grave spirit. But this impression of Nietzsche is not balanced. A very different concern is evident in his correspondence of this traumatic period, a deep concern with images.

Nietzsche's written expression, even in his letters, is filled with powerful images: "The old Europe of the Great Flood" threatens; he longs to escape to "the plateaus of Mexico."[38] He wishes he had the money "to build a sort of ideal dog kennel around me—I mean, a timber house with two rooms, and it would be on a peninsula which runs out into the Sils lake and on which there used to be a Roman fort."[39] He describes himself as "the incarnate wrestling match" who feels, in response to some reponse to some requests made by Overbeck's wife; "as if someone were asking old Laocoön to set about it and vanquish his serpents."[40]

The imagistic character of all Nietzsche's writing is striking, and it is particularly prominent in *Zarathustra*. Nietzsche's imagistic self-expression in letters suggests that imagery is not a rhetorical enhancement of his writing, but a fundamental condition of the way he thinks. While dark concerns are more prominent in his letters of the *Zarathustra* period, Nietzsche's concern with images—beautiful and/or strong images—is nonetheless manifest.

This concern—and Nietzsche's general concern with beauty—will be more in evidence in the discussion of *The Birth of Tragedy* in Chapter 2. I mention it here because it is crucial to a picture of Nietzsche's basic preoccupations at the time he wrote *Thus Spoke Zarathustra*. The man behind the philosophy expressed in that work was deeply serious, hypersensitive, nearly obsessed with the problems of suffering and the meaning of life, but enraptured by the beautiful images that filled the world he perceived. With some sense of this person and the background of the next two chapters, we will be in a position to consider *Thus Spoke Zarathustra*, the book of which he writes: "It contains an image of myself in the sharpest focus, as I am, *once I have thrown off my whole burden.*"[41]

2 Nietzsche's Conception of Tragedy and the Tragic Worldview

Classical scholarship as knowledge of the ancient world cannot, of course, last forever; its material is exhaustible. What cannot be exhausted is the perpetually new adjustment of our own age to the classical world, of measuring ourselves against it. If we assign the classicist the task of understanding *his own* age better by means of the classical world, then his task is a permanent one. — This is the antinomy of classical scholarship. Men have always, in fact, understood *the ancient world* exclusively in terms of *the present*—and shall *the present* now be understood in terms of *the ancient world?* More precisely: men have explained the classical world to themselves in terms of their own experience; and from what they have acquired of the classical world in this way, they have *assessed,* evaluated their own experience. Hence experience is clearly an absolute prerequisite for a *classicist.* Which means: the classicist must first be a man in order to become creative as a classicist.[1]

NIETZSCHE DEVOTED the period of his schooling and ten years as a Basel professor to classical philology. Eventually his sympathies with his profession—and his profession's sympathy with him—dwindled to such an extent that his ultimate resignation from his position for reasons of health struck him as no great disappointment.[2] Silk and Stern observe that Nietzsche "had been at odds with conventional philology and philologists even before he took the chair at Basel."³ But Nietzsche's estrangement from his field does not indicate that he fell out of love with what first excited him about classics.

As late as 1888, his final year of writing, Nietzsche entitled a section of *Twilight of the Idols* "What I Owe to the Ancients' and devoted another to 'The Problem of Socrates."⁴ Nietzsche's concern with classics both during and after his professional involvement was intense but unconventional. Throughout his mental life, he employed the ancients—primarily the Greeks—as foils for thought about more contemporary matters and about human existence in general. As the passage at the beginning of this chapter indicates, Nietzsche believed that use of the ancients as foils for contemporary thought is the enterprise that classical philology is really all about.

Because this point of view was not shared by many of Nietzsche's fellow classicists, the profession was less than enthralled by Nietzsche's first major contribution to classical philology, *The Birth of Tragedy*. From a scholarly standpoint the book is bizarre. It lacks footnotes; it is clearly bedazzled by Nietzsche's nineteenth-century heroes, Schopenhauer and Wagner; one-third of the book refers continuously to the contemporary musical scene in Germany; and in general the book's rhetoric and stylistic maneuvers could be described as wild. For instance, the book opens with a discussion of the significance of the Greek gods Apollo and Dionysus, and Nietzsche appeals to the reader to consider the physiological states of dreams and intoxication in order to gain a sense of what these gods represent.⁵ In other words, he appeals to his readers to consider their own experiences with drugs and dreams, and this in an era before Freud had made dreams respectable to the scholarly community.

It is not surprising that *The Birth of Tragedy* was skeptically received by the philological community, particularly because Nietzsche had been viewed by his colleagues as something of a wunderkind from whom they could expect a splash.[6] The most hostile response to the book was also one of the most immediate; it took the form of a pamphlet by Ulrich von Wilamowitz-Moellendorff. Silk and Stern note, "It is not easy to summarize what Wilamowitz objected to in *The Birth of Tragedy*, except with one word, *everything*."[7]

The philological criticisms raised against *The Birth of Tragedy* are worth looking at if one's purpose in reading the book is to gain a historically correct account of the origin and mechanism of Attic tragedy,[8] but the purpose of this chapter is to help the reader gain insight into what Nietzsche was looking for when he set out to examine Greek tragedy, and to determine what he came to understand as tragedy's significant features. Nietzsche's analysis of tragedy will prove important to our understanding of his objectives in *Thus Spoke Zarathustra*, which he characterizes as a tragedy. It will also help us identify some central problems of Nietzsche's work in general that figure prominently in *Zarathustra*.

To gain a sense of Nietzsche's objective in analyzing tragedy, let us return to the passage cited at the beginning of this chapter. The orientation toward classics expressed there—the perspective that the value of classical philology lies in what it can reveal about the classicist's own time—is thematically evident in *The Birth of Tragedy*. The book's basic analysis of tragedy, which is focal only through section 12 of the book's 25 sections, is employed to ground a critique of the Socratic tradition of Western philosophy as it develops into the modern age. In his preface to the second edition of *The Birth of Tragedy*, which appeared sixteen years after the book was originally written, Nietzsche made it clear that the employment of theory in service of actual living was the basic concern of the book. "The task which this audacious book dared to tackle for the first time" is "*to look at science in the perspective of the artist, but at art in that of life.'*[9]

This perspectivist formula is rather opaque as an explanation of the book's project, at least until one reads it in its entirety. The text elaborates Nietzsche's understanding of the artistic and scientific perspectives, and the characterization of life as a chaotic force underlying all phenomena, which is central to the text, is not obvious in the formula, but it is crucial to interpreting it. For our purposes, however, it is enough that we observe that Nietzsche sees science (which, as a translation of the German *Wissenschaft*, is to be understood as scholarly investigation in general) as inextricably linked to artistic activity and that Nietzsche sees creative human activity, whether artistic or scientific, as significant only in its relationship to life.[10]

The Birth of Tragedy is not the only work in which Nietzsche insists that no theoretical enterprise is of value unless it has relevance to actual human life. For instance, in his essay entitled "On the Advantage and Disadvantage of History for Life," he assesses three perspectives on history and evaluates them on the basis of their capacity to provide insight of value to living in the present and the future.[11] *The Birth of Tragedy*, however, is a particularly salient example of Nietzsche's applying his principle to his own theoretical pursuit. The subject lends itself to a display of the relationship between theory and life—for tragedy is an art form that is perhaps uniquely inextricable from life outside of art. However controversial the issue of tragedy's proper pleasure may be, few would contend that the proper response is absolutely divorced from the kind of emotional reaction we have to terrible events in actual life. Even Schopenhauer, who sees aesthetic response to tragedy (and to art in general) as primarily intellectual, links the insights to be gained from tragedy to an enhancement of the viewer's power to feel compassion.[12] Tragedy has something to do with its viewer's affective responses to the actual.

THE PROBLEM OF TRAGIC SUFFERING

But the actual to which tragedy is related is not the world of actual events of all varieties. The province of tragedy is related to an extreme subset of the actual—the part of actual human experience that is painful and not susceptible to relief through analysis.

The small pains and irritations that accompany everyday life can often be soothed through thinking about the situations that produce them. If you are hurt because you feel slighted by a friend, for example, you might reflect that your friend is busy or preoccupied with his or her own problems—and this thought will probably make you feel better. The slight, you come to realize, is not aimed at you personally. Or you might reflect on how your rapport with this friend could be improved, again with the consequence that you feel better. You come to feel that you can act to prevent the recent hurt from becoming part of a pattern in your relationship. "Thinking things over," as we say, mitigates a considerable portion of human pain. The province of the actual with which tragedy is concerned is not this province in which thinking can remedy suffering.

The kind of suffering from which tragedy draws its material is not remedied by thinking the situation through. The suffering of a mother who loses a child to a stray bullet in a store robbery is not mended by her thinking through the scenario a number of times. If anything, thinking about the situation is likely to intensify her pain and to make her more aware of the senselessness of her child's death. Tragedy deals with situations that produce pain of this sort. Its purpose, in Schopenhauer's formulation, is "the description of the terrible side of life."[13] Nietzsche reflects the quality of human suffering with which tragedy is concerned when he associates, in the previously cited letter to von Stein, the "tragic problem" with the "heartbreaking and cruel character" of human existence.

The heartbreaking character of life with which tragedy deals calls the value of human existence into question. Unlike typical, everyday human pain, which can often be minimized by thought directed toward action, tragic suffering not only resists soothing thought but also provokes painful lines of thought on its own. It moves one to ask, "Is there no safety from senseless horrors like the accidental death of one's child?" and to ask the even more unsettling "If something so hideous can happen without warning, what good is it to be alive?"

Nietzsche's discussion of tragedy is focused on these weighty questions. Early in the text, he observes that Greek mythology reveals a darker side than that evident in the triumphantly vital gods and goddesses of Olympus. This darker side is evident in the legend of Silenus, which Nietzsche relates as follows:

> There is an ancient story that King Midas hunted in the forest a long time for the wise Silenus, the companion of Dionysus, without capturing him. When Silenus at last fell into his hands, the king asked what was the best and most desirable of all things for man. Fixed and immovable, the demigod said not a word, till at last, urged by the king, he gave out a shrill laugh and broke out into these words: "Oh, wretched and ephemeral race, children of chance and misery, why do you compel me to tell you what it would be most expedient for you not to hear? What is best of all is utterly beyond your reach: not to be born, not to *be*, to be nothing. But the second best for you is—to die soon."[14]

Silenus' claims about the valuelessness of human life are claims that tragic events tempt us to believe. One of Nietzsche's basic arguments in *The Birth of Tragedy* is that Greek tragedy provided an answer to Silenus' charges.

The basic problem that Nietzsche is concerned with in his investigation of what tragedy does, then, is not so much an historical or even directly an aesthetic one. Instead it is a version of the problem of evil: How can human life be said to be meaningful in the face of enormous evils—both humanly and naturally caused—that inflict suffering on the undeserving? Nietzsche investigates Greek tragedy in an effort to answer this question. In considering this investigation, we will discover that Nietzsche saw the problem of meaning that tragedy raises to be an inevitable consequence of being a human individual. After this elaboration of Nietzsche's problem, we will be in a better position to understand the details of what he took to be its solution.

TRAGIC SUFFERING AND HUMAN INDIVIDUATION

Early in *The Birth of Tragedy*, Nietzsche makes reference to Schopenhauer's account of the principle of individuation—the principle that makes it possible to distinguish individuals, whether people, animals, or things, from one another. Schopenhauer's account holds that the principle of individuation, to which Schopenhauer refers with the Latin *principium individuationis*, is essential to the way we perceive the world. Our ability to distinguish things and animate beings from one another allows us mentally to order our environment, and this ordering puts us in a position to appropriate the things around us.

Schopenhauer contends, however, that the *principium individuationis* gives us a picture of reality that is ultimately illusory. The more fundamental truth about the

21

world is that the things and creatures we perceive as distinct entities are all intimately connected in the life of the whole of which they are parts. The life of the whole is the only reality and this whole is a chaotic cauldron of driven energy that expresses itself phenomenally in the willfulness of animate beings and the self-preservative tendencies of inorganic things. The fundamental reality behind all phenomenal things is willful, and Schopenhauer calls this fundamental reality "the will."[15]

Schopenhauer's theory involves an ethical dimension. If our usual perception of things in the world as individuated is erroneous, we are using a fiction as our guide in orienting our behavior. This fiction, according to Schopenhauer, is not merely an inaccuracy. It is a vision that exerts a pernicious influence on our relationships to other people. Because we see other individuals as separate from ourselves, we imagine that we can benefit ourselves by exploiting and manipulating them. All evil that is perpetrated by one human being against another is premised on the view that the fates of individuals are separate and that one can hurt another without hurting oneself.

Seeing through this mistaken opinion—penetrating the illusion formed by the *principium individuationis*—is the key to ethical enlightenment, according to Schopenhauer. Once one discards this illusion and recognizes one's essential identity with the selves of others, one's response to other human beings—and to other animate beings in general—will be characterized by compassion.

I have devoted so much attention to Schopenhauer's account of individuation because Nietzsche builds his analysis of tragedy on the Schopenhauerian model. Apollo in Nietzsche's discussion is the divine representative of the *principium individuationis*, while Dionysus represents the chaotic life-force that underlies the apparent world of individuated things. In other words, Schopenhauer's duality of the apparent, individuated world and the will as fundamental reality recur in Nietzsche's images of Dionysus and Apollo. This recurrence of Schopenhauer's themes does not exhaust Nietzsche's images, a matter that we will consider shortly, but it is important to note that Schopenhauer's dualistic model of individuation serves as a basis for Nietzsche's duality of Apollo and Dionysus. The relationship of Nietzsche's Apollo and Dionysus is important: they emblemize interpretations of human individuation which, in relation to one another, are crucial to Greek tragedy's solution to the problem of tragic suffering.

The connection between tragic suffering and human individuation is perhaps not obvious. In the late twentieth century we know well that tragic suffering can afflict masses of people in contexts in which a single victim's individual existence seems scarcely a matter of concern. In a sense, however, such situations reveal the connection between individuation and tragic suffering all the more strongly because they disregard the human individual. A situation in which one is brutally harmed without regard for individuality displays strikingly how vulnerable we all are as individuals, and it shows how susceptible our individual efforts are to being thwarted by outside influences.

Nietzsche's association of Schopenhauerian concerns for individuation and the problem of Greek tragedy derives from his awareness of this kind of vulnerability. As individuals we are all vulnerable to kinds of suffering that are impervious to any effort we might make. Being a human individual essentially involves being radically insecure. The plans and projects by which we direct our lives, the very standards by which we judge our own successes, might be undercut at any moment by forces that are independent of us: natural disasters, political and economic events, disease, accidents, even the surfacing of repressed psychic material. And ultimately our most successful efforts to secure comfort, satisfaction, and happiness will be undercut by death.

We are not safe. With this observation, Nietzsche reminds us that our existence as individuals makes each of us subject to the tragic. Perhaps, in accordance with the wisdom of Silenus, we would have been better off not to have been born at all. That, at least, Nietzsche tells us, is the possibility that the ancient Greeks faced squarely. And yet, he goes on, they overcame the Silenic vision of the horrors of existence—and they achieved this overcoming through art.[16]

THE PERSPECTIVES OF ART: APOLLO AND DIONYSUS

Nietzsche's conception of art is not a narrow one. He classifies as art not only Greek tragedy but also the Greeks' invention of the Olympian gods. Perhaps the only common denominator of art for Nietzsche is that art is a product of human creative activity with an existence in the external world, an existence that allows it to be experienced by others besides its inventor. This vague description should be sufficient for our present purposes. The distinction between the Apollonian and Dionysian modes of art is crucial to Nietzsche's analysis of the mechanism of tragedy. Furthermore, this distinction hinges on the divergent ways in which Apollonian and Dionysian art inhabit the external world.

The visual, Apollonian arts, according to Nietzsche, can be compared to dreams. He goes so far as to suggest that the visual arts owe their existence in part to the fact that human beings naturally have dream experiences.[17] Dream experience demonstrates that beautiful images are deeply satisfying and that this is so even though they are illusions.

So much do we enjoy dreaming, he goes on, that "perhaps many will, like myself, recall how amid the dangers and terrors of dreams they have occasionally said to themselves in self-encouragement, and not without success, 'It is a dream! I will dream on!' "[18] We know that the dream is not real, and yet for this reason we enjoy it all the more. We are not deceived by its images—instead we take pleasure in their form.

The dream world is a fragile but ordered world, and it finds an appropriate patron in Apollo. Apollo is the god of sunlight, and thereby of illumination and vision, and also the god of order and restraint. Nietzsche associates the visual arts, primarily sculpture, with Apollo, and as I have suggested he sees these art forms as being similar to dreams. As representational media, painting and sculpture produce images that resemble but do not counterfeit things in the external world.[19] We do not mistake them for reality outside the art world; in fact, our enjoyment stems in part from our recognizing these images as illusions. We are delighted by visual artistic representations—we enjoy their proportion, their form, their order, and we find them soothing, a welcome respite from our everyday world.

Not all art is like this, however, even when we restrict our consideration to the fine arts. Far from soothing us with tranquil illusions, the Dionysian art of music arouses us.[20] It incites us "to the greatest exaltation of all ... [our] symbolic faculties." Our emotions are powerfully affected; we are moved to dance. We feel a sense of union with something outside ourselves, a union that Nietzsche describes as "oneness as the soul of the race and of nature itself."[21] Music intoxicates us—and Nietzsche likens its effect to that of wine. Although we take music into our bodies by listening to it, we feel transported by it.

Dionysus is appropriately the patron of dithyrambic music, along with wine, revelry, and sexual frenzy. He emblemizes the various potencies that take us outside of ourselves. What Dionysus represents is best understood as a kind of experience. The Dionysian experience involves a collapse of the usual restraints that are involved in out comportment as individuals through the world. In our everyday lives, we project relatively consistent personalities that others can rely upon, but this involves considerable restraint, control, and even dissimulation. In the Dionysian experience, self-control is abandoned, and with it the boundaries between individuals. The result is the characteristic feeling that one is intimately connected with one's fellow human beings, even with all of nature. The Woodstock rock concert—at least as mythologized—is a more recent example of the kind of experience that Nietzsche associates with the Greeks in their worship of Dionysus.

As Nietzsche draws the distinction, Apollo and Dionysus represent very different perspectives on the external world. The Apollonian perspective, which focuses on images, can be directed beyond the art world to the world of everyday experience. Extended in this manner, it perceives objects in the world in accordance with what Schopenhauer identifies as the *principium individuationis*. In other words, the Apollonian perspective on the external world interprets it as being composed of distinct things that can be ordered, classified, and differentiated from one another. The Apollonian view focuses on the form of a thing, the characteristic by which a thing can be enjoyed as beautiful, and also the characteristic by which a thing is distinguished from everything else. The external world seen from this perspective is a world of boundaries.

The Dionysian perspective, by contrast, attends to the flow of elements in a dynamic whole. This is the perspective that allows a listener to appreciate music. By extension, such a perspective can be directed toward the external world. This perspective focuses on the movement of the whole environmental configuration, rather than on the individuated entities that produce it. By comparison with the serenely ordered world of the Apollonian perspective, the world of the Dionysian perspective is more chaotic, punctuated by the transient tensions and resolutions of tension that arise among its elements instead of being structured by stable forms that are clearly arranged. The Dionysian world is a world in which no boundary is secure. Its elements are directional impulses that are continually undergoing transformation by virtue of their interaction with one another.

As perspectives on the external world, both the Apollonian and the Dionysian perspectives presuppose someone for whom they are perspectives. And as modes of one's orientation toward external reality, they also represent modes of orientation toward oneself. Nietzsche's analogous physiological phenomena—dreams and intoxication—provide hints as to what these modes of self-understanding are like. The Apollonian mode of self-understanding resembles that implicit in most of our dreams. Images present themselves to us. Although we are actively engaged in the dramatic scenarios of many dreams, Nietzsche focuses on their display of representations for our viewing. Implicitly, the self that dreams is a captive audience, a self that stands at a distance from what it sees, just as the audience of a visual artwork assumes a position of distance as a precondition for enjoying it. The self of the Apollonian perspective on the external world, in keeping with the dream analogy, stands at a distance from what it observes. One might conceive of oneself as related to the external world while assuming the Apollonian perspective; nevertheless, one understands oneself as separate from the things that one observes, just as these things are separate from each other. The Apollonian mode of self-understanding is essentially the same as the conception of one's individual existence that is entailed by the Schopenhauerian *principium individuationis.*

The Dionysian mode of self-understanding, as I suggested above, involves the breakdown of the typical sense of oneself as independent and separate from the rest of one's environment. Just as the boundaries that separate entities from one another are blurred by the Dionysian perspective on the world, so the boundaries between the self and the environment are blurred as well.

The experiences that are paradigmatically associated with the Dionysian experience—those of music and sexuality—provide models of the mode of self-understanding that the Dionysian perspective affords. Music, which conditions the entire environment, draws the listener into an experience that is shared in its basics by anyone in the vicinity. Although it affects one's emotions—usually viewed as individual, if anything about oneself is—music produces similar effects on the emotions of others as well. What is normally seen as private is shared in the musical context. Of course, the musical model is most suggestive when we consider the ideal listening experience—but the ideal need not be the most common encounter with music in order for the model to help us understand the Dionysian perspective of the self.

The same holds for a consideration of sexuality as a model of the Dionysian perspective on the self. In the ideal sexual encounter, an emotionally rapturous and immediate experience of the individual is shared with another individual. It is even preconsciously understood to be shared with the other, and shared in all its intensity. As in the case of music, feelings of sorts that are usually considered individual and private—both physiological and emotional— are experienced as shared with another. In both cases, Apollonian awareness of oneself as a distinct individual is surrendered to a recognition that one experiences some of one's most deeply felt nuances of emotion and sensation in common with someone else.

This recognition corresponds in certain ways to what Schopenhauer describes as the recognition that everyone and everything manifests the same will as oneself. Both recognitions, at any rate, involve as an essential feature of one's self-understanding a sense of essential identity with another self or selves. But the character of the breakdown of the everyday sense of oneself as a separate individual differs in the accounts of Schopenhauer and Nietzsche. For Schopenhauer this breakdown leads to the insight that sympathy with others is the only course appropriate to our own ontological status; and the ethical behavior that stems from this insight, if one assimilates it well enough, is the renunciation of willfulness in one's actions and the adoption of an attitude of passive acquiescence toward the rest of the world. For Nietzsche, as we shall see in our discussion of tragedy, the consequence of the breakdown of the Apollonian perspective is considerably less somber; it involves an orientation in one's behavior that is more akin to *joie de vivre* than to saintliness.

We are about to consider how tragedy, on Nietzsche's analysis, effects the breakdown of the usual Apollonian stance toward oneself, but before we leave our discussion of the distinction between the Apollonian and the Dionysian, we should make two more observations. One is that the Apollonian and Dionysian perspectives, if they are appropriately compared to dreams and intoxication, seem to represent aberrant orientations toward the self and external reality. The statements "It was a dream" and "I was drunk" strike our ears as excuses, explanations for why someone's perceptions and judgments were faulty. Does Nietzsche mean to suggest that both the Apollonian and Dionysian orientations toward self and world are distortions?

In a sense, he does. Both perspectives are important to

a human individual. We each need the Apollonian illusion that the world is orderly and manageable, if only to have the minimum sense of security necessary to assert ourselves in our behavior, and the very fact that we dream indicates that our minds find a kind of nurturance in images. On the other hand, we are actually always vulnerable to forces beyond our control on all levels of our lives. The price of forgetting this Dionysian wisdom is to become even more vulnerable, for when one associates one's own well-being with the continued smooth operations of the orderly world around one, disaster is certain. Something as natural and predictable as the death of an elderly relative is likely to provoke doubts about the value of being alive.

Neither the Dionysian nor the Apollinian perspective gives us the "right" picture of the world, therefore, and in that sense the picture provided by either is something of a distortion. This is one point that we should observe about Nietzsche's distinction. A second and particularly interesting observation is that the perspectives represent *imcompatible* orientations toward self and world—but at the same time *we have all experienced both.* We may adamantly repress the threatening truths that are inherent in the Dionysian orientation, and yet anyone of us who has ever been influenced by wine knows an experience in which the everyday boundaries between self and world have been altered. In our own experience, each of us has fluctuated in our perspective on our world and our relationship to it. Nietzsche draws on this characteristic of our experience in his account of how Greek tragedy works, to which we will now turn.

GREEK TRAGEDY'S SOLUTION

Greek tragedy, in Nietzsche's view, provides a solution to the problem of meaning posed by tragic suffering. This problem of meaning involves a sense that there is no justification for certain kinds of human suffering, however much the frequency of such suffering convinces us that suffering is a part of the order of the world. Nietzsche summarizes the kind of solution to this problem that tragedy provides: "For it is only as an *aesthetic phenomenon* that existence and the world are eternally justified" (italics in the original).[22]

With this remark, Nietzsche distances his account of tragedy from those accounts of tragic suffering that seek a moral solution to the problem of meaning involved. Among these are such Christian accounts as that of Augustine, who claims that despite appearances God arranges things so as to maximize good. Free will, which admits the evil of sin into the world, makes the world better than it would be if we lacked the power to choose. Many of the "evils" in the world are the fault not of God's creation but of our misuse of free will, which is good in itself. Furthermore, apparent evils that are the results of human sin may provide the preconditions for some greater good, which God alone may be able to see.[23]

Nietzsche objects to this solution to the problem of evil, believing that it substitutes a fictitious interpretation of events for a perception of the jarring actuality of the world. The illusion that the world, despite appearances, is morally ordered represents a disguised antipathy toward life, for it prefers to substitute a cheerful fiction for life's actuality. A serious application of moral standards to life as it actually is, however, would judge life harshly. Nietzsche makes this point in his preface to the second edition of *The Birth of Tragedy*: "For, confronted with morality (especially Christian, or unconditional, morality), life *must* continually and inevitably be in the wrong, because life *is* something essentially amoral—and eventually, crushed by the weight of contempt and the eternal No, life *must* then be felt to be unworthy of desire and altogether worthless" (italics in the original).[24]

Efforts to make tragic suffering make sense in a rational moral scheme of things are doomed to failure, Nietzsche tells us. Tragic suffering *cannot* be rationalized. One can resolve the problem of meaning it poses in an honest and humane manner only by appealing to a part of one's being that is more basic than one's rationality: the vital emotive center of a healthy person that finds satisfaction just in the fact of being alive. One can, says Nietzsche, find consolation in "the metaphysical comfort... that life is at the bottom of things, despite all the changes of appearances, indestructibly powerful and pleasurable."[25]

The power of Greek tragedy stems from its ability to draw us into this perspective from which life is justified. The state to which it is designed to induce its audience simultaneously involves an awareness of the hideous in life, the subject matter with which tragedy deals, and a peaceful and even joyous recognition that one is part of a life that is rich and powerful. This state involves a combination of the Apollonian and the Dionysian perspectives on self and world that we have considered. The Apollonian perspective sees with horror the world-order's cavalier unconcern with the individual's well-being. Yet the Dionysian perspective redeems the horrible vision by reminding us that the world is not a force that threatens us externally, but a dynamic unity that our very persons express. The object of tragedy is to move the members of the audience to this dual perspective.

It might appear that the solution to the problem of tragic suffering might be achieved through exclusive adoption of the Dionysian perspective, without the disturbing Apollonian vision. In a sense, this is so. Nietzsche's suggestion is that tragic suffering arises because the usual Apollonian illusion—that the world is an orderly place that can be navigated safely—is undermined by some hideously unrationalizable event. The Dionysian perspective, with its ecstatic sense of involvement in the dynamic flux of life, is the restorative element in the formula of the Greek tragedy's effect, for it affirms life regardless of life's horrors.

But in Nietzsche's view the Dionysian state is deficient precisely because of this lack of regard for life's horrors. So far is Nietzsche from being a proponent of the exclusive pursuit of Dionysian experience that he makes a point of denouncing the barbarian Dionysian orgies—those "centered in extravagant sexual licentiousness, whose waves overwhelmed all family life and its venerable traditions" and unleashed "the most savage natural instincts," "including even that horrible mixture of sensuality and cruelty which has always seemed to me to be the real 'witches' brew.' "[26] Dionysian excess, without a balancing Apollonian awareness of the real cruelty that it implies, is not, according to Nietzsche, a tenable resolution of the problem of tragic suffering. The human being who is captivated by Dionysian experience remains in a very real sense an individual, for he shares a world that in most everyday contexts is understood as being composed of individual people or things. Although this Apollonian perspective is not ultimately in keeping with the basic reality of the world, it is an essential component of human reality. The barbaric Dionysian orgiast negates his own individuality, and his mode of doing so violates the individuality of others. In his orgiastic state he is not disposed to attend to the humanly fundamental problem of tragic suffering, but he has not by assuming this state eliminated the problem.[27]

What a solution to the problem of tragic suffering requires is a religious transformation of perspective, in the sense that a concern with what is ultimately important is "religious." Greek tragedy operates to effect such a religious transformation.

The key to the effectiveness of the mechanism of Greek tragedy is its ability to move the individual audience member to identify with someone else. The drama's power to move its viewer to identify with its hero is simultaneously the power to alter the audience member's perspective on himself or herself. By affording the viewer the occasion for identifying with another, the drama precipitates a breakdown of the viewer's everyday sense of himself or herself as a detached individual.

Greek tragedy is particularly powerful in this achievement because it sets the mood for the viewer to overcome his or her distance from others, a distance presupposed by the everyday Apollonian perspective, *before* the viewer has become acquainted with the tragic hero. The tragedy does this by employing the chorus, which represents a throng of dancing and singing satyrs. The satyr, a creature who is half-human and half-animal, is "the archetype of man," combining animal vitality with capacity for rapturous religious emotion.[28] The satyrs are, mythologically, the ecstatic worshipers of the god Dionysus. Nietzsche's account of why the chorus of reveling satyrs captivated the Greeks deserves to be quoted at length even though it includes the previously cited statement of the nature of tragedy's metaphysical consolation.

> I put forward the proposition that the satyr, the fictitious natural being, bears the same relation to the man of culture that Dionysian music bears to civilization. Concerning the latter, Richard Wagner says that it is nullified by music just as lamplight is nullified by the light of day. Similarly, I believe, the Greek man of culture felt himself nullified in the presence of the satyric chorus; and this is the most immediate effect of the Dionysian tragedy, that the state and society and, quite generally, the gulfs between man and man give way to an overwhelming feeling of unity leading back to the

very heart of nature. The metaphysical comfort—with
which, I am suggesting even now, every true tragedy
leaves us—that life is at the bottom of things, despite all
the changes of appearances, indestructibly powerful and
pleasurable—this comfort appears in incarnate clarity in
the chorus of satyrs, a chorus of natural beings who live
ineradicably, as it were, behind all civilization and remain eternally the same, despite the changes of genera-
tions and of the history of nations.[29]

The chorus of satyrs presents the tragic audience with
an impression of the character of life as it is understood
from the Dionysian perspective, for the chorus is a unity
that is dynamic, chaotic, and wondrous. Nietzsche accepts
the established view that the chorus is the original form of
tragedy, and he concludes that the Dionysian perspective
that the chorus represents is the central component of what
Greek tragedy conveys.[30] He does not, however, see the
chorus as performing an exclusively representational function for the audience. Instead, the purpose of the chorus is
to draw the audience into the state that it simultaneously
depicts. At the height of Attic tragedy, says Nietzsche,
"there was at bottom no opposition between public and
chorus: everything is merely a great sublime chorus of dancing and singing satyrs or of those who permit themselves
to be represented by such satyrs."[31] The spirit of the chorus
of satyrs contagiously affects the audience. When the chorus
has the intended effect, the viewer is disposed to surrender
the stance of an individual who is at a distance from what
is observed. He or she feels immediately engaged in the
activity that occurs on stage. The excited sense of oneness
of the chorus is communicated to the audience, and by
virtue of this identification "we have a surrender of individuality and a way of entering another character." The
abandonment of the perspective of the isolated individual
is reinforced by the fact that the audience is itself a group

phenomenon. "A whole throng experiences the magic of this transformation."[32]

Already in its experience of the chorus, the audience is incited to a simultaneous assumption of both Apollonian and Dionysian perspectives. It sees a throng of individuals before it, and yet it is provoked to feel a part of what it sees. In this way the tragic chorus returns the individual audience member to a simultaneous awareness of both the communal and the individual aspects of himself or herself.

This awareness puts the audience in the appropriate frame of mind for comprehending the intended significance of the tragic hero. In Nietzsche's view the tragic hero is always an appearance of Dionysus in his form as the god who suffers from his dismemberment into individuals.

> The hero is the suffering Dionysus of the Mysteries, the god experiencing in himself the agonies of individuation, of whom wonderful myths tell that as a boy he was torn to pieces by the Titans and now is worshiped in this state as Zagreus. Thus it is intimated that this dismemberment, the properly Dionysian *suffering*, is like a transformation into air, water, earth, and fire, that we are therefore to regard the state of individuation as the origin and primal cause of all suffering, as something objectionable in itself.[33]

Nietzsche speaks here in mythological language, but his point is that when a tragedy succeeds in its aim the audience sees the hero's situation as one instance of a universal human condition: the condition of absolute individual vulnerability. The audience recognizes the hero's predicament as its own, and their surrender of individual distance in identifying with the hero makes them literally vulnerable to tragic suffering, although in this case vicariously.

The vicarious nature of this suffering indicates something else that is contained in Nietzsche's suggestion that the audience recognizes Dionysus in the tragic hero. The audience perceives not only their own suffering in the tragic hero, but also the same life. The audience of *Oedipus Rex* perceives awesome vitality in the tragic hero Oedipus, who comes to a kind of resolution, albeit a resolution without hope, in the wake of the traumatic experiences. That Oedipus contiunes at all when he has lost everything is a striking reminder that, despite the appearance that contingent things grant value to our lives, we ultimately value life itself as good unconditionally. This Dionysian insight can occur only in consequence of tragic loss, whether one's own or that of someone with whom one identifies. Tragic loss reveals our basic disposition toward life when all its contingent charms have fled. What we may discover, when our Apollonian sense of security has failed us, is that we love life anyway and that the worst of fate is powerless to make us regret being a part of it.

This metaphysical comfort is hardly superficial exuberance; instead it involves a kind of deep joy. This joy is the rapture of the tragic audience whose everyday perspective on self and world has been transformed to the tragic perspective, which is paradoxically Apollonian–Dionysian. The tragic perspective is undeceived about the murky facts of human life. It recognizes that the individual is constantly exposed to no-win situations, hideous pains that are not compensated with resulting greater satisfactions, and insecurities whose only certain resolution is death. But the tragic perspective also appreciates life as the common support of both the individual and the world, and it sees life as wondrous for the diversity it contains and sustains in continuously fluctuating relationships.

The person who has assumed the tragic perspective feels awe in observing that the same impulse of life is infused through the whole, and feels satisfied to be himself or herself an expression of that very impulse. That person's pleasure stems from seeing the world as a vibrant unity that underlies all diversity and contradiction. It depends, in other words, on his or her seeing the world on the model of a work of art. The aesthetic prespective on the world that allows that person to recognize the basic unity in diversity, the unity represented by Dionysus, is essential to what Nietzsche sees as the solution to the problem of meaning that Greek tragedy provides. The tragic solution sees life aesthetically and, by virtue of this vision, it sees life as justified.

Nietzsche's account of tragedy suggests a perspective on human life that sees life as meaningful despite the existence of tragic suffering, but does not provide us with assurance that everyone who identifies with the suffering of a tragic hero will reach the insight that life is joyous and powerful anyway. At most his account explains why the vicarious experience of the hero's tragic suffering can remind us of a love of life that we feel deeply. But perhaps this basic belief is not universal. The mechanism of tragedy, as Nietzsche describes it, depends for its effectiveness on a prior unconscious faith that life is worthwhile, however painful. Nietzsche cannot show that Greek tragedy will move any of us who observe it to the tragic perspective and its solution to the problem of tragic suffering. He can show only that Greek tragedy facilitates the experience of this perspective for those who have the necessary spiritual predisposition.[34]

Mention of this limitation of Greek tragedy on Nietzsche's account does not denigrate that account, for Nietzsche's prespective on images and their function entails this limitation. The Apollonian image, the vision beheld at a distance, can be a focus that helps to recall its viewer to a spiritual state. This is what the image of the chorus of satyrs is designed to do, and the tragic hero provides a focus that facilitates the recollection of the nature of individuated existence as it is emblemized in the suffering Dionysus.

These images, or icons, are powerful to the extent that they facilitate the experience of the spiritual states they are designed to elicit. But the "magic" of these images obtains only when they are charged by the appropriate spiritual disposition in their observers. The spectacle of a Greek tragedy can effect a transformation of religious worldview in a viewer who is open to it, but if an audience member is not receptive to such a transformation, the tragedy's icons remain mere images, and the tragedy is just a play. An icon does not literally possess magical powers.

This being Nietzsche's view, it is not surprising that he devotes a considerable portion of *The Birth of Tragedy* to warning the reader about the dangers of the Apollonian illusion that safety from the tragic dimension of life is in principle attainable. This illusion, as precarious as it is in the actual business of living, is solidly lodged in the everyday thinking of most members of the modern Western world, according to Nietzsche. But it is disastrously self-defeating. It renders those in its spell particularly liable to despair and trauma when the tragic dimension interferes with the safe interpretation of life on which they have come to depend. Simultaneously, it makes them insusceptible to the tragic perspective that might heal despair, for it has accustomed them to a systematic avoidance of the recognition that the individual is radically vulnerable, a recognition that is essential to tragic insight. In Nietzsche's view, the illusion of attainable safety abets the nihilistic perspective that life has no value. And yet its spell reigns over most people whom he observes. The project of seeking safety is both strongly motivated by the painfulness of life's insecurity and dominant in Nietzsche's culture. He therefore sees it as singularly worthy of attack in all its manifestations. The phenomenon that Nietzsche considers the most powerful and pernicious expression of this project in the modern world is the phenomenon of Christian morality.

3 Nietzsche's Case Against Christian Morality

On reading the *Morgenröte* and *Fröhliche Wissenschaft*,
I happened to find that hardly a line there does not
serve as introduction, preparation, and commentary to
the aforesaid *Zarathustra*. It is a *fact* that I did the commentary *before* writing the *text*.[1]

NIETZSCHE'S OPPOSITION to Christianity is well publicized. In the modern Western world he is, perhaps along with Marx, the paradigmatic atheist. And his rabid outcries against love of neighbor, pity, and altruism have tended to cast him, in the imaginations of many, as a gleefully cruel egomaniac who opposed Christianity because he had a sadistic dislike of other human beings.

Such a picture is wildly at odds with the image of Nietzsche that I sketched in Chapters 1 and 2. Particularly, it is contrary to the idea that Nietzsche's is deeply concerned with the problem of human suffering. If Nietzsche is the humanist that I have suggested, why does he oppose Christianity, with its concern for the suffering of the world, so stridently? And why does he aim so much of his attack at precisely those ethical objectives of Christianity—love of neighbor and compassion—that would seem to respond to the problem of suffering in this world and not merely in the hereafter?

I have already hinted at the answer. Nietzsche sees Christianity as providing an escapist solution to the problem of tragic suffering in a number of ways, most overtly by minimizing the importance of this life and offering eternal reward as compensation for earthly suffering. The effect is that Christianity implicitly trivializes the significance of tragic suffering, and in doing so fails in the very virtue that it most strongly promotes—compassion.

This chapter will consider the details of Nietzsche's critique of Christianity as an antitragic religion. The range of Nietzsche's arguments against Christianity should demonstrate that an alternative worldview, and not merely doctrinal revision, would be necessary to correct what Nietzsche finds objectionable. This point will prove important to our understanding of *Zarathustra*, for while that book includes many speeches in which Zarathustra is promoting alternative doctrines, we would be misled to assume that Nietzsche simply wants us to adopt some specific nontraditional beliefs. After analyzing Nietzsche's theoretical rejection of the entire Christian worldview, we should be in a better position to recognize the kind of radical transformation of outlook that is basic to Zarathustra's message.

Because my discussion of Nietzsche's position on Christianity is offered as background to *Zarathustra*, I offer no criticisms of Nietzsche's account in this chapter. Certainly Nietzsche's views might be criticized along a number of lines. One might, for instance, object that the picture he presents of Christian morality is an unfair caricature, or that it applies only to a certain interpretation of Christianity that one need not adopt, or that it attacks hypocritical uses of Christian doctrine instead of Christianity's spirit or essence. And I do not indicate the points at which Nietzsche's account is vulnerable to these lines of criticism; readers inclined to adopt a critical perspective will be tacitly observing these points themselves.

I am also not presenting a defense of Nietzsche's view of Christian morality. Instead I provide a more descriptive account, relying primarily on Nietzsche's *Daybreak:*

Thoughts on the Prejudices of Morality as a source. Unlike Nietzsche's more famous and vitriolic anti-Christian writings, *Twilight of the Idols* and *The Antichrist*, *Daybreak* makes its statements quietly. I shall say more about the book's communicative strategy later, but for now I observe that *Daybreak* lends itself to the project of presenting a descriptive overview of Nietzsche's position better than the more shrill alternatives.

The decision to focus on Nietzsche's arguments in *Daybreak* has another rationale. Published in 1881, *Daybreak* predates *Zarathustra*, which was written in the period spanning 1883 and 1885. The more notorious anti-Christian writings, however, were both products of Nietzsche's last year of writing, 1888. The significance of focusing on *Daybreak* is that it reveals that Nietzsche had analyzed Christian morality thoroughly and formulated his basis for opposing it before *Zarathustra* was written. It demonstrates, then, that we can presuppose this formulated opposition as part of the theoretical context in which Nietzsche brings *Zarathustra* to life.

DAYBREAK'S MODE OF CRITICISM

Daybreak's style is unusual among Nietzsche's works. Here the strategy of the typically flamboyant Nietzsche is to presuade by quietly fueling his readers' doubts, usually doubts about the status and ultimate value of the morality in which they have been raised. An aphoristic work, the book exploits the technique of juxtaposition as a means of drawing the reader into sympathy with Nietzsche's standpoint.

Nietzsche's basic strategy in *Daybreak* is to disarm the reader by offering relatively palatable analyses of such things as the evolution of scientific theory and the nature of the psychological gratification afforded by subtle moves

43

in social intercourse. Then, by interspersing these discussions with comments on morality, he implies that morality, like science, has evolved, that the rewards of morality are akin to those attainable in shrewdly conducted social maneuvers, and so on. But I shall say more about Nietzsche's strategy below.

A discussion of its contents cannot fully exploit *Daybreak's* strategy of juxtaposition. For a direct experience of the effect of Nietzsche's strategy, the reader can only turn to the book itself, a step that I recommend. In a more limited sense, however, a discussion such as this can exploit Nietzsche's strategy in *Daybreak.* As a consequence of the work's reliance on juxtaposition, we find terse, pointed comments on various aspects of Christian morality that will suit our purpose of gaining a quick overview of Nietzsche's opposition. Furthermore, even a description of Nietzsche's strategy in *Daybreak* will give us a sense of his attention to context in the arrangement of aphorisms. This will be of value to us because this facility is fundamental to *Thus Spoke Zarathustra.*

In the preceding chapter I suggested that in Nietzsche's view Christianity represents the quest for safety as a response to tragic suffering, and my discussion of *Daybreak* will center on a justification of this claim. In order to see exactly what Nietzsche is contending, however, we should take a closer look at the manner in which Nietzsche sets up his discussion. Nietzsche's case is not exclusively propositional. As in his other writings, Nietzsche is not content to display his reasoning in *Daybreak;* he also wants to move his readers to his perspective.[2] In this effort *Daybreak* first aims at convincing the reader that the Christian worldview is not necessarily the truth.

This objective guides the quiet beginning of the book. Immediately morality is implicitly attacked by Nietzsche's artfully juxtaposed comments on a variety of familiar modes of thinking. Among the early aphorisms, we find discussions of the imaginative nature of the interpretation of our world involved in such diverse spheres as those of language (which, in the case of German and many other languages, assigns gender to common nouns,[3] custom,[4] and popular medicine.[5] Nietzsche implies by these remarks that many practices that appear entrenched in the nature of things are merely long-practiced habits. He insinuates that the same is true of morality—by interspersing among these comments discussions of the nature of morality and its relation to tradition.[6] The implication is that morality too may be unfounded as a means of interpreting experience, just as popular medicine is unfounded as a means of interpreting disease.[7] Nietzsche suggests, furthermore, that the moral interpretation of experience has consequences that are as harmful as unscientific accounts of disease may prove to be. "Morality is a hindrance to the creation of new and better customs; it makes stupid."[8]

Nietzsche's effort here is to insinuate a different overall perspective on morality into the minds of his readers, not simply to offer them argumentative grounds for rejecting traditional morality.[9] And this strategy is consistent with his understanding of what morality is. If, as Nietzsche suggests, morality is a deeply entrenched system of habits of world interpretation, arguments against specific moral platitudes will be insufficient to uproot it. A habit retains its sway over our feelings and general outlook long after our intellect has become convinced that we should change it. What is required for a change in our habits is a new practice or pattern of practices that can replace those that are currently habitual. The smoker who wants to stop smoking is thus more likely to succeed if he exploits this character of habit by developing substitute rituals—such as chewing gum when he wants a cigarette—than if he simply convinces himself that smoking is harmful to his health.

Nietzsche seeks to dislodge some of our most basic intellectual habits, those involved in our practice of passing moral judgments. "We have to *learn to think differently*," says Nietzsche, writing explicitly about our habitual moral judgments, "in order at last, perhaps very late on, to attain even more: *to feel differently*."[10] He offers *Daybreak's* kaleidoscope of aphorisms as a demonstration of a different way of thinking, one that contrasts with our morally colored habits of interpreting human activity. In this way he suggests that an alternative to these habits is quite possible, even if it is unfamiliar to us.

As we read the book, we become increasingly habituated to Nietzsche's novel way of looking at human behavior and its disregard for inherited moral standards. The book is designed to give us an *experience* of thinking extramorally. The daybreak it heralds, if it succeeds in its project, is the dawn of our realization that moral categories are dispensable.

The aphoristic strategy of *Daybreak* is the context in which the arguments against Christian morality occur; in this sense the arguments that we shall be considering presuppose Nietzsche's authorial effort to extricate us from our mental habits. We now turn to the arguments themselves. While Nietzsche's style in *Daybreak* tries to show that extramoral thinking is possible, his specific comments on morality try to demonstrate that there are good reasons to move beyond thought that is informed by Christian morality.

WHY ABANDON CHRISTIAN MORALITY?

I have suggested that Nietzsche uses style in *Daybreak* to insinuate that Christian morality may be as unfounded as the advice of folk medicine, but the contents of many of the book's passages do more than insinuate. Nietzsche straightforwardly advances the view that the morality we have received as an inheritance depends on an imaginary world of causes and effects. He cites as an example the ritual ablutions that certain communities employed in response to evil chance occurrences. Demonic causes of such events, Nietzsche reports, were merely assumed, as were the supernatural effects—the propitiation or provocation of the deity—that were supposed to result from one's ritual. In the end, Nietzsche concludes, "One accords reality a value only *insofar as it is capable of being a symbol.* Thus, under the spell of the morality of custom, man despises first the causes, secondly the consequences, thirdly reality, and weaves all his higher feelings (of reverence, of sublimity, of pride, of gratitude, of love) *into an imaginary world:* the so-called higher world." The higher world assumed by modern people, Nietzsche argues, is of the same order—it is an imaginary world that comes into play "whenever a man's feelings are *exalted.*" "It is a sad fact," he concludes, "but for the moment the man of science has to be suspicious of *all higher feelings,* so greatly are they nourished by delusion and nonsense."[11]

Nietzsche does not limit the influence of imaginary constructions to the province of overtly Christian concepts. Nevertheless, other comments make it clear that he sees many basic concepts of the Christian moral worldview as paradigm instances of deluded interpretations founded on an imaginary world. "Man created sin," he asserts in section 81.[12] On sacrifice he comments, "Christians have never ceased to discharge their dissatisfaction with themselves on to a *sacrifice.*[13] Punishment and guilt are similarly inventions of the Christian moral imagination: "Only in Christendom did everything become punishment, well-deserved punishment: it also makes the sufferer's imagination suffer, so that with every misfortune he feels himself morally reprehensible and cast out."[14] In general, Nietzsche sees moral judgments of all sorts, including those asserted by Christianity, to be based on the fictitious: " 'To deny morality' ... can mean: to deny that moral judgments are based on truths.... This is *my* point of view."[15]

Not only the negative concepts of moral evaluation, but also the positive terms employed by Christendom are, in Nietzsche's view, fictitious constructs. Nietzsche discusses revelation, for instance, as follows: "How can a person regard his own opinion about things as a revelation? This is the problem of the origin of religions...."[16] Of the miraculous, Nietzsche writes, "Throughout the whole Middle Ages, the actual and decisive sign of the highest humanity was that one was capable of visions—that is to say, of a profound mental disturbance."[17] And Nietzsche sees the Christian view of the end of the world as a fiction developed from political motives: "Christianity welded together Rome, the 'world' and 'sin' into *one* sensation; it avenged itself on Rome by imagining the sudden destruction of the world to be near at hand."[18] The concept of God is treated in *Daybreak* as a projection of personal egoism:

> How many there are who still conclude: "life could not
> be endured if there were no God!" ... —therefore there
> *must* be a God...! The truth, however, is merely that
> he who is accustomed to these notions does not desire a
> life without them: that these notions may therefore be
> necessary to him and for his preservation—but what
> presumption it is to decree that whatever is necessary
> for my preservation must actually *exist!* As if my pres-
> ervation were something necessary![19]

Even this brief roster of Nietzsche's comments on Christian concepts demonstrates that he considers much of the Christian conceptual apparatus to be fictitious. It is also apparent that he views these fictions as instrumental to a very morbid perspective on life. "Indeed," as Nietzsche puts his point in yet another passage, "what a dreadful place Christianity had already made of the earth when it everywhere erected the crucifix and thereby designated the earth as the place 'where the just man is *tortured* to death'! ... Let us never forget that it was Christianity which made of the *deathbed* a bed of torture."[20] Nietzsche later makes the point that Christianity is built on morbid imaginings in the more hyperbolic voice for which he is well known.

> In Christianity neither morality nor religion has even a single point of contact with reality. Nothing but imaginary *causes* ("God," "soul," "ego," "spirit," "free will"—for that matter "unfree will", nothing but imaginary *effects* ("sin," "redemption," "grace," "punishment," "forgiveness of sins"). Intercourse between imaginary *beings* ("God," "spirits," "souls"); an imaginary *natural* science (anthropocentric; no trace of any concept of natural causes); an imaginary *psychology* (Nothing but self-misunderstandings, interpretations of agreeable or disagreeable general feelings—for example, of the states of the *nervus sympathicus*—with the aid of the sign language of the religio-moral idiosyncrasy: "repentance," "pangs of conscience," "temptation by the devil," "the presence of God"); and imaginary *teleology* ("the kingdom of God," "the Last Judgment," "eternal life").[21]

Nietzsche goes on to consider the psychological problem raised by the dismal character of these categories: Why would someone interpret the world in categories that make the world appear more depressing than it would without them? His answer is interesting, and it suggests a sense in which Christianity is directly antithetical to a tragic interpretation of life: "Who alone has good reason to lie his way out of reality? He who suffers from it. But to suffer from reality is to be a piece of reality that has come to grief."[22]

The morbid character of Christian concepts is not, as it might seem, an indication of the Christian's willingness to confront the harshest reality. The only psychologically convincing explanation, says Nietzsche, is that these concepts somehow offer a world interpretation that is more palatable than the more obvious one suggested by the reality we confront. Let us now return to *Daybreak* to see how Christian morality functions to offer what Nietzsche takes to be an escapist interpretation of life.

Christian Morality as a Quest for Safety

Nietzsche concerns himself in *Daybreak* with the motive of Christian morality. This concern is novel, for even to ask the question of motive presupposes that this morality is ultimately optional, something that human beings can do without. In his taunting challenge to Christians, Nietzsche suggests more directly that Christian morality is optional:

> They owe it to themselves to try for once the experiment of living for some length of time without Christianity, they owe it to *their faith* in this way, for once to sojourn "in the wilderness"—if only to win for themselves the right to a voice on the question of whether Christianity is necessary... Only if you are driven back, not by homesickness but by *judgment* on the basis of a rigorous *comparison*, will your homecoming possess any significance![23]

The motive Nietzsche sees behind the Christian moral worldview, despite the depressing stance implicit in its categories, is the Christian's desire for self-protection.[24] But how does the Christian moral framework function to satisfy this desire? In *Daybreak*, Nietzsche isolates a number of aspects of Christian moral thinking, and the mythology behind it, that serve to foster the believer's sense of personal security.

One aspect of Christianity that serves this function is its basis for self-escape in the mythology of oneness with God. In a section entitled "Flight from Oneself," Nietzsche claims that a gloomy disposition toward oneself inspires many to seek to "dissolve into something 'outside.' " For the Christian, God provides assurance that such a longing can be satisfied. Belief in God fortifies Christians who long for self-escape by assuring them that one can lose oneself in God and "become wholly at one with him."[25]

A second characteristic of Christianity that enhances the believer's sense of safety, according to Nietzsche, is its assurance that one can take a short cut to perfection. "Christianity wanted to free men from the burden of the demands of morality by, as it supposed, showing a *shorter way to perfection*. . . . It was an error . . . —yet nonetheless a great comfort to the exhausted and despairing in the wilderness."[26] The idea that Christianity is a religion of quick moral results might strike the reader as strange, particularly if he or she is well versed in such scriptural maxims as "It is easier for a camel to go through the eye of a needle than for a rich man to enter the kingdom of heaven."[27] Without discounting the rhetoric of Christianity's difficulties,[28] Nietzsche contends that Christianity makes the question of salvation unrealistically simple. Christianity does this by interpreting one's status in regard to salvation in terms of absolutes and unconditionals. With the concept of eternal salvation and eternal damnation, it "brought into life a quite novel and limitless *perilousness*, and therewith quite novel securities, pleasures, recreations and evaluations of all things."[29]

In one sense the Christian concepts of heaven and hell exacerbate the individual's sense of risk in life. The risk is that one will suffer torment endlessly, a threat which, to

51

most imaginations, sounds like a worse fate than simple extinction in death. But there is a trade-off for admitting this terrifying prospect into one's imagination, Nietzsche claims. Just as one can be eternally damned, according to the Christian doctrine, one can also be eternally saved. Salvation is achieved, when it is achieved, absolutely—and the route to salvation is also clear. The attainment of salvation depends also on one's unconditional surrender, or lack thereof, to a single deity. One's standing with God is the only determinant of personal salvation. Turning to God with unconditional trust is therefore the only course of true self-interest.

The formula of unconditional surrender to God as the recipe for unqualified, limitless happiness strikes Nietzsche as an offer of a short cut. It suggests that a single transformation of one's moral orientation can transform one's destiny from eternal suffering to eternal bliss.

> In the sphere of morality Christianity knows only the miracle: the sudden change in all value-judgements, the sudden abandonment of all customary modes of behavior, the sudden irresistible inclination for new persons and objects. It conceives this phenomenon to be the work of God and calls it a rebirth, it accords it a unique, incomparable value: everything else which calls itself morality but has no reference to this miracle thus becomes a matter of indifference to the Christian.

For reasons that we shall discuss more fully below, Nietzche views the Christian "rebirth" to the path of salvation with skepticism.

> What such a sudden, irrational and irresistible reversal, such an exchange of the profoundest wretchedness for the profoundest well-being, signifies physiologically (whether it is perhaps a masked epilepsy?)—that must

be determined by the psychiatrists, who have indeed
plenty of occasion to observe similar "miracles" (in the
form of homicidal mania, for example, or suicide
mania). The relatively "*more pleasant consequences*" in
the case of the Christian make no essential difference.[30]

Whatever one may think of its physiological significance,
the notion of rebirth clearly signifies assurance to the Christian. It promises that eternal bliss is attainable and that a
single spiritual step is sufficient to gain it. This promise is
what Nietzsche refers to when he claims that Christianity
promises a shortcut.

A third aspect of Christianity that offers security to the
Christian is a corollary to this promise. Along with the offer
of eternal happiness as a reward for devotion, the Christian
is offered a vicarious sense of power by virtue of his or her
relationship to God.

> "Enthusiastic devotion" "sacrifice of oneself"—these are
> the catchwords of your morality. . . . By devoting your-
> selves with enthusiasm and making a sacrifice of your-
> selves you enjoy the ecstatic thought of henceforth
> being at one with the powerful being, whether a god or
> a man, to whom you dedicate yourselves: you revel in
> the feeling of his power, to which your very sacrifice is
> an additional witness. The truth of the matter is that
> you only *seem* to sacrifice yourselves. . . . In short, it is
> you who want intoxication and excess.[31]

Alliance with God means alliance with the most powerful
being. By forging this alliance through devotion, the Christian is able to overcome vicariously the insecurities and
displeasures of his or her limitations as a finite individual.

A fourth aspect of Christianity that serves as a means
of self-protection is also a corollary to the concept of the
immortal soul and the vision of attainable eternal salvation.

53

SCCCC - LIBRARY   WITHDRAWN
4601 Mid Rivers Mall Drive
St. Peters, MO 63376

Quite simply, Christianity promises an escape from death. Nietzsche discusses the doctrine of personal immortality as egotistical, in the extreme. In a section entitled "To the Dreamers of Immortality," he mocks the Christian's arrogance in this regard:

> So you want this lovely consciousness of yourself *to last forever?* Is that not immodest? Are you not mindful of all the other things which would then be obliged to *endure you* to all eternity, as they have endured you up to now with a more than Christian patience? Or do you think to inspire them with an everlasting sense of pleasure at your existence? A single immortal man on earth would be enough to drive everything else on earth to a universal rage for death and suicide out of *satiety with him!*[32]

More obliquely, Nietzsche suggests that the belief in "the absolute importance of eternal *personal* salvation"[33] is ultimately an expression of cowardice."*Final argument of the brave.*—'There are snakes in these bushes.'—Good, I shall go into the bushes and kill them.—'But perhaps you will be their victim, and not they yours!'—What do I matter![34]

The Christian Worldview Versus the Tragic

Already it is apparent how antithetical the promises of Christianity are to the tragic vision of life discussed in Chapter 1. The tragic worldview confronts what it takes to be several dark truths about human reality: (1) the individual is essentially vulnerable to catastrophic suffering, which cannot be mitigated by intellectual reinterpretation; (2) the individual will inevitably die; and (3) no effort of the individual can secure him or her from his or her essential vulnerability and mortality. The Christian worldview, on Nietzsche's account, denies these premises of the tragic perspective. According to the Christian worldview, the in-

BGGC · LIBRARY
4601 Mid America Blvd
St. Louis, MO 63129

dividual is not essentially vulnerable to tragic suffering; whatever suffering one might confront in life can be cured by the bliss of the afterlife. Because the personal soul is immortal, the individual who dies merely appears to die. Many Christian denominations—including the Lutheran faith, in which Nietzsche was raised—argue that faith rather than good works is crucial to salvation; nevertheless, the implication is that the individual can, at least passively, give himself or herself over to unconditional faith in God, thereby directing his or her own efforts toward the attainment of salvation.[35] The observations about life that are the starting point of what Nietzsche calls the tragic worldview are simply denied by Christianity.

So far I have cited four aspects of Christianity that make it serve as a vehicle for the believer's achievment of a sense of personal security: (1) it provides a means of selfescape through fostering a sense of oneness with God; (2) it promises a shortcut to perfection and complete happiness in the concept of rebirth; (3) it provides a derivative sense of power by allowing the Christian to associate himself or herself with an omnipotent God; and (4) it promises personal immortality and endless bliss for the devout. These offers to the believer depend, Nietzsche claims, on fictional concepts—"God," "eternal life," "immortality of the soul," and "rebirth"—and on believers accepting these fictions as true because the offers are attractive. The motivation that inspires believers to adopt such gloomy concepts as "sin" and "eternal punishment" remain to be indicated. The connection between Christianity's "uglier" concepts and the quest for personal safety is evident if we consider two further aspects of Christianity that offer protection to the believer.

The Concept of Guilt as Antitragic

One of these aspects is that Christianity allows the believer to deflect his or her sense of personal failure. It does this by providing the notion of "guilt" as a basic interpretive concept for analyzing the situation in which one feels a failure.

"Guilt is always sought wherever there is failure; for failure brings with it a depression of spirits against which the sole remedy is instinctively applied: a new excitation of the *feeling of power*—and and this is to be discovered in the *condemnation* of the 'guilty.' "[36]The concept of guilt allows one to feel superior to those labeled guilty, and the person who feels a failure is the one most likely to crave an easy route to a sense of personal superiority. Nietzsche discusses this mechanism of deriving a sense of superiority from one's stance in moral judgment as an expression of vindictiveness.

> Here is a morality which rests entirely on the *drive to distinction*—do not think too highly of it! For what kind of drive is that and what thought lies behind it? We want to make the sight of us *painful* to another and to awaken in him the feeling of envy and of his own impotence and degradation.... There stands a great artist: the pleasure he anticipated in the envy of his defeated rivals allowed his powers no rest until he had become great—how many bitter moments has his becoming great not cost the souls of others! The chastity of the nun: with what punitive eyes it looks into the faces of women who live otherwise! How much joy in revenge there is in these eyes!

Far from being a manifestation of the delicacy of conscience, Nietzsche argues, a morality that interprets human behavior in terms of guilt is really an indication of joy in cruelty."The theme is brief, the variations that might be played upon it might be endless but hardly tedious—for it is still a far too paradoxical and almost pain-inducing novelty that the morality of distinction is in its ultimate foundation pleasure in refined cruelty." [37]

The Christian is willing to interpret human behavior in terms of the concepts of sin and guilt because these concepts serve to foster a sense of personal superiority. The gain resulting from use of these concepts does not stem directly from applying them to one's own behavior. Instead it results from one's use of these same concepts to describe the behavior of others. The person who adheres to Christian morality is, with every successful avoidance of sin, able to feel superior to those who "give in to temptation." He or she is also able to gain this sense of moral superiority through sheer passivity, simply by *not* doing the things that have been designated as sinful.

Although the Christian may claim to abhor his or her own sinfulness, Nietzsche finds these claims suspicious. The Christian's real motive, in his view, is the desire to justify himself or herself to others. The Christian's magnification of his or her own faults is simultaneously a magnification of the faults of others, and this latter magnification is so agreeable that it affords a hook by which Christianity gains acceptance for its doctrine of human sinfulness.

The concepts of sin and guilt, Nietzsche goes on to argue, are expressions of human brutality that we should make effort to surpass.

> What a relief it would be for the general feeling of life if, together with the belief in guilt, one also got rid of the old instinct for revenge, and even regarded it as a piece of prudence for the promotion of happiness to join Christianity in blessing one's enemies and *to do good* to those who have offended us! Let us do away with the concept *sin*—and let us quickly send after it the concept of *punishment*. [38]

Not only does the Christian view that behavior should be understood in terms of guilt foster deceitful smugness on the part of the believer; it also promotes a sense of qualmlessness in inflicting suffering in the context of administering punishment. Nietzsche is not arguing that Christians, in particular, are responsible for the institutions of punishment that are established by the criminal code, but he does maintain that in promoting an outlook on human behavior that focuses on guilt, Christianity fosters the spirit of retaliation that institutions of punishment traditionally reflect. Nietzsche contends that all punishment practices are motivated by the spirit that fuels a lynch mob. "He who is punished is never he who performs the deed," argues Nietzsche. "He is always the scapegoat."[39]

Punishment serves no positive function in Nietzsche's view. It neither expiates crime[40] nor moves the criminal to conscience.[41] He concludes that the real function of punishment is to gratify those who take part in afflicting it. But this purpose expresses and feeds the spirit of revenge. Punishment and the concept of guilt should therefore be abolished."Men of application and goodwill assist in this one work: to take the concept of punishment which has overrun the whole world and root it out! There exists no more noxious weed!"[42]Insofar as Christianity promotes the concept of guilt in its moral outlook, it feeds vindictiveness in believers and justifies attitudes toward other people that are the reverse of Christian compassion."Misfortune and guilt—Christianity has placed these two things on a balance: so that, when misfortune consequent on guilt is great, even now the greatness of the guilt itself is still involuntarily measured by it."[43]

Christian morality deflects the believer's sense of personal failure through its use of the concepts of guilt and sin. The smugness, vindictiveness, and punitive spirit that these concepts encourage are among what Nietzsche sees as the pernicious consequences of the Christian moral worldview, which will be our next focus. But first, we should observe one further aspect of Christianity that, in Nietzsche's understanding, offers security to the believer. This aspect is Christianity's ability to justify a timid spirit in morality. One need not be a moral hero or an acrobat of spiritual exertion in order to be, by Christian standards, a good person.[44] One need only exercise the feeble spirit of sympathy that is described with the expression "love of neighbor." Nietzsche contends that even Christianity's high evaluation of such sympathy is motivated by a concealed yearning for personal safety.

> Behind the basic principle of the current moral fashion: "moral actions are actions performed out of sympathy for others," I see the social effect of timidity hiding behind an intellectual mask: it desires, first and foremost, that *all the dangers* which life once held should be removed from it, and that *everyone* should assist in this with all his might.[45]

The compassion urged by Christianity is in practice entirely self-referential and selfish. In a discussion of the concept of *Mitleid*, variously translated as "compassion" or "pity," Nietzsche comments:

> The truth is: in the feeling of pity . . . we are, to be sure, not consciously thinking of ourself but are doing so *very strongly unconsciously*. . . . An accident which happens to another offends us: it would make us aware of our impotence, and perhaps of our cowardice, if we did not go to assist him. Or it brings with it in itself a diminution of our honour in the eyes of others or in our own eyes. Or an accident and suffering incurred by another constitutes a signpost to some danger to us; and it can have a painful effect upon us simply as a token of

> human vulnerability and fragility in general. We repel
> this kind of pain and offence and requite it through an
> act of pity... But it is *only this suffering of our own*
> which we get rid of when we perform deeds of pity.[46]

The morality of sympathy benefits one's sense of security
and potency in the world. It also makes a sense of personal
effectuality compatible with minimal exertion and avoidance of life's dangers. Christian morality, despite its claims,
makes it easy to fulfill the requirements for being a good
person. In Nietzsche's view it is the morality of the me-
diocre. Little exertion is demanded, and the accomplish-
ments that are demanded have the recompense of making
one feel less vulnerable than others.

The aspects of the Christian moral worldview that cater
to the individual's desire for safety provide a clear hook for
gaining acceptance of its worldview. As noted in Chapter
2, Nietzsche considers the desire for safety an understandable response to the insecurity that is inherent to human
existence. Nevertheless, he views Christianity's palliatives
to be ultimately harmful to vitality, happiness, and humane
interaction with others.

We have already seen that the Christian worldview denies the basic insights of the tragic worldview that
Nietzsche takes to be fundamental to the individual's understanding of his or her actual position with respect to the
world. This denial of tragedy's basic insights involves com-
mitment to beliefs that are basically false, but this is not
Nietzsche's primary objection to this denial.[47] Nietzsche's
basic concern is that the threatening character of life will
inevitably intrude upon the individual who believes that
his or her doctrine has brought personal safety. The believer's response will mostly likely be continued tenacious belief—but this amounts to a denial of reality, which will
render the believer all the more mentally inflexible and

vulnerable to disorienting occurrences. In worse circumstances, the believer may be so shattered by his or her confrontation with the cruel character of life that the believer will despair entirely, nihilistically concluding that life is not really worthwhile.

OTHER PERNICIOUS EFFECTS OF THE CHRISTIAN MORAL WORLDVIEW

The conflict of orientation between Christian doctrine and tragic insight is fundamental to Nietzsche's objection to the Christian moral worldview. Because this conflict will be at least the implicit focus of many of Zarathustra's comments, it should be prominent in our attention when we attempt to make sense of *Zarathustra.* But Nietzsche and his character Zarathustra also contend that Christianity harms the believer even before tragic experience provokes a crisis. And so, before closing this discussion of his objections to Christian morality, I turn to Nietzsche's arguments that Christian belief damages the believer's ability to navigate in the larger world. We shall look at five ways in which Christianity, in Nietzsche's interpretation, does this. According to Nietzsche, Christianity is pernicious because it (1) promotes, on a nonsuperficial level, the believer's sense of failure; (2) whets the believer's spirit of cruelty and revenge; (3) necessitates dissimulation and dishonesty; (4) promotes hatred of life in the world; and (5) inculcates a false view of individuality.

Christianity Promotes a Sense of Failure

The claim that Christianity promotes the believer's sense of failure may seem to contradict the earlier assertion that Christianity helps the believer to deflect a sense of failure, but these claims are not incompatible. As Nietzsche sees it, both are true, and their conjunction creates a more alarming picture of Christianity than either would convey individually.

How, on Nietzsche's view, does Christianity promote the believer's sense of failure? It does so by establishing standards of morality that are impossible to fulfill. The moral exemplar, Christ, is designated as a model whom the believer cannot fully imitate. The Christian law of love, on the other hand, proposes a goal of absolute self-denial and unselfishness, a goal that is incompatible with even the minimal degree of self-interest that is essential to continued existence as a self. Because no one can obey the law of love perfectly, the believer is set up to believe he or she is a moral failure. And this is how Christianity instills the motive for throwing oneself unconditionally into a spirit of submission to God.

> In the New Testament, the canon of virtue, of the ful-
> filled law, is set up: but in such a way that it is the
> canon of *impossible virtue:* those still *striving* after mo-
> rality are in the face of such a canon to learn to feel
> themselves ever *more distant* from their goal, they are
> to *despair* of virtue, and in the end *throw themselves on
> the bosom* of the merciful.[48]

Nietzsche sees appeal to God's mercy as an abdication of assertive effort to direct one's life. This condition weakens the believer's general state of vitality. But the impossible goal of Christian morality has a more drastic adverse effect. It enforces on the believer an interpretation of one's own activity and the activity of others that judges human effort in general to fail inevitably.

> How often the individual is advised to set himself a
> goal that he cannot reach and is beyond his strength, so
> that he will at least reach that which his strength is ca-
> pable of *when put to the farthest stretch!* But is this

> really so desirable? ... When as a result one sees noth-
> ing but struggling athletes, tremendous efforts, and no-
> where a laurel-crowned and triumphant victor, does
> that not envelop the world in a grey veil of *failure*?[49]

If he or she takes the Christian moral stance seriously, the Christian's reflection on his or her personal moral efforts and on human effort in general leads to the depressing conclusion that one is bound to fail. The thrust of Nietzsche's claim is perhaps more applicable to the doctrine of Lutheranism, the brand of Christianity with which Nietzsche was most familiar, than with that of certain other Christian denominations. Lutheranism emphasizes the ineffectuality of human effort.[50] But Nietzsche believes that the basic Christian doctrines of an unfulfillable law of love and the sinful imperfection of human beings result inevitably in the believer's sense of personal failure.

By promoting a sense of failure, Christianity establishes the believer's need for its palliatives. And this explains why it is not contradictory to assert simultaneously that Christianity promotes a sense of failure and that it provides means for deflecting this sense. Because the Christian is forced by Christian morality to feel inadequate, he or she is motivated to deflect this feeling by looking for guilt in others. And the orientation that judges the moral terrain in terms of guilt is precisely that of the Christian moral perspective. Christianity provokes a sense of failure and thereby motivates the believer to analyze others, as well as himself or herself, in terms of guilt.

This analysis may still sound circular. Am I saying that Nietzsche argues that Christianity makes the believer feel inadequate and that as a result he or she is motivated to feel inadequate? No. The motivation that is provided when Christianity fosters a sense of failure is the desire to deflect this feeling. Christianity also offers a means to satisfy this desire; it suggests that it is often possible to blame someone for the problems one perceives. Christianity teaches its believers to look for guilt wherever there is pain or difficulty. Its conceptual framework thus imposes an interpretive overlay of sordidness on much human behavior.

What begins as a sense of the inadequacy of one's own and all human efforts—a feeling that Christianity's "law of love" forces on the believer's attention—is quietly transformed to a feeling that oneself and others are *guilty*. Christian doctrine interprets human behavior generally by reference to the concept of guilt. It also endorses interpretations that utilize the concept of guilt as providing the correct perspective on one's feelings of inadequacy, although it helped force these feelings on the believer's awareness in the first place. The Christian moral worldview creates a self-perpetuating cycle of feeling a failure and looking for guilt.

Christianity Promotes Vindictiveness

The concept "guilt" imaginatively amplifies one's sense of personal inadequacy, but the interpretation of one's own behavior in terms of guilt also ensures interpretation of the behavior of others by the same measure, as we have discussed. Because the psychological gain to be made by focusing on the guilt of others is high—increasingly high, as one feels more guilty oneself—the Christian is motivated to attend to "guilt" in others. It is perhaps not startling that Nietzsche claims that Christianity has "invented the repellent flaunting of sin...introduced into the world sinfulness *one has lyingly made up.*"[51]

From the vision of others' guilt that the Christian view of one's own guilt motivates, a spirit of vindictiveness is a short step. What Nietzsche takes to be the facility of Christian morality for prompting subtle cruelty and revenge in the believer's attitudes toward others has been discussed above. This propensity of Christianity is a second ground for Nietzsche's insistence that Christian moral belief is pernicious.

Christianity Promotes Dissimulation

A third objection turns Christian morality back on itself. Christianity appears to praise honesty and truthfulness, but Nietzsche contends that Christian belief itself provides incitement to dishonesty and dissimulation. By being dishonest about itself, it encourages dishonesty. It claims to offer unchanging truth, and yet it spread by adapting itself to vernacular, heathen customs.[52] It claims unabashedly that the truth of its doctrine can be deduced from the courage of its early adherents, but that claim is undisguisedly groundless.[53] And it makes doctrinal claims that all evidence seems to refute, for example, the passage, "But seek ye first the kingdom of God, and his righteousness, and all these things shall be added unto you."[54] Christianity's misrepresentations of itself and the false claims of its doctrines encourage Christians to be equally dishonest at least with regard to the grounds of their beliefs.

More important, however, is the fact that Christianity's judgmental perspective on human conduct itself promotes dishonest appraisals of oneself and others. Its moral categories for interpreting conduct provide both the incentive and the means for dissimulating concealment of one's real motivations. The dissonance between the manifest doctrines of love and compassion, and the vindictiveness spawned by Christian moral theory, can be intellectually navigated only by the overt denial of the latter. Christianity consigns to unconsciousness the vindictiveness that it fosters by offering self-righteous ways of thinking of one's pursuits. In so doing, it functions in a manner that is consistent with its other efforts to make the world appear less threatening than it is. A veneer of politeness and concern for others unifies the style of "Christian conduct," but the concealed purpose of this veneer is to camouflage the less charming impulses behind it.[55]

Christianity Promotes Hatred of Life

A fourth objectionable consequence of Christian moral belief is its promotion of dissatisfaction with the basic character of being a human being. By denigrating the passions and objecting to all motives of self-interest, Christian morality urges the believer to take objection to essential components of his makeup, and this, says Nietzsche, is calamitous. "The passions become evil and malicious if they are regarded as evil and malicious . . . Is it not dreadful to make necessary and regularly recurring sensations into a source of inner misery, and in this way to want to make inner misery a necessary and regularly recurring phenomenon *in every human being?*" Taking sexual passion as an example, Nietzsche suggests the extent to which Christianity's antipathy toward humanity's passional nature has introduced ugliness into the world:

> The sexual sensations have this in common with the sensations of sympathy and worship, that one person, by doing what pleases him, gives pleasure to another person—such benevolent arrangements are not to be found so very often in nature! And to calumniate such an arrangement and to ruin it through associating it with a bad conscience![56]

Elsewhere, Nietzsche extends this point to claim that this attitude of Christianity indicates a general antipathy toward life. "It was Christianity, with its *ressentiment* against life at the bottom of its heart, which first made something unclean of sexuality: it threw *filth* on the origin, on the presupposition of our life."[57]

Christianity encourages habits of hostility toward our fundamental makeup, but these are fortunately remediable. Discussing his position that altruistic actions are of the same sort as egoistic actions, Nietzsche admits that the hitherto valued actions, those of the former category, will probably be performed less often as a consequence of the adoption of his view.

> But our counter-reckoning is that we shall restore to men their goodwill toward the actions decried as egoistic and restore to these actions their *value—we shall deprive them of their bad conscience!* And since they have hitherto been by far the most frequent action, and will continue to be so for all future time, we thus remove from the entire aspect of action and life its *evil appearance!* This is a very significant result! When man no longer regards himself as evil he ceases to be so![58]

Christianity Distorts Individuality

A fifth objectionable consequence of Christian moral doctrine is that it inculcates a faulty view of the nature of individual existence. We have already observed that Christian moral doctrine denies fundamental tragic insights that Nietzsche takes to be essential to a genuine perspective on the individual's status in the world. Christian morality also lies about its own relationship to the individual's well-being. While offering imaginary rewards that seem to respect and benefit the individual directly, Christianity actually urges the individual to abdicate whatever characteristics he has that are genuinely individual. Christian moral theory ultimately offers bribes for conformity, and delusional bribes at that.

> *Insofar* as the individual is seeking happiness, one ought not to tender him any prescriptions as to the path to happiness: for individual happiness springs from one's own

67

unknown laws, and prescriptions from without can only
obstruct and hinder it.—The prescriptions called "moral"
are in truth directed against individuals and are in no
way aimed at promoting their happiness.[59]

Christian morality, like all communally prescribed moralities, promotes behavior that accords with convention.[60]
It is, in other words, finally a morality of habits, specifically
habits that resist individual originality. "The critic of customs" is "the antithesis of the moral man," and he is treated
as such by those who subscribe to the Christian moral
worldview.[61] "What is wanted—whether this is admitted or
not—is nothing less than a fundamental remoulding, indeed
weakening and abolition of the *individual*."[62] The social
consequences of this attitude are negative. It harms the
vitality of the individual who is naturally at odds with custom,[63] and it promotes stagnation of communities and
nations.[64]

The Christian moral worldview, besides obscuring the
actual nature of individual existence, denigrates the means
by which human beings can take satisfaction in their individual characters—that of utilizing them to have some
impact on the larger world. By promoting conformity, the
Christian moral worldview precludes the possibility of the
believer's taking pride in his or her uniqueness or unusual
achievements. In this way the Christian moral worldview
helps lay the groundwork for deep doubts about the value
of life—the condition Nietzsche calls "nihilism"—if ever
the believer should falter in his or her faith that God is a
"bulwark never-failing."[65]

CONCLUSION

Daybreak is primarily a critical work that urges the
abolition of much of the conventional Christian moral

worldview. Nietzsche acknowledges both the difficulty and the risk involved in the cultural and psychological transformations he is advocating,[66] but he suggests the positive consequences of embarking on this endeavor. Moving beyond Christianity might force us to look at the tragic character of existence, which we have conventionally veiled from ourselves. But such a move would also bring in its wake the realization that our lives are full of promise in a way that was also obscured by Christian moral doctrine, with its simplistic analysis of human action in terms of sin. With the elimination of the principles of Christian moral evaluation, we might be able to interpret our lives as pregnant with options.[67] "There is absolutely no eternal necessity which decrees that every guilt will be atoned and paid for," says Nietzsche near the end of the book. "It is not *things,* but opinions *about things that have absolutely no existence,* which have so deranged mankind!"[68]

Daybreak serves as a kind of invitation to explore the unconventional possibilities of nonmoral thinking and pursuing a life that is informed by this different kind of thought. Nietzsche's assessment that the people of his culture should wake up to these possibilities and his judgment that tragic insights reveal the actual condition of the human being are the central observations of his own worldview as it was formulated when he set out to write *Thus Spoke Zarathustra.* Having gained a sense of the world as Nietzsche sees it, it is time to become acquainted with the fictional hero that Nietzsche inserts into it.

4   Why Zarathustra Speaks

With sounds our love dances on many-hued rainbows.[1]

HAROLD ALDERMAN observes that the very title of *Thus Spoke Zarathustra* indicates that the book is concerned with communication.[2] Zarathustra, it tells us, is someone who speaks. And the first section of the book reinforces this picture of Zarathustra as a speaker. The first of his actions that we behold is an act of speech, and in fact an act of speech about speaking. He addresses the sun as a comrade in the need to communicate: "You great star, what would your happiness be had you not those for whom you shine?" And Zarathustra throughout the book is in the role of a speaker. Even at the end of the book, having given up those few disciples he had hopes in, he continues to speak, addressing the sun once again. "Rise now, rise, thou great noon!"[3]

This very frame of Zarathustra's speeches should suggest something peculiar about Zarathustra's role as a speaker. We observe that he speaks whether or not he has a human audience. Often too, sections portraying Zarathustra in solitary reflection end with the refrain "Thus spoke Zarathustra."[4] The presence of an audience appears not to be crucial to the speaking that the book's title brings into focus. The book's subtitle, furthermore, reinforces this observation. Zarathustra's reported speeches, we are told, constitute "A Book for All and None."

The countergestures involved in both the complete title

and in the monologues are problematic, and they raise the question of authorial motive. We are told before opening the book that Zarathustra speaks. But *why* does he speak? And, more fundamental, why does Nietzsche make Zarathustra speak?

These questions do not admit of simple answers. Zarathustra's motive as a speaker undergoes transformation almost as soon as he ends his prayer to the sun. And Nietzsche's authorial intentions are problematic in a number of respects. What does he mean in general terms when he addresses this volume to all and to none? And what kind of story is he telling with this strangely formed work of literature—part parody, part fictional biography, and, by Nietzsche's own account, a kind of tragedy? Finally, why does Nietzsche choose a fictional form for this book? This chapter considers these questions sequentially. I shall begin with a discussion of the character Zarathustra's developing motivation through the Prologue.

ZARATHUSTRA'S MOTIVATION: THE PROLOGUE

The Opening Invocation

Zarathustra's opening invocation to the sun, gives us insight into Zarathustra's motive as a communicator. Having found wisdom and happiness in his solitary life in a mountain cave, he dedicates himself to communicating his discoveries to others.

> Behold I am weary of my wisdom, like a bee that has gathered too much honey; I need hands outstretched to receive it.
>
> I would give away and distribute, until the wise among men find joy once again in their folly, and the poor in their riches.[5]

He calls himself "the cup that wants to overflow," that "wants to become empty again."[6] And this indicates Zarathustra's motivation. The project that the book will chronicle is Zarathustra's project of sharing what he most values with others. In this respect, Zarathustra parallels the philosopher of Plato's Myth of the Cave, whose descent for the purpose of sharing his insight is parodied by Zarathustra's venture.

The parody of the Platonic Myth in the opening section is worth probing at this juncture, for it can help us gain perspective on what Zarathustra is up to, and also on what Nietzsche has in mind in presenting him to us. To those familiar with *The Birth of Tragedy*, the allusion to Plato is informative. In conjunction with the material from that work considered in Chapter 2, Nietzsche attacks Socrates, casting him as an emblem for the antitragic perspective on life. Socrates, in Nietzsche's view, was the primary cause of the death of Attic tragedy. He was the originator of the optimistic worldview built on the beliefs that thought can save us from the tragic in life and that every perplexity can be made rationalizable.[7] This worldview, Nietzsche claims, has come to dominate the West, and as the innovator behind this development, Socrates is "the one turning point and vortex of so-called world history."[8]

One would expect that Nietzsche's initial allusion to Plato in *Thus Spoke Zarathustra* would be continuous with his earlier attach on Socrates. And this is exactly what we discover. The parallel between Zarathustra and the philosopher of Plato's Myth of the Cave casts Zarathustra as a rival of Socrates and an opponent of his worldview. While Zarathustra is like Plato's mythic character in emerging from a cave into sunlight and in contemplating the communication of his insights, the other points of resonance between them are primarily points of contrast.

Zarathustra's original flight from his former home did

not amount to a flight from a cave into the sun, but from a valley illuminated by the sun to his own cave. Zarathustra's cave is high in the mountains, much closer to the sun than is the valley of the community. Zarathustra's home symbolizes the dark, Dionysian powers of the earth, but at the same time it represents a closer point of access to the sun, the source of Apollonian insight. It symbolizes a rejection of the Platonic Myth's opposition of Apollonian rationality and earthly existence, and it stands as an indication that Zarathustra's home, where he is most truly himself, is built of both Apollonian and Dionysian elements.

Zarathustra's insight is born in this place, where he understands his place in the world through both Apollonian and Dionysian modes of experience. At the beginning of the book, Zarathustra is moved by this insight to return to the community of other human beings. The Apollonian and Dionysian modes of self-understanding, each of which relates the individual to his or her world, together inspire Zarathustra with a feeling of love that wants to express itself actively.

In *The Birth of Tragedy*, Nietzsche portrays Socrates as a thinker who does not sufficiently respect the Dionysian character of life and who believes that the truly terrible in life can be "cured" through rational thought. But Nietzsche makes much of another side of Socrates, a side revealed in Socrates' final days as they are reported in Plato's *Phaedo*. In that dialogue, Socrates tells his disciples that he has had a recurrent apparition in a dream which, as Nietzsche reports it has "always said the same thing to him: 'Socrates, practice music.' "[9] Until his final few days, Socrates had believed that this apparition was encouraging him to continue the philosophizing he was already doing, philosophy being the highest work of the Muses. But Socrates, on the edge of death, as he is portrayed in the *Phaedo,* begins to doubt the correctness of his interpretation:

> Ever since my trial, while the festival of the god has been delaying my execution, I have felt that perhaps it might be this popular form of the art that the dream intended me to practice, in which case I ought to practice it and not disobey. I thought it would be safer not to take my departure before I had cleared my conscience by writing some verses in honor of the god whose festival it was. When I had finished my hymn, I reflected that a poet, if he is to be worthy of the name, ought to work on imaginative themes, not descriptive ones, and I was not good at inventing stories. So I availed myself of some of Aesop's fables... and I versified the first of them that suggested themselves.[10]

The god to whom Socrates wrote a hymn was Apollo, yet Nietzsche takes this whole incident as an indication that Socrates was dimly aware that his rational gospel was not the last word on reality. Although Socrates' musical efforts appear feeble, he was nonetheless making an unprecedented concession to Dionysus, the god of music. In *The Birth of Tragedy,* Nietzsche concludes his discussion of this with the suggestion that there could perhaps be a "musical Socrates," a philosopher who was balanced in appreciating both Apollonian and Dionysian perspectives.

Zarathustra begins his mission as a philosophical teacher in a manner reminiscent of Socrates—he addresses the sun, the physical representation of Apollo, with a hymn of praise. From the very first, then, Zarathustra is identified in Nietzsche's portrait as "the Socrates who practices music," the paradigmatic art of Dionysus. Zarathustra is the philosopher who begins his mission at just the point at which the mission of the historical Socrates of the Platonic

dialogue ends.[11] Socrates ends his mission with a mild suspicion that the Apollonian project needs a Dionysian com-
plement. Zarathustra begins with a recognition of the
importance of the Apollonian/Dionysian synthesis, and this
recognition is the basis of the message, that he is moved to
communicate to others.

As a character in his own right, however, Zarathustra
is motivated in a complex manner. While his description
of his aim at times suggests abundance and gratuitous generosity, it also hints at an underlying need on Zarathustra's
part. In his opening statement, where he asks the sun what
its happiness would be without those for whom it shines,
Zarathustra suggests that this happiness would be meaningless if uncommunicated. And he goes on, as we have
seen, to compare the sun's metaphorical predicament with
his own. In a straightforward way, then, the first section of
the Prologue indicates a sense in which the book that follows is, as the subtitle claims, "A Book for All and None."
Zarathustra offers his message to everyone, and yet in a
sense his speaking is not *for* those to whom he speaks, but
for himself.

Zarathustra's Audience

Almost immediately, however, this extreme formulation of Zarathustra's perspective on his audience becomes
problematic. Despite the nebulousness of Zarathustra's
conception of his audience, any audience that he can address
will be composed of a finite number of specific human individuals. Much of the Prologue following the invocation
is concerned with the question of who Zarathustra's appropriate audience is. It addresses this question by depicting
Zarathustra, who is nearly bursting with the message he
wants to communicate, in various encounters with an as-
sortment of other people.

The first encounter occurs in the second section, where

76

Zarathustra, meets a saintly hermit. The hermit has stopped interacting with other human beings, he claims, because he needs only his animals for company, and God above to praise. Zarathustra recognizes that the saint's sense of self-sufficiency stems from his belief in a worldview that Zarathustra does not share. "Could it be possible?" he asks himself after leaving the saint. "This old saint in the forest has not yet heard anything of this, that *God is dead!*"[12]

The abruptness of this announcement of God's death, couched as it is in a subordinate clause, is startling. But this grammar is pointed. Zarathustra takes the idea that God is no longer a living force in the world completely for granted. The death of God is not the culmination of Zarathustra's gospel, but its starting point.

Because Zarathustra believes that God is no longer a living force in the world, he sees the saint as leading a life that is uncommunicated and meaningless. The saint, however, is immune from doubts about his life's meaning because he believes that he is heard by God. Zarathustra sees this and says to the saint, "What could I have to give you? But let me go quickly lest I take something from you!"[13]

The community that Zarathustra seeks to address, unlike the saint, has put aside belief in God, whether consciously or not. Zarathustra meets this community in the third section of the Prologue, where it becomes obvious that even among those who share the atheism of his worldview, he is not going to find communication an easy project. Filled with enthusiasm for sharing his insights, Zarathustra bursts into a crowd and begins a speech on his vision of the meaningful life. "*I teach you the overman*," he begins abruptly.[14] The crowd, to his disappointment, assumes that Zarathustra is part of the show for which it has gathered, and it understands his speech as a bombastic prelude to the arrival of the show's tightrope walker.[15] "When Zarathustra had spoken thus, one of the people cried: 'Now we have heard enough about the tightrope walker; now let us see him too!"[16]

Zarathustra's Message

Zarathustra's speech fails to communicate to the crowd, but it forecasts the basic themes of his gospel for the benefit of the reader. Expanding on the idea of the overman, the speech directly addresses the question of the meaning of life in an atheistic context. Zarathustra explains the importance of the idea of the overman in terms of meaning: "The overman is the meaning of the earth. Let your will say: the overman *shall be* the meaning of the earth!" That the meaning of the earth is to be understood in the absence of God becomes evident in the sentence that immediately follows. "I beseech you, my brothers, *remain faithful to the earth*, and do not believe those who speak to you of otherworldly hopes!"[17] Zarathustra elaborates on the timeliness of this message. "Once the sin against God was the greatest sin; but God died, and these sinners died with him. To sin against the earth is now the most dreadful thing, and to esteem the entrails of the unknowable higher than the meaning of the earth."[18] God is dead, Zarathustra reiterates to the crowd. And yet God's death should not be mourned as the loss of meaning in human life.

The real threat to the ability of human beings to find meaning in life stems not from the death of God but from the tendency of many to persist in demanding an otherworldly ground for meaning. Those who continue to expect such a ground in a world in which God is dead risk being forced to confront the condition of nihilism. Nietzsche defines nihilism elsewhere: "The highest values devalue themselves. The aim is lacking: 'why?' finds no answer."[19] Nihilism involves the conviction that one cannot find meaning in life, a conviction that is unavoidable if one does not believe that an otherworldly ground of meaning exists, but clings to the belief that meaning can be grounded only in something outside this life. Nihilism is intolerable for human beings; those who confront it must respond to it, though this response might take the form of resignation and avoidance of the question of meaning altogether. And this is the response that Zarathustra sees as typical among his contemporaries. "But you, too, my brothers, tell me: what does your body proclaim of your soul? Is not your soul poverty and filth and wretched contentment?"[20]

Zarathustra urges his audience to seek something higher in their lives than the contentment with which they numb themselves:

> What is the greatest experience you can have? It is the hour of the great contempt. The hour in which your happiness, too, arouses your disgust, and even your reason and your virtue.
>
> The hour when you say, "What matters my happiness? It is poverty and filth and wretched contentment. But my happiness ought to justify existence itself."[21]

The quest for comfort is not the only psychologically tenable response to the nihilism that has descended upon modern culture as a consequence of God's death, but it is the response that Zarathustra sees as pervasive among his contemporaries. He uses a parable to suggest the hideousness of the life in quest of soporifics. I quote this parable in its entirety because it provides a powerful image of the malaise against which Zarathustra's gospel is offered as a cure:

> Alas, the time of the most despicable man is coming, he that is no longer able to despise himself. Behold, I show you the *last man*.
>
> "What is love? What is creation? What is longing? What is a star?" thus asks the last man, and he blinks.
>
> The earth has become small, and on it hops the last

man, who makes everything small. His race is as inerad-
icable as the flea-beetle; the last man lives longest.

"We have invented happiness," say the last men, and
they blink. They have left the regions where it was hard
to live, for one needs warmth. One still loves one's
neighbor and rubs against him, for one needs warmth.

Becoming sick and harboring suspicion are sinful to
them; one proceeds carefully. A fool, whoever still
stumbles over stones or human beings! A little poison
now and then: that makes for agreeable dreams. And
much poison in the end, for an agreeable death.

One still works, for work is a form of entertainment.
But one is careful lest the entertainment be too harrow-
ing. One no longer becomes poor or rich: both require
too much exertion. Who still wants to rule? Who obey?
Both require too much exertion.

No shepherd and one herd! Everybody wants the
same, everybody is the same: whoever feels different
goes voluntarily into a madhouse.

"Formerly, all the world was mad," say the most refined, and they blink.

One is clever and knows everything that has ever
happened: so there is no end of derision. One still quar-
rels, but one is soon reconciled—else it might spoil the
digestion.

One has one's little pleasure for the day and one's little pleasure for the night: but one has a regard for
health.

"We have invented happiness," say the last men, and
they blink.[22]

The modern age is radically questioning the meaning of
human existence, and a common response is to pursue the
lifestyle of the last man—these are Zarathustra's premises.
His message is offered as a more positive alternative response to that questioning than that of his comfort-craving
contemporaries. The aim not only of Zarathustra's Prologue

speech but also of his teachings generally is to communicate this alternative.

Zarathustra's positive message is premised on the idea of the overman. The overman, according to Zarathustra's address, is to be the new goal for human beings. The overman represents something that in principle is unattainable by the merely human: "And man shall be just that for the overman: a laughingstock or a painful embarrassment."[23] The overman's mode of being is continuously creative; the overman's present being and all that he carries over from the past are squandered in acts of creativity toward the future. The overman's existence is the erotic mode of being *par excellence,* and while it surpasses human capacity for resilient self-transcendence, it establishes a project for human beings by serving as this capacity's ideal. Zarathustra believes that his project can itself serve as a basis for meaning in human life.

It is significant that the overman is by definition a goal that human beings will always fail to achieve.[24] "Man is something that shall be overcome."[25] "Man is a rope, tied between beast and overman."[26]

And yet the details of one's life can be seen as steps and experiments toward this goal. The project itself—which includes the entirety of a life dedicated to its pursuit—is valuable, according to Zarathustra, so much so that it transfigures the inadequacies of the present that call the meaning of life into question. The relationship between the ideal of the overman and the tragic perspective is suggested by Zarathustra's depiction of pursuit of the overman as intrinsically valuable. Zarathustra uses his vision of the overman as a means of transfiguring the negative insight that human existence, in the details of its present actuality, does not always seem sufficient to justify itself.

The interpretation of one's individual life that the overman provides can transfigure one's view of one's personal failure, but this interpretation is not a purely private one. The goal of the overman is a communal goal. It emblemizes a vision of greatness that has not yet appeared on earth but that should nevertheless be brought into being. This goal of greatness is a goal that all individuals can share, even to the extent of inspiring one another's efforts.[27] Zarathustra observes in his speech on friendship, "You cannot groom yourself too beautifully for your friend: for you shall be to him an arrow and a longing for the overman."[28] But at the same time, the overman is a goal that each individual can pursue in individual actions. Advising a youth who feels alienated from others when pursuing the longings of his inner soul, Zarathustra encourages fidelity to his individual dream in terms that refer to the overman ideal. "Do not throw away the hero in your soul! Hold holy your highest hope!"[29]

The overman can thus serve as a key to interpreting one's own behavior as having significance and relevance to a more universal project. The importance of the overman as a goal that links individual pursuits and more general human aspiration will become clearer after Zarathustra's function as a tragic hero is considered. For now, it should be noted that the overman is a key to a comprehensive vision of the activities of one's life, and that this vision links one's own activities to those of others.

The relevance of understanding one's activities in a communal context to a sense of meaning in life becomes evident if the implications of God's death are fully considered. If the meaning of the individual's life must be established here on earth, it must be established in a context in which the individual does not find himself or herself alone, but with others. The energetic, vibrant involvement with the life of the world demanded by the project of aspiration toward the overman necessarily involves interaction with other human beings. Zarathustra's decision to descend from his cave and preach his insights is not peripherally related to the content of those insights; on the contrary, his vision of the meaningful human life is inseparable from vital participation in the social world in which one finds oneself. Human interaction is, in Nietzsche's view, problematic, as even our brief consideration of the Prologue suggests. But human interaction does not pose a problem that anyone seeking meaning within this life can evade.

These considerations indicate the significance of the theme of communication for the field of the book's concern. *Thus Spoke Zarathustra* is focused sometimes on the nature of human communication and sometimes on the problem of meaning in human life. The two concerns are essentially related to one another. The problematic of communication is central to the book because it is central to the problem of the meaningful human life, the problem on which Zarathustra's insights are focused.

If the relationship between Zarathustra's message about the meaningful life and the theme of human communication is kept in mind, the significance of the various communicative failures recounted in the remainder of the Prologue also becomes apparent. These failures are not simply comical, as their narrative context might lead the reader to believe. They are significant threats to Zarathustra's ability to implement his gospel in his life, particularly because the vocation through which he is attempting to pursue the project of generous greatness, represented by the overman, is the vocation of a teacher.

Zarathustra's efforts to confront his communicative failures refine his sense of what his teaching vocation entails in practice. They also develop his understanding of what preconditions are necessary for any kind of communication to occur.

Zarathustra responds to his initial failure to communicate to the crowd by modifying the style of his presentation. His abstract speech in section 3 has resulted in the crowd's uncomprehending jeers, so he shifts to a discourse that is more dependent on metaphor and parable. His speech in section 4 is an imagistic litany that plays on the metaphors of "going over" and "going under" (*übergehen* and *untergehen*). (*Untergehen* has the double meaning of "to go under," used to refer to the sun's setting, and "to perish." Nietzsche utilizes this double meaning in section 4, and the reader should be alert to his punning in this section.)[30]

> I love him who works and invents to build a house for the overman and to prepare earth, animal, and plant for him: for thus he wants to go under....
>
> I love him who makes his virtue his addiction and his catastrophe: for his virtue's sake he wants to live on and to live no longer.
>
> I love him who does not want to have too many virtues. One virtue is more virtue than two, because it is more of a noose on which his catastrophe may hang.
>
> I love him whose soul squanders itself, who wants no thanks and returns none: for he always gives away and does not want to preserve himself.
>
> I love him who is abashed when the dice fall to make his fortune, and asks, "Am I then a crooked gambler?" For he wants to perish.
>
> I love him who casts golden words before his deeds and always does even more than he promises: for he wants to go under....[31]

While this rhetorical litany retains an abstract content as its major point, Zarathustra's images are designed to concretize the kind of self-investment that the quest for the overman involves. Similarly, the parable of "the last man" in section 5, evokes a series of concrete images that help to render the mode of life that Zarathustra despises in a vivid fashion.

Zarathustra Confronts Tragedy:
The Tightrope Walker's Accident

Zarathustra's imagistic discourses in sections 4 and 5 may successfully enrich *our* understanding of his gospel of the overman, but they seem to do nothing for the crowd. They shout: "Give us this last man, O Zarathustra . . . Turn us into these last men! Then we shall make you a gift of the overman!" And the people in the crowd "jubilated and clucked with their tongues."[32] Zarathustra remains a failure as a teacher at the beginning of section 6, which provides an account of the tightrope walker's show. To this point, Zarathustra has recognized his failure and has responded with efforts to improve the packaging of the insights he intends to teach. In section 6, which portrays the tightrope walker's fatal accident, Zarathustra's reflections on failure become more profound. Here we see Zarathustra confronting the genuinely tragic in human life, and the reflections provoked by this confrontation lead Zarathustra to revise not only the methods of his teaching vocation but also his basic perspective on it.

The typical reaction to a first reading of the tightrope walker's story is to be uncertain as to what is going on. The tale is certainly weird. The performing tightrope walker loses his balance and falls to his death after being leaped over and taunted by a malicious but clearly talented jester. The detail is complicated and worth in-depth consideration for what it summarizes about the book's overall messages. Although I disagree with some details of Alderman's commentary, I recommend it as an indication of the extent of the symbolic richness of the passage.[33] Because my purpose here is to provide a survey of the Prologue rather than a detailed commentary, I shall only comment briefly about this story. One thing worth noting is that the jester's taunts resemble those that might be made of anyone who attempts a break with tradition. The jester suggests with the epithet "Lamefoot" that the tightrope walker is like Oedipus, the paradigmatic father-killer, and he jeers, "Forward, lazy-bones, smuggler, pale-face, or I shall tickle you with my heel! What are you doing here between towers? The tower is where you belong. You ought to be locked up; you block the way for one better than yourself."[34]

The jester's taunts are, in effect, the voice of tradition confronting the individual who departs from the security of its doctrines. As we observed in Chapter 3, Nietzsche recognizes the psychological difficulty involved in any effort to escape the orientation of the traditional worldview, and he also recognizes the risks that accompany any success in this effort. The perspective of conventional morality solidifies its entrenched authority for those who inherit it by passing judgment on those who come to grief. Like the jester jeering at the tightrope walker, the conventional moral perspective claims that the moral experimentalist who meets disaster has only gotten what he or she should have expected. He or she should have stayed where it was safe instead of engaging in such risky business.[35]

The tightrope walker's way of life represents, in certain respects, a practical instantiation of the lifestyle that Zarathustra advocates abstractly. The tightrope walker is not cowed by danger, but instead exposes himself to risk of such magnitude that he ultimately succumbs to it. He is, in the words of Zarathustra's litany, willing "to perish." His orientation is far removed from that of "the last man," whose highest ambitions are comfort and security. The tightrope walker's vocation is not directed toward the attainment of any static goal, but instead is focused on the activity of graceful, balanced movement. He is, as the German *Seiltänzer* (tightrope walker) makes clear, a "rope-dancer." Zarathustra's gospel, as we will increasingly observe, advocates graceful movement instead of goal-achievement as fundamental to a meaningful life.[36] Already Zarathustra's way of being has been associated with the tightrope walker's profession: the saint of section 2 describes Zarathustra as one who walks "like a dancer."[37]

A discrepancy between Zarathustra and the tightrope walker has been indicated before section 6 as well. We see the crowd as mistaken in the belief that Zarathustra's speech pertains to the tightrope walker. The apparent implication is that the mundane reality of the tightrope walker's work is far removed from Zarathustra's glowing vision of aspiration toward the overman. Furthermore, the tightrope walker and Zarathustra are in competition for the crowd's attention throughout the portions of the speech included in section 4 and 5, for we are told that the tightrope walker, believing that Zarathustra has been speaking of him, begins his performance at the end of section 3.[38]

The simultaneous association and discrepancy between Zarathustra and the tightrope walker reflect a central problem involved in Zarathustra's developing work as a teacher. Zarathustra's abstract doctrines about life do not appear to stand in easy relation to the actual living of life. We are, to some extent, given both sides of a story in the Prologue. We see the crowd of the marketplace as a gang of petty simpletons, but at the same time we see Zarathustra as hopelessly out of touch with the community's actual life. The reparation of the schism between Zarathustra's ideas and his audience is crucial to his teaching project. It is also crucial to his gospel's having wider significance as an answer to the question of how human life can be seen as meaningful in a Godless world.

The fact of this schism is brought home to Zarathustra as a consequence of the tightrope walker's accident. The jester, who has been taunting the tightrope walker, has been running toward him on the rope.

> But when he was but one step behind, the dreadful
> thing happened which made every mouth dumb and
> every eye rigid: he uttered a devilish cry and jumped
> over the man who stood in his way. This man, however,
> seeing his rival win, lost his head and the rope, tossed
> away his pole, and plunged into the depth even faster, a
> whirlpool of arms and legs. The market place became as
> the sea when a tempest pierces it: the people rushed
> apart and over one another, especially at the place
> where the body must hit the ground.[39]

Zarathustra, however, stays beside the dying man. In a role
that is reminiscent of a priest who administers the last rites,
Zarathustra paradoxically eases the tightrope walker's angst
by converting him to atheism. In response to the dying
man's raving about hell and the devil, Zarathustra tells him,
"By my honor, friend, ... all that of which you speak does
not exist: there is no devil and no hell. Your soul will be
dead even before your body: fear nothing further."[40]

The tightrope walker's first response is to conclude that
if Zarathustra is right, his life has been meaningless. His
reply is probably the initial response of most members of
Nietzsche's culture to his claim that God is dead: "If you
speak the truth, ... I lose nothing when I lose my life. I am
not much more than a beast that has been taught to dance
by blows and a few meager morsels." Zarathustra, however,
reassures him: "You have made danger your vocation; there
is nothing contemptible in that. Now you perish of your
vocation: for that I will bury you with my own hands."
Zarathustra's words seem to have secured a deathbed conversion. The Prologue reports that the tightrope walker
"moved his hand as if he sought Zarathustra's hand in
thanks" in the final gesture before his evidently peaceful
death.[41]

Zarathustra's words to the tightrope walker reflect
Nietzsche's theoretical position: The move to a worldview

that counters the traditional Socratic-Christian worldview is difficult, perilous, and vulnerable to hostility from those who adhere to inherited values. We should not be surprised, Nietzsche tells us, if we encounter grief in the effort to transform our own minds and hearts, and even more in the effort to transform those of others. Risk and troubles are inherent elements of the project, but painful and tragic consequences that follow upon this project are not, as the moral tradition will tell us, an indication that the project is misguided. Quite to the contrary, mishap and pain are exactly what the moral experimenter should expect, and risk that sometimes ends in fatality is an inseparable correlate of the nobility of his vocation.

When he consoles the dying man, Zarathustra is a mouthpiece for Nietzsche's thoughts on this matter. But Zarathustra is a living reflection of the difficulty of Nietzsche's view when we overhear his thoughts in the sections that follow the tightrope walker's death. Cool while in the role of the dying man's counselor, Zarathustra is afterward seriously shaken. "Human existence is uncanny and still without meaning: a jester can become man's fatality," he reflects.[42] He meditates on his failure to communicate to "the dark cloud of man": "I am still far from them, and my sense does not speak to their senses."[43] The jester who drove the tightrope walker to his fatal fall reappears in section 8 and jeers threateningly at Zarathustra:

> Go away from this town, Zarathustra; . . . there are too
> many here who hate you. You are hated by the good
> and the just, and they call you their enemy and de-
> spiser; you are hated by the believers in the true faith,
> and they call you the danger of the multitude. It was
> your good fortune that you were laughed at; and verily,
> you talked like a jester. It was good fortune that you
> stooped to the dead dog; when you lowered yourself so
> far, you saved your own life for today. But go away

from this town, or tomorrow I shall leap over you, one living over one dead.[44]

Zarathustra subsequently meets some gravediggers, who cheerfully and superstitiously heckle him further.

Through these sections Zarathustra is wrestling with the tragic implications of the human predicament. Accidents can bring life to an end; communication can be impeded by the chasms of understanding between individuals; and the person who attempts to find meaning in his life in an innovative fashion in perennially at risk, the more so because traditionalists may be tempted to attack while he is vulnerable. But Zarathustra's traumatic reflections are interrupted by biological need; he notices that he is hungry. Nietzsche seems to be playfully suggesting that, however profound one's reflections, one's life is a practical, "earthly" project.

Zarathustra's quest for food is comic. While still carrying the corpse of the tightrope walker, he knocks on the door of a hermit whose home he has come upon in the forest. The hermit is obliging and offers Zarathustra bread and wine, but he insists that the dead man eat too. When Zarathustra points out how unlikely it is that the corpse will cooperate with his host, the hermit "peevishly" retorts, "I don't care...Whoever knocks at my door must also take what I offer."[45] This hermit's indiscriminate generosity to other human beings comes off as more absurd than the saintly hermit's absolute avoidance of others, but Zarathustra's encounters with both hermits present caricatures of human interaction gone awry.

By the end of section 8, it appears that virtually all of Zarathustra's communicative efforts have been catastrophic. Zarathustra's single success was achieved only at the moment in which his auditor expired—a dubious communicative success. Zarathustra's initial, glowing dream seems to have come to nothing. The character we see before us at the end of this section is a bumbling eccentric who is "used to walking at night" because he likes "to look in the face" of all who sleep. Zarathustra finally decides to go to sleep at dawn, and with this decision he "buries" his dead companion in a tree.

Beyond Catastrophe

But this is not the end of Zarathustra's chronicle; it is only the beginning. Sleep seems to help Zarathustra assimilate the events of his turbulent first day as a teacher, for he awakes in a buoyant mood.

> He rose quickly, like a seafarer who suddenly sees land, and jubilated, for he saw a new truth. And thus he spoke to his heart:
> "An insight has come to me: companions I need, living ones—not dead companions and corpses whom I carry with myself wherever I want to. Living companions I need, who follow me because they want to follow themselves—wherever I want."

Perhaps as a consequence of meeting the absurdly indiscriminate hermit, Zarathustra concludes that he himself has been too indiscriminate when he addressed the mob in the marketplace. He decides that he will change his teaching strategy by seeking companions instead of masses of followers.

> An insight has come to me: let Zarathustra speak not to the people but to companions. Zarathustra shall not become the shepherd and dog of a herd.
> To lure many away from the herd, for that I have come. The people and the herd shall be angry with me: Zarathustra wants to be called a robber by the shepherds.[46]

This resolution represents a major change of strategy in response to failure. Zarathustra has failed in the objective that he set for himself, at least as he initially conceived it; he has not communicated his insights to others. The Prologue ends with Zarathustra's reconsideration of his project. He has failed, he concludes, because he has not sufficiently recognized that the contents of his message impose constraints on the methods that can communicate it. His revolutionary message is a call for individuals to depart from the traditional way of thinking, which focuses on another world as a ground for meaning. An appeal to the masses is an inappropriate approach because the masses form the community that teaches this way of looking at things. From now on, Zarathustra vows, he will seek companions, individuals who can be lured "from the herd." At this juncture, he appropriates his failure by considering it a setback that instructs him on making his future efforts more realistic.

As we will see, Zarathustra's further confrontations with failure recurrently employ this tactic of reevaluating it as an ingredient in the forward movement of his basic project. Thus far, however, we have already seen that Zarathustra's communicative mission is directly concerned with the possibility of a meaningful human existence, which suggests that the theme of failure will remain central in the narrative account of Zarathustra's activities. And this theme is naturally related to Zarathustra's concern with meaning in a world without God. An afterlife, if it existed, might rebaptize human failures as unobvious spiritual successes and guarantee that death is not really a form of failure. But in the absence of such an afterlife, human failures pose a *prima facie* threat to any easy claim that life is meaningful. Zarathustra's message, focused as it is on providing an earthly basis for existential meaning, must address the threat posed by failure, and this necessity is underscored by the fact that Zarathustra, so far, has met only with failure in the arena of his own quest for meaning, the arena of the social world.

By the end of the Prologue, we also have the outline of Zarathustra's message regarding meaning in human life. In short, meaning is attainable through an integrative vision of the events of one's life as all being involved in one's project toward a goal, the goal of greatness that Zarathustra sketches in his account of the overman.

We have also seen Zarathustra apply this formula practically in the course of confronting the failures that accompany his early teaching efforts. Seeing the goal of communicating his insights as integral to his personal project of aspiring toward greatness, Zarathustra analyzes his failures as informative setbacks that can assist his project as a whole.

The Prologue ends with Zarathustra's reassessment that he should seek an audience of kindred spirits instead of the masses. In section 10 he is fortified in this resolve by the arrival of his animals, the eagle and the snake which represent his pride and his wisdom. The implication seems to be that Zarathustra feels the correctness of his reassessment so strongly that multiple dimensions of himself converge in endorsing it.

NIETZSCHE'S INTENTION: A BOOK FOR ALL AND NONE

We have seen the development of the character Zarathustra's motivations in speaking. Over the course of the Prologue, he has transformed himself from one who seeks to communicate to all to one who seeks to communicate to a few who can understand him. This very development, however, seems to distinguish Zarathustra's motivations in the text that follows from the motivations of Nietzsche himself, who maintains paradoxically that he writes the book "for all and none." I shall turn now to the question of what Nietzsche as an author is doing when he causes Zarathustra to speak. This question of the author's motives ambiguously considers why he writes for all and none, what kind of book he is writing, and why he uses a fictional character as a mouthpiece.

What does Nietzsche mean by subtitling his book "A Book for All and None"? And does this subtitle mean that Nietzsche's own motives are radically different from those of his character? One might construe the subtitle as Nietzschean pretentiousness at its worst. On this reading, Nietzsche would be emphatically reminding us that despite the book's generous dissemination of his insights, he does not believe that he has any worthy readers. Martin Heidegger's reading of the subtitle, although sympathetic, interprets it as an elitist comment of this sort. In a translation that renders the subtitle "For Everyone and No One," we find Heidegger commenting thus:

> *For Everyone* means for each man as man, insofar as his essential nature becomes at any given time an object worthy of his thought. *And No One* means for none of the idle curious who come drifting in from everywhere, who merely intoxicate themselves with isolated fragments and particular aphorisms from this work.[47]

This account is inadequate for several reasons. Heidegger's definition of "For Everyone" omits the necessary information of when and in what manner each person's essential nature becomes an object worthy of thought. Through reference to "each man," Heidegger emphasizes the individuality of each person being addressed, but he then seems to rescind this emphasis by stating that each person is addressed in that humanity which is shared with all human beings. As we have observed, however, Nietzsche considers the recognition of the uniquely individual aspect of the person to be an essential component of healthy self-understanding of the sort that he consistently hopes to inspire in his readers. Heidegger's analysis of "For Everyone" ignores regard for the individual.

Heidegger's analysis of "And No One" is even more inadequate. Heidegger denies that Nietzsche means "no one." He asserts that Nietzsche is simply demanding that his readers prove their worthiness by piecing Zarathustra's puzzle of aphorisms together on their own. Nietzsche does often place elitist demands on his readers, but in attempting to read this into the subtitle, Heidegger assumes that Nietzsche does not really mean what he says. He does not support this assumption with argument. And this account would seem to be more appropriate if Nietzsche had claimed to be addressing "a few" rather than "no one."

An interpretation of the subtitle should begin with the assumption that Nietzsche does mean what he says in both of its paradoxical halves. The book is for all, but it is also for none. If this claim, however, is to make any sense, it must be "for all" in a sense different from that in which it is a book "for none."

The sense in which the book is for all is not deeply problematic; books written for publication address an unspecified general public. Nietzsche's book is "for all" in the same sense that Zarathustra speaks "to all" at the beginning of the Prologue. Nietzsche, in writing this book, is presenting his insights to the general public.

The sense in which the book is for no one is more problematic. What does it mean to publish a book "for no one"? If Nietzsche's objective of publicly presenting his insights is suggested when he calls *Zarathustra* a book for all, the second half of the subtitle suggests that he has another objective as well. And the book certainly has another purpose besides the direct communication of Nietzsche's insights. This other purpose is suggested not only by the subtitle but also by Nietzsche's inclusion of sections that present Zarathustra's introspective meditations, sections which, like those that report Zarathustra's speeches, conclude with the refrain "Thus spoke Zarathustra." Not all of Zarathustra's speeches are for an audience. Sometimes Zarathustra's speeches are for himself.

Zarathustra's private meditations are, from the standpoint of his own motivations, "for no one." But what of Nietzsche's motivation in presenting them to us? Their function cannot be the direct transmission of insight through the mouthpiece of his speaker, but they do serve a dramatic function in the depiction of Zarathustra as a fictional hero.[48] The significance of this function will be analyzed in the following chapter. But the dramatic function of Zarathustra's offstage musings calls to mind the dramatic character of the book as a whole. While the book does attempt to communicate directly some of Nietzsche's insights about the human condition, it is also a gesture of an indirect sort. *Thus Spoke Zarathustra* is not only a series of speeches directed to us as an audience; it is also a narrative that has an internal integrity and is written *for* an audience only in an indirect way.

Alderman's interpretation develops this notion that the subtitle shows Nietzsche's concern with indirect communication in the book. He explicates the subtitle by referring to a statement made by Zarathustra in Part IV:

> In Section I of "The Higher Men," Zarathustra remembers the folly of his first attempt to teach in the market place: "When I spoke to everyone, I spoke to no one." Thus are we given Nietzsche's meta-reflection on the publication of the book itself, which, by virtue of being made public, is for everyone and because of its deliber-

ately metaphorical, dramatic, and compressed style is
for no one except those who have the courage and the
patience to deal with its cryptic density and masks.

Like Heidegger, Alderman emphasizes Nietzsche's elitism
in his interpretation of "for no one," and to the extent that
he does, his interpretation is subject to the same criticism
that I made of Heidegger's. However, Alderman makes an
important point about the manner in which Zarathustra
communicates: "Every doctrine is intimately connected
with its mode of expression and dissemination . . . Every idea
is a *voiced idea,* and we hear it well only if we hear the
tonal particularities of the language in which it is
expressed."[49]

The implication of the subtitle to which Alderman alludes in this passage is important: All speaking is intimately
expressive of the individual nature of the speaker. We hear
in an act of speech not just its propositional content, but
also the voice, tone, and diction in which the content is
expressed. Zarathustra's speech is no exception. As a consequence, Zarathustra's speaking is in a sense "for no one."
He is speaking through his own voice as an individual—in
other words, he is speaking, for himself and for no one else.
Through speech he represents his own way of being. In this
sense his speeches reveal the fictional person whose story
we are reading, and in this sense they are not *for* us as
readers.

The tension between Zarathustra as Nietzsche's mouthpiece, who speaks to us, and Zarathustra as a fictional character in his own story recalls a tension involved in every
act of communication. This tension is the ambivalence between an individual speaker's effort to express himself and
his effort to tailor his words to the understanding of his
audience. These two ambitions motivate not only Zarathustra when he speaks, but also any nonsolipsistic speaker.

The subtitle indicates, therefore, that *Thus Spoke Zarathustra* will address the paradox involved in human communication, the paradox that communication must bridge the chasm between individual experience and communal understanding. The subtitle also indicates that *Thus Spoke Zarathustra* will not only address this paradox, but also instantiate it. Through Zarathustra, Nietzsche will simultaneously attempt the self-expression of his deepest insights and a kind of interpersonal communication.

But this formula is familiar. This bridging of the individual and the communal is precisely the goal that successful tragedy, on Nietzsche's account, achieves. The person who communicates successfully, therefore, must attain a kind of synthesis between individual and communal perspectives similar to that ideally achieved by the tragic audience. And because communicating with others is essential to the work of a teacher, such as Zarathustra, a teacher in particular must achieve the sort of balance between individual and communal perspective that Nietzsche has emphasized from his earliest writings.

So the problem of achieving a tragic perspective has the same essential form as the problem of communicating with others and this will prove continually significant to our discussion. The isomorphism of the structure of the problems of tragic perspective and human communication enables Nietzsche to address both simultaneously in the plot of *Zarathustra*.

WHAT KIND OF STORY IS *THUS SPOKE ZARATHUSTRA*?

Our discussion has suggested strongly that Nietzsche's authorial project is multidimensional. I have just suggested that the book tells a story that grapples simultaneously with the tragic dimension of human life and with the practical problems of human communication. Earlier I suggested that Zarathustra plays the role of a parodic counterpart to Plato's Socrates. Implicitly, too, my discussion of the Prologue treated Zarathustra as a counterpart of Christ imparting a new gospel. How can we make sense of these multiple projects that seem to be embedded in Nietzsche's text? Why, when he speaks through Zarathustra, does Nietzsche tell this particular structurally complicated tale?

A cursory inspection of the text does not reveal easy answers. As a work of fiction, the book is peculiar, especially by nineteenth-century standards. It is not much like a novel. The plot is discontinuous. It is probably not uncommon among first-time readers of *Zarathustra* scarcely to notice that there is any plot through Parts I through III. (Part IV represents a literary form that is structured very differently, as I shall discuss later.) The fact that the Prologue, for all the bizarreness of its story, does reveal a connected plot might suggest that Nietzsche intends a continuous plot throughout but bungles the project. Minimal reflection on Nietzsche's obsession with control of literary form, however, eliminates this possibility.[50]

So we are left perplexed about Nietzsche's intention in the structure of the text beyond the Prologue. The pastiche of disparate materials in Part I can be lumped under the heading "Zarathustra's Speeches" only with the broadcast construal of what a speech is supposed to be. We encounter songs, lectures, parables, and narratives that involve Zarathustra's speeches, dreams and dream interpretations, occasional interactions with walk-on characters, and visions. If the juxtaposed diversity of material resembles anything else in literature, it is probably the Bible, which, as I noted earlier, also involves a pastiche of reports, narratives, short conversations, parables, songs, and visions. And Nietzsche does seem to want to remind us of the New Testament, from the first sentence of the book, where he recalls Christ's experience in the desert by telling us that Zarathustra left his home and went into solitude at the age of thirty.[51] But observing this parallel hardly explains Nietzsche's project, nor does it exhaustively describe even the surface character of the text's structure. We have already seen that the opening passage also makes reference to Plato.

As a preliminary step in making sense of the text's complexities, I shall follow Alderman's cue when he focuses on *Zarathustra* as a story.[52] A story has continuous, unified structure. By focusing on the unified narrative structure of *Zarathustra*, we can determine which aspects of Zarathustra's story are fundamental to the project throughout.

But which *aspect* of the story should we take as fundamental? Is that not precisely our problem?

We can conceive of the book as a tragedy,[53] a parody of the New Testament, a parody of the Platonic dialogues, a story about a philosophical teacher, or a *Bildungsroman* (the German "novel of education"). Which of these schemes offers us the most fundamental interpretive clue? While this question may seem to be the obvious response to the structural diversity of Zarathustra's story, it is not the best one. The many layers of the story that the various interpretive schema suggest operate simultaneously. Allusions to Plato and to Scripture are scattered throughout the book—neither the parody of the New Testament nor that of the Platonic dialogues ultimately proves to be the more dominant parody. Zarathustra remains a teacher from start to finish, and the portrayal of his development toward maturity, after the fashion of a *Bildungsroman*, is a description that can be applied to the entire narrative. All these models seem to apply to the whole book. One is not more fundamental than the others.

But it is possible to gain a sense of what is fundamental to Zarathustra's story. Each of these models contributes cooperatively to what is fundamental in the *Zarathustra* narrative, and each adds depth to the picture of *Zarathustra* which is suggested by the others. I shall focus on the models of parody, tragedy, and *Bildungsroman*, in turn, in order to indicate the centrality of each to the Zarathustra story. At the same time I shall indicate how, in the case of each of these models, the aspects of the story revealed by the other models reinforce the aspect illuminated by the model under discussion.

Zarathustra *as Parody*

The parodies of Christ and Socrates work as natural counterparts to the aspect of the story that focuses on Zarathustra as a teacher. Christ and Socrates are the teachers with the greatest influence on how we in the West confront questions regarding the basic meaning of human life. Zarathustra is drawn as a philosophical teacher who advocates a fundamentally different approach to these questions, and his role as this kind of teacher is underscored by the fact that he is a parodic counterpart of Socrates and Christ. Zarathustra's gospel is in effect a parodic gospel—for it is to be taken by the reader as similar in scope to the gospel of the West's two great teachers but diametrically opposite to those gospels in much of its import.

The character of *Zarathustra* that resembles the *Bildungsroman*, which portrays the maturing process of the hero,[54] enhances the impact of this parody. Both Socrates in the dialogues and Christ in the New Testament are portrayed as individuals who develop over time.[55] In their stories, however, the point of their development is to reach the position of attained maturity from which they can speak authoritatively. Zarathustra's story parodies this perspective on maturity that seems implicit in the earlier teachers' stories. In Zarathustra's story the "education for life by life itself"[56] that the maturing process involves is not merely a necessary preliminary to his ability to teach others. Zarathustra's growth into increasing maturity is the substance of his teaching. Zarathustra is an exemplar after the fashion of Socrates and Christ, but he does not resemble them in presenting a model of the ultimate goal of maturity. Instead he is a model of one who is engaged in the process of development. In Heidegger's expression, Zarathustra is a teacher who "teaches by showing."[57]

Zarathustra as Tragedy

The tragic structure of *Zarathustra* draws the interpretive threads together while also depending on them. Tragedy, as we have seen, represents in Nietzsche's view a worldview diametrically opposed to that of Christianity. At the same time its worldview also opposes that of the Western philosophical tradition that began with Socrates. By choosing to write *Zarathustra* in a form modeled on Greek tragedy, Nietzsche solidifies the image of Zarathustra as an opponent of Christ and Socrates.

That Nietzsche does deliberately choose to model *Zarathustra* on Greek tragedy is evident from a number of comments that he makes in various works. In *The Gay Science*, Nietzsche suggests that *Thus Spoke Zarathustra* is appropriately viewed as a tragedy, for there he publishes the passage that will begin "Zarathustra's Prologue" under the title *"Incipit tragoedia"*, "The Tragedy Begins."[58] In *Ecce Homo*, Nietzsche reiterates the suggestion that *Zarathustra* is a tragedy. Describing what he calls "the type" of Zarathustra, Nietzsche repeats another passage from *The Gay Science*: "It is perhaps only with him that *great seriousness* really begins, that the real question mark is posed for the first time, that the destiny of the soul changes, the hand moves forward, the tragedy *begins*."[59] Nietzsche goes on in his *Ecce Homo* discussion to call the type of Zarathustra "the concept of Dionysus himself." Nietzsche consistently links his notion of Dionysus to his conception of tragedy, not only in *The Birth of Tragedy* but in later writings as well.[60] It seems clear that Nietzsche intends that Zarathustra's tale be viewed as a tragedy.

Given Nietzsche's conception of the nature of tragedy, it is easy to see suggestions of the tragic form in his mode of presentation in *Zarathustra*. Zarathustra, for instance, is a figure who, although presented as somewhat larger than life even in the Prologue, is nevertheless intended as someone with whom we can identify. Being a written rather than a performed work, *Thus Spoke Zarathustra* cannot rely on the excitement generated by the tragic chorus to secure this identification. But Nietzsche's use of novelistic devices (e.g., bringing us inside Zarathustra's mind, allowing us to see Zarathustra off the stage of his public speeches) establishes a kind of identification which resembles that felt by the tragic audience toward the hero. Most significant, Zarathustra is portrayed as undergoing failure, the paradigmatic situation of the tragic hero and the vehicle that effects our sense that the hero's predicament is relevant to our own. We shall observe that Zarathustra's basic concern is the question of what constitutes the meaningful individual life, and *Thus Spoke Zarathustra's* conformity to tragic conventions reflects Nietzsche's selection of a genre that is appropriate to this problem. As a tragic hero, Zarathustra is presented as one who comes to terms with the question of meaning in the manner of tragic heroes: by living through certain difficult experiences and achieving a new understanding of what kind of meaning he, as an individual, can find in his life.

Zarathustra's biography involves a quest for a tragic sense of meaning in life, and in this respect it is antithetical to both the Christian and Socratic perspectives on meaning in human existence. The tragic structure of Zarathustra's story therefore reinforces the book's parodies of Plato's dialogues and the New Testament. In addition, the tragic structure reinforces the story's *Bildungsroman* dimension—or perhaps it would be more apt to say that the *Bildungsroman* dimension is exploited as a means of creating the tragic structure.

Zarathustra *as* Bildungsroman

The element that links the tragic and the *Bildungsroman* aspects of the story is the pattern of recurrent failure that occurs in Zarathustra's life. Failure provides the occasion both for the radical self-doubt and questioning of life's meaning that is essential to Zarathustra's role as a tragic hero, and for the strides forward toward maturity that mark him as the protagonist of a *Bildungsroman*. The *Bildungsroman*-like story of Zarathustra's maturing experiences and of the development of his ability to incorporate what he learns from failure into the ongoing movement of his life is essential to his function as a tragic hero.

The *Bildungsroman* character of the book harmonizes also with Nietzsche's effort to pose Zarathustra as a rival of Christ and Socrates. Nietzsche attempts to demonstrate the superiority of his alternative to the Christian and Socratic worldviews, which he criticizes as poorly adapted to the actuality of human existence; and this effort must, if he is to be consistent, focus on the effect of his worldview on the practical project of living a human life. The fictional biography of Zarathustra, which involves Zarathustra in maturing experiences, provides a demonstration of the experiential consequences of adopting Nietzsche's alternative worldview. It also depicts vividly the radical difference between Zarathustra as a teacher and his rivals. He is a radically new kind of teacher on questions of the meaning of life, not so much because his doctrines conflict with those of Christ and Socrates, but because his mode of confronting these questions in his own life differs radically from theirs.

WHY DOES NIETZSCHE WRITE FICTION?

I have considered the objectives that Nietzsche has in writing a book in Zarathustra's unusual form. But why did Nietzsche choose to write a *fictional* work in the first place? I have already suggested something of an explanation. Nietzsche intends to employ indirect communication in *Thus Spoke Zarathustra*, and the book's fictional format makes this kind of communication possible. But why is Nietzsche concerned with indirect communication? I shall close this chapter with a consideration of Nietzsche's views on human communication that inform his decision to treat this theme through a fictional format.[61]

The Limitations of Universal Discourse

Nietzsche's basic view that the social basis of language impedes the communication of uniquely personal experience is evident in both section 354 of *The Gay Science* and in "On Truth and Lies in a Nonmoral Sense." Although both accounts are subject to criticism for their cursory treatment of the subject of linguistic communication, Nietzsche articulates the same view again and more adequately in *Thus Spoke Zarathustra*. Zarathustra argues that naming one's own virtue with a common name is inappropriate because what he calls "virtues" stem from individual passions. He plays on the female gender of the German *die Tugend* ("the virtue", saying that when one refers to his own virtue with a common name, one "now ... [has] her in common with the people and ... [has] become one of the people and herd with ... [one's] virtue." Zarathustra does not claim that one should never speak of one's own virtue, but he asserts, "If you must speak of her, then do not be ashamed to stammer of her."[62] Virtues and passions are inexpressible, and the honest individual should be able to admit that there can be no direct communication of what

105

these virtues and passions are. Since virtues and passions are part of what makes the individual a unique person, communicating them directly to other individuals is in principle impossible. If one individual could completely transmit the aspects that were uniquely his or hers to another, those aspects would not be his or hers uniquely. The implication of Zarathustra's warning against naming virtues with universal names is that when one attempts to speak of private experience in universal terms, one puts oneself into a position in which it does not matter which individual is speaking.

If all discourse were to be conducted with reference only to the universal aspects of experience, then the individual behind the speaking mask would never be a matter of importance in communication. Insofar as the individual desired to express himself or herself within discourse, his individuality would be effaced from what he communicated. Insofar as the individual understood *himself* through universal terms, his existence as an individual would have no significance. The individual might still have inner, personal experiences, but if the individual found these personal experiences to be meaningful, he would, to that extent, be a solipsist. The meaning of those experiences would be dissociated from the realm of common discourse.

Such considerations help to show the rationale behind Nietzsche's concern that philosophy acknowledge itself as the insights of great individuals, derived from their experiences, rather than continue its pose as a bastion of universally valid observations. Although philosophy, according to Nietzsche, is always the unconscious autobiography of a strong individual, its refusal to admit this prevents it from discussing and evaluating the significance of individuality, even the significance of the role of individuality within a larger social world. The universal mode of discourse which philosophy has usually utilized as its only mode of communication, at least since Descartes, is therefore incapable of elaborating an overview in which the significance of individuality in relation to the larger whole is understood.

Nietzsche contends that universal, univocal discourse is inappropriate for the discussion of certain sorts of things, such as virtues, personality, and certain aspects of inner experience. These things pertain to the individual aspect of experience, which is not identical for all persons. The expression of these things through language is difficult, for words necessarily group together things that differ in certain particulars. The use of generalizing terms to refer to partially private experience is problematic, and this is a problem with which Nietzsche must deal. His way of doing this differs sharply from that of Ludwig Wittgenstein, who claims, "Whereof one cannot speak, thereof one must be silent."[63] Nietzsche concludes that not to speak of things that pertain to the individual nature of human experience would not be "true to the meaning of the earth." The earth as it can be understood by human beings is always understood by individual persons with some characteristics and combinations of characteristics that uniquely differentiate them from other individuals. The effort to communicate these aspects of experience is essential if the earthly life as actually experienced by human beings is to have meaning. For Nietzsche, the question is not whether one should speak of these things, but rather *how* one should speak of them.

Communication of the Personal

Section 374 of Nietzsche's *Human, All-Too-Human,* Volume I, discusses conversation in a manner that reveals the nature of the nonuniversal sort of discourse that Nietzsche considers suitable to these more individual aspects of the human person:

A dialogue is the perfect conversation because everything that the one person says acquires its particular
color, sound, its accompanying gesture *in strict consideration of the other person* to whom he is speaking; it is
like letter-writing, where one and the same man shows
ten ways of expressing his inner thoughts, depending
on whether he is writing to this person or to that. In a
dialogue, there is only one single refraction of thought:
this is produced by the partner in conversation, the mirror in which we want to see our thoughts reflected as
beautifully as possible. But how is it with two, or three,
or more partners? There the conversation necessarily
loses something of its individualizing refinement; the
various considerations clash, cancel each other out; the
phrase that pleases the one, does not accord with the
character of the other. Therefore, a man interacting with
several people is forced to fall back upon himself, to
present the facts as they are, but rob the subject matter
of that scintillating air of humanity that makes a conversation one of the most agreeable things in the
world.[64]

Nietzsche here sees the "individualizing refinement" of
conversation as related to stylistic considerations. The implication of this passage is that every individual produces
a different refraction of thought and that this production
has less to do with the facts being expressed in conversation
than with the style in which facts are conveyed. The inherently individual aspect of communication seems, from
Nietzsche's discussion, to communicate itself through
style; the absence of a clear projection of style implies the
withdrawal of the individual, as a unique person, into himself. Yet style also appears to be necessarily something that
is projected outward, since its particular coloring and tone
arise as a result of consideration for the person addressed.
This outward projection is individual in its focus to such a

degree that stylistic dissonance may occur when a number of different individuals are present.

Style, however, responds to the individual characteristics of the person addressed and does not simply reflect the characteristics of the person who is speaking. This suggests that a pure representation of the uniquely individual characteristics of the speaker is not transmitted even in the "perfect conversation" occurring between two individuals in privacy. Nonetheless, the implication of the quoted passage is not that the radical differences between one individual and another are a barrier to communication. On the contrary, the implication is that these differences are the means through which a deeper sort of communication can take place.

These considerations suggest why the vehicle of a fictional work strikes Nietzsche as appropriate for the communication of philosophical insight. Zarathustra, a fictional spokesman with an eccentric biography, cannot easily pose as a spokesman for universal, unaltering truth, but he can and does speak for himself. He attempts to articulate insights that he has discovered through individual experience. At the same time, Zarathustra incorporates Nietzsche's observations on style into his efforts to reach others. He modifies his speaking style to accommodate his various auditors in the Prologue—the saint, the crowd, and the tightrope walker, for example. Later in the text, one of his auditors even chides him for speaking differently to different audiences.[65]

Other comments that Nietzsche makes concerning style reveal that he views it as a means of taking into account not only essential differences between individual human beings, but also the temporary differences in individual perspectives caused by moods. As early as *Human, All-Too-Human*, Volume II, Nietzsche links style to the transference of moods from one human being to another and suggests that the best style finds "expression for the most desirable human moods, the communication and transference of which one desires most."[66] "*Good* is any style that really communicates an inward state," he remarks later in *Ecce Homo*, and he proceeds to discuss the excellence of *Thus Spoke Zarathustra* in this regard.[67]

Again, Nietzsche's portrayal of Zarathustra is informed by his theoretical observations. Nietzsche shows Zarathustra experiencing a variety of inward states. Zarathustra's thoughts, as we shall see, undergo many vicissitudes as a consequence of his varying emotional states. We are led to recognize the effect of mood on thought through this portrayal. However, the more basic result of Nietzsche's depiction of Zarathustra's moods is that we confront the latter's thought as fundamentally bound to experience. In order to think along with Zarathustra, we have to engage ourselves in his inner states of experience. And this is precisely what Nietzsche is aiming at.

Nietzsche recognizes the importance of mood as a tool in a writer's efforts to communicate, but at the same time he recognizes that the reader's state of mind is an important factor in the success of indirect, stylistically assisted communication of personal experience. He comments in *Ecce Homo:* "Ultimately, nobody can get more out of things, including books, than he already knows. For what one lacks access to from experience one will have no ear."[68] This claim is problematic. It is also important, for it suggests a general difficulty with Nietzsche's recourse to stylistic maneuvers as a means of communicating his individual insights. If one's stylistic transmission of inner experience succeeds only with those individuals who have already had similar experiences, Nietzsche does not seem to have expanded his communicative resources through his conscious attention to stylistic device. On the contrary, it would seem that indirect stylistic communication is much more limited than universal discourse; the former requires something close to an ideal chemistry between the experience of the reader and the style employed, whereas the latter is designed to penetrate the communicative barrier posed by the diversity of individuals' biographical experiences.

Nietzsche is able to resolve this apparent paradox by appealing to the temporal context of human communicative acts, the context to which the comment about books draws attention. The individual who has not had the kind of experience that provides access to what a book attempts to communicate will not understand the book, but this is a matter of the reader's previous employment of his or her temporal situation. The reader, after reading the book, will presumably continue to have experiences, some of which may equip him or her to understand the communicative act that the book represented. Nietzsche observes in *Human, All-Too-Human*, Volume II, that the reader who calls a book harmful when putting it down "perhaps one day . . . will confess that the book did him a great service by thrusting forward and bringing to light the hidden disease in his soul." The book itself may condition a reader's later experience in such a way that it first assists his or her individual development through time and afterward proves to be comprehensible. The book can thus serve as a hidden influence before the reader is in such a state of self-understanding that he or she can really "hear" what the book is saying. Nietzsche goes on to point out that this hidden influence of books does not infringe on respect for the reader's individuality: "Altered opinions alter not at all (or very little) the character of a man: but they illuminate individuated facets of his personality, which hitherto in another constellation of opinions, had remained dark and unrecognizable."[69]

The access to a book that a reader's experience provides is therefore considerably greater than Nietzsche's comment about needing ears to be able to hear might seem to imply. The reader need not have experienced the very state that the author's style reflects. Even a reader who is not attitudinally receptive to a book at the time of reading might have had experiences that make his or her less-than-conscious inner being responsive. With regard to communicating his or her individual insights, time is on the author's side. And time also provides the vehicle for navigating the obstructions that more temporary moods and frames of mind might pose for the reader's understanding of the author's insights. Memory, rereading, and subconscious responsiveness all enhance the author's chances of reaching any particular reader, regardless of the latter's temporary state of mind at the time of reading.

Nietzsche's comments on the delayed effects of books suggest a theory of communication as an open-ended phenomenon. The act of reading can have unexpected reverberations at a considerably later point in time. A verbal act of communication would seem to have the same potential as a written act for provoking unexpected rethinking on the part of the recipient. The written act of communication, however, may have the advantage of affording opportunity for its recipient to return to it in a frame of mind different from that in which he or she first encounters it.[70]

Communication or Manipulation?

Nietzsche's concern with communicative style has another potentially disturbing consequence, one that appears to be more problematic. As we have seen, Nietzsche warns that externally imposed frameworks can inhibit healthy self-awareness on the part of individuals. But this suggests that the philosopher's appropriate function, when he or she discusses individual existence, must be to help readers liberate themselves from categories of self-understanding that are foreign to their inner character. If the philosopher's insights about individuality are to have value to others, the philosopher must somehow address readers *as individuals,* and thus without imposing on them*externally developed modes of self-understanding.

But does not the conscious employment of stylistic devices in the fashion that Nietzsche describes amount to a kind of manipulation of individuals? Doesn't Nietzsche's deliberate employment of mood-influencing devices impose an external form of self-understanding on the reader akin to that foisted on one by the domination of socially imposed categories? The manipulative potential of stylistic appeals is a matter that Nietzsche's view of philosophical communication must address.

Nietzsche does attempt to answer these apparent problems in his understanding of philosophical style. He acknowledges that employing manipulative stylistic devices can be a part of the actor's art instead of the honest communication that he advocates for the philosopher. But Nietzsche's argument that stylistic concerns are essential for philsophical communication suggests that stylistic devices can be used both honestly and dishonestly; they need not be tools of manipulation. Nietzsche employs Zarathustra, his ideal philosopher, to show how stylistic devices and individualistic references can be used effectively without resort to the deception of the actor.

The distinction between Zarathustra and the actor is made evident in Zarathustra's encounter with the Magician in Part IV of *Thus Spoke Zarathustra.* In the course of that encounter, the Magician occasionally says things that resemble remarks of Zarathustra. He manages to deceive Zarathustra into believing that he is distressed, and then laughs at Zarathustra for being taken in by his act. Zarathustra, however, exposes the Magician as a person who is so equivocal that his words are no longer genuine.

You ... have to deceive: that far I know you. You have
to be equivocal—tri-, quadri-, quinquevocal. And what
you have now confessed, that too was not nearly true
enough to suit me. ... You would rouge even your disease when you show yourself to your doctor. In the
same way you have just now rouged your lie when you
said to me, "I did all this *only* as a game." There was
seriousness in it too. ... I solve your riddle: your magic
has enchanted everybody, but no lie or cunning is left
to you to use against yourself: you are disenchanted for
yourself. You have harvested nausea as your one truth.[71]

The Magician's dishonesty does not affect only those
whom he deceives; it characterizes his relationship to himself as well. As one who is practiced in self-deception and
role-playing, he has become unavoidably confused about
what sort of person he really is. He appears ambiguously to
himself as all things and as no particular thing. Because he
does not know what he actually is, he cannot become enchanted with anything about himself. He attempts to fit
too many roles, so that his audience can recognize him as
matching a role that is familiar to them and enjoy their own
recognition. The Magician's self-understanding amounts to
a confused nausea.

Zarathustra, by contrast, is presented throughout the
book as one who engages in honest introspection. He returns to solitude recurrently, not as a means of retreat-
ing from his work but as an essential part of his work.
During periods of solitude, Zarathustra comes to a self-
understanding that is not pressured by the considerations
of adapating his discourse to other individuals. Just as
Nietzsche says that the private conversation is the most
perfect, so the most perfect means of attaining an understanding of oneself appears in *Thus Spoke Zarathustra* to
be the unmediated conversation of oneself with oneself. As
Heidegger observes, the portrayal of Zarathustra's discourse

with himself calls to mind the Platonic doctrine that "the essence of thought resides in the soul's conversation with itself."[72] Zarathustra is unlike the Magician, for the latter never comes to a clear understanding of his own individuality. He therefore deceives others, partly for the reason that he actually has no alternative.

The introspective periods of Zarathustra's life contribute to his teaching by allowing him independence from his normal state of involvement with the community, so that he can observe his own role and the community itself with a certain degree of detachment.[73] The evident importance of these periods of introspection reveals the importance of a strong individualism in the philosopher as Nietzsche understands him, but it also reveals the importance of the temporal dimension of philosophical teaching. Because teaching occurs within a temporal context, the insights that Zarathustra experiences in solitude at one point in time can be communicated to others at a later point. And because Zarathustra is a fictional character, and not simply a speechmaker, we are able to see the relationship between these moments because we are allowed to observe Zarathustra in both.

The Importance of Individual Insight

In presenting Zarathustra in both moments, Nietzsche underscores his view that the philosopher must detach himself or herself from the opinions of his or her community in order to gain the individual insights upon which philosophy depends. The individual who defines all thought and personal experience exclusively in the standard vocabulary of the herd cannot articulate an insight which is novel, communication of which might be beneficial to the community. Because that person interprets experience in terms of categories that are common to everyone, he or she focuses only on the familiar, general aspects of the experience and not on those that are not so familiar, perhaps only because they are not commonly expressed. Nietzsche recognizes that human beings take for granted those things that are most familiar to them:

> What is it that the common people take for knowledge?
> ...Nothing more than this: Something strange is to be
> reduced to something *familiar*. And we philosophers—
> have we really meant *more* than this when we have
> spoken of knowledge?...Error of errors! What is famil-
> iar is what we are used to; and what we are used to is
> most difficult to "know"—that is, to see as a problem;
> that is, to see as strange, as distant, as "outside us."[74]

The individual who does not suspend dependence on familiar interpretations and terminology from time to time inhibits his or her own receptiveness to insights that might occur spontaneously in their absence. But the suspension of this dependence requires that the individual take leave of the community in some fashion. Nietzsche observes that the individuals who spends all their time in conversation with others will continually attune the formulation of their thoughts to those with whom they attempt to communicate. An individual can hear the most profound insights that arise from within only if there are occasions when both the linguistic conventions of the community and the stylistic considerations relevant to his or her particular audience are not demanding the individual's attention.[75] Such occasions can contribute to the development of the community, but only because there are other occasions during which this individual is actively communicating with others.

The implication of this analysis is that any significant communication—particularly philosophical communication—depends upon the temporal dimension of human life for its effectiveness. Nietzsche's employment of Zarathustra, a fictional character whose experiences and communicative acts have temporal extension, suitably reflects the project of teaching Nietzsche's insights on communication "by showing." Zarathustra, as a character in the midst of a fictional life-story, demonstrates what Nietzsche takes to be the typical pattern of significant communication, a pattern whose vicissitudes include both moments of individual isolation and communal interaction.

The vicissitudes of Zarathustra's demonstrative teaching have yet to be considered in detail; they will comprise the subject matter of Chapter 5.

The Ambivalence of Zarathustra's Doctrine

A little revenge is more human than no revenge.[1]

"ZARATHUSTRA'S SPEECHES" is the heading for the remainder of Part I after the Prologue. And true to report, we are presented with a barrage of sermons on a wide variety of topics. The content is antitraditional, but the tone, in keeping with the heading, is sermonizing. After his excursion into an unappreciative mob, Zarathustra seems to have found his audience, and he appears to be preaching doctrines that are clear to him and fully developed. Even during the intermission in the speeches afforded by "On the Tree on the Mountainside," where we see him converse with a young man who idolizes him, Zarathustra retains the mystique of a full-blown wise man. He has the right words for advising the discouraged. We do not sense that there is any discrepancy between Zarathustra's confident words and what is going on in his mind until the final section of Part I:"When Zarathustra had said words, he became silent, like one who has not yet said his last word; long he weighed his staff in his hand, doubtfully. At last he spoke thus, and the tone of his voice had changed."[2]

The discrepancy hinted at here—the discrepancy between Zarathustra's confident statements and his fluctuating attitude toward his doctrines—will be the focus of this chapter. The irony that emerges is a structural component that is crucial to making sense of the body of the book.

Zarathustra's doctrines are presented as approximate

119

formulations for insights that involve a vital attitudinal aspect as well as cognitive content. Statements that report the cognitive content of insights may fail to communicate those insights if they are not supported by more indirect modes of communicating a spiritual or attitudinal state. We saw such a situation in the Prologue. Although the crowd in the marketplace made some propositional sense of Zarathustra's words about tightropes and overmen, their attitudinal orientation prevented them from seeing the full meaning behind Zarathustra's words. The irony of the crowd's belief that they have understood some of Zarathustra's meaning is highly significant. It alerts us to the possibility that we ourselves may misunderstand the real import of Zarathustra's statements as well.

The irony that will be the focus in this chapter is akin to the irony of the crowd's misunderstanding. But the irony I shall emphasize in this chapter is more subtle. This irony is a matter of Zarathustra's own misunderstanding of his doctrines. Zarathustra can, as a human being with fluctuating spiritual states, lose his sense of the attitudinal component of his insights and retain only their propositional formulations. When this happens, his doctrine loses its value for living and becomes a petrified formula that is as likely to prejudice his perspective as to enhance it.

I refer to this double-edged potential of Zarathustra's doctrines as "ambivalence." This chapter argues that Nietzsche portrays Zarathustra as falling prey to this ambivalence in order to make a point about the value that any doctrine (or theory) can have. The value of any doctrine, Nietzsche contends, depends on its ability to help human beings navigate through the world. Because the world is in a continuous state of flux, rigid adherence to the letter of a doctrine is likely to interfere with this project in many situations. As Nietzsche sees it, doctrine can be of general value to human beings only if it is applied to one's life with a lightness of touch and with recognition of the incommensurability of any firmly formulated statement with the dynamic project of living.

In portraying Zarathustra's own moments of confusion about the significance of his doctrine, Nietzsche shows how a sometimes useful doctrine may become a harmful distraction. And perhaps even more important, he shows how this problem can be overcome. Zarathustra recurrently recognizes that his doctrine and his life are out of sync and afterward succeeds in reestablishing a healthy interplay between the two. In this respect especially, he performs the function for us that Heidegger describes as "teaching by showing." And it is significant that Zarathustra can perform this function as a direct consequence of his own mistakes and confusion. (The importance of this last point will be emphasized in Chapter 7.)

Communication of inner states is best achieved, in Nietzsche's view, by indirect means. How then does Nietzsche communicate the inner states that Zarathustra passes through, sometimes to the detriment of his perspective on his doctrine? He does this largely by reporting various projections of Zarathustra's subjective states—dreams, songs, visions, and emotionally distraught behavior. These are related to Zarathustra's inner, subjective state much as the manifest content of a dream is related to the latent content in Freud's analysis.

Much of this chapter examines such reports and considers what they suggest about Zarathustra's current attitudinal orientation. On the basis of what we discover about Zarathustra's subjective states, we will be able to recognize when Zarathustra loses touch with the spirit of his doctrines and when, on the other hand, his full recollection of the insight of his doctrines is restored. Before focusing on the inner states behind the words of Zarathustra's doctrines, however, we consider something about the overt content of Zarathustra's speeches. The first section of this chapter will make some suggestions about reading Zarathustra's speeches in Parts I through III. We shall look at problems that the reader may encounter as a consequence of the general character of the speeches as well as problems that may arise in the context of certain difficult sections.

ZARATHUSTRA'S SPEECHES, PARTS I–III

The Content of Zarathustra's Doctrines

Zarathustra's speeches comprise a large percentage of the book as a whole, but they are particularly dominant in Part I. They present in detailed form the implications of the anti-Christian *Gestalt* of Zarathustra's (and Nietzsche's) worldview for a wide variety of topics. Most of these have to do with the practical matters of living, both personal and social. Zarathustra comments on marriage, friendship, the modern European state, perspectives on the body, crime, war, sex, institutions of punishment, education, common views on what makes someone a good person, death, and so on. At times Zarathustra's remarks have definite targets in the philosophical tradition. For example, Schopenhauer is attacked in the satirical section entitled "On the Teachers of Virtue," where Zarathustra hears and mocks a sermon that praises sleep as the central goal in life.[3] But the sermons are not styled as statements in a philosophical debate. Instead they offer essentially what was advertised in the Prologue: suggestions for how one can "remain true to the meaning of the earth."

Seen as clarifications of what Nietzsche means by this expression, the pedestrian character of some of the topics discussed in Zarathustra's speeches need not be viewed as remarkable. In a sense the speeches are addressed to the pedestrian, and as a collection they offer much day-to-day advice for someone who wants to live an earthbound existence. This character of Zarathustra's maxims is in keeping with the spirit of Nietzsche's lifelong insistence that the value of theories and doctrines depends on their applicability to the practical conduct of life. In *Ecce Homo: How One Becomes What One Is*—a work that is again a kind of handbook, but one that is more effectively self-ironical than *Zarathustra*—Nietzsche summarizes his perspective on the diverse and mundane details of which everyone's life is full:

> One will ask me why on earth I've been relating all these small things which are generally considered matters of complete indifference: I only harm myself, the more so if I am destined to represent great tasks. Answer: these small things—nutrition, place, climate, recreation, the whole casuistry of selfishness—are inconceivably more important than everything one has taken to be important so far. Precisely here one must begin to *relearn*. What mankind has so far considered seriously have not even been realities but mere imaginings—more strictly speaking, *lies* prompted by the bad instincts of sick natures that were harmful in the most profound sense—all these concepts, "God," "soul," "virtue," "sin," "beyond," "truth," "eternal life."—But the greatness of human nature, its "divinity," was sought in them.—All the problems of politics, of social organization, and of education have been falsified through and through because one mistook the most harmful men for great men—because one learned to despise "little" things, which means the basic concerns of life itself.[4]

If Zarathustra's sermons are to be faulted for their content, they should probably be faulted for their level of abstraction rather than for their subject matter. The abstraction is sometimes a bit airy, but a compensating

123

grace is that Zarathustra shares Nietzsche's pleasure in images. The following passage from Zarathustra's speech "On Reading and Writing" is an example of Zarathustra's characteristic insertion of visually striking images into an abstract discussion. This comment follows a rebuttal to those who claim that "life is hard to bear." Speaking for those who oppose the self-indulgence implicit in this cliché, Zarathustra comments:

> True, we love life, not because we are used to living but because we are used to loving. There is always some madness in love. But there is also always some reason in madness.
>
> And to me too, as I am well disposed toward life, butterflies and soap bubbles and whatever among men is of their kind seem to know most about happiness. Seeing these light, foolish, delicate, mobile little souls flutter—that seduces Zarathustra to tears and songs.[5]

The abstraction that characterizes much of "Zarathustra's Speeches" (Zarathustra, Part I) is somewhat mitigated by such imagistic insertions. The dissonance between the abstraction involved in any formulation of insight and that insight's application to life is a serious concern of the remainder of the book, however. And since Nietzsche himself argues that abstraction can become harmfully out of touch with the reality of what it aims to describe, we are warranted in asking whether Zarathustra, Part I, is flawed from the author's own perspective.

The points at which the speeches in Part I seem farthest removed from tangible reality are exactly those points at which Zarathustra's doctrine of the overman is most in evidence as a doctrine. While the extreme abstraction that sometimes characterizes Zarathustra's speeches may be too excessive to be consistent with his earthbound emphasis or to be effective for communicating with his audience, the abstraction of Zarathustra's speeches about the overman is appropriate for expressing what Zarathustra means by this concept. We now turn to some of Zarathustra's comments on the overman in order to demonstrate that Zarathustra's abstraction is sometimes essential to his point.

The following are some passages from Zarathustra's speeches that refer to the overman:

> Where the state ends—look there, my brothers! Do you not see it, the rainbow and the bridges of the overman?[6]

> Bitterness lies in the cup of even the best love: thus it arouses longing for the overman; thus it arouses your thirst, creator. Thirst for the creator, an arrow and long- ing for the overman: tell me, my brother, is this your will to marriage? Holy I call such a will and such a marriage.[7]

> The friend should be the festival of the earth to you and an anticipation of the overman.... Let the future and the farthest be for you the cause of your today: in your friend you shall love the overman as your cause.
>   My brothers, love of the neighbor I do not recommend to you: I recommend to you love of the farthest.[8]

Such passages do not seem particularly informative about the state, marriage, or friendship, and perhaps for this reason they seem undesirably abstract. But this criticism is unfair, because the overman is an emblem for the goal of human development toward greatness, and as such it is an essen- tially abstract and formal concept. The concept is neces- sarily abstract because it is not instantiated, and also because various lives that aspire toward it might have only general characteristics in common. The abstraction of the quoted passages is therefore appropriate to their content. Furthermore, the passages, while not very informative with respect to the state, marriage, or friendship, *are* informative with respect to the concept of the overman. They indicate points of contact between everyday aspects of our social experience and the vision of human greatness that "the overman," in Nietzsche's vocabulary, represents. By suggesting this connection, Nietzsche is asking provocative questions about the extent to which our ideals inform our interpersonal relationships and our political institutions. At the same time, Nietzsche is indicating the multifaceted character of the goal of greatness that he signals with the term "overman." Abstraction, even extreme abstraction, is appropriate in these passages. The goal of the overman is necessarily abstract because, as Nietzsche characterizes it, it is a goal that is overarching with respect to every aspect of our lives.

Allusions

In discussing the overt content of Zarathustra's speeches, I should say something about Nietzsche's use of allusions. Nietzsche has a veritable mania for allusions. He alludes again and again to the New Testament and Plato, but he also alludes to the Old Testament, Goethe, Shakespeare, Luther, Schopenhauer, Kant, Sophocles, Homer, Apuleius, and Greek mythology. In addition to such scholarly and intersubjectively valuable allusions, he makes self-indulgent allusions to friends and former friends.[9]

My effort in this book is not to provide a detailed commentary on *Zarathustra* but to indicate the general sweep of that text. I do not catalog Nietzsche's allusions to earlier texts, because such an effort is not in keeping with the thrust of my project. The proverbial perspective of looking at the trees instead of the forest has, in my view, only too frequently been applied to Zarathustra with the effect that the significant role of fictional movement has been largely ignored or underemphasized.[10] Nietzsche's allusions may be rampant, but for the most part they are not obscure.

Minimal familiarity with the New Testament and Plato's dialogues should enable the reader to recognize the most evident strands of allusion, those that refer to Scripture and to the dialogues. The majority of other allusions refer to well-known statements from earlier works and historical contexts. The pun on Luther in "Among Daughters of the Wilderness," for example—

> And there I stand even now
> As a European;
> I cannot do else; God help me!
> Amen.[11]

refers to Luther's most famous line.

An exception to my basic claim that Nietzsche's allusions are not particularly obscure appears in a systematic pattern of allusions to Apuleius, which occurs in *Zarathustra*, Part IV. Chapter 7 treats this pattern in detail, first because it is not obvious to the reader who has not read Apuleius' *Golden Ass*, a work that is not currently a part of the standard American curriculum, and second because this pattern helps to reveal the structural importance of Part IV, which does not much resemble the earlier parts of the book.

Nietzsche does not make his allusions do his work for him. The allusions to the New Testament reinforce the reader's recognition that Zarathustra is an antagonist of Christianity[12] but the substance of Zarathustra's claims in passages that make such allusions is usually clear in its anti-Christian tenor independently. The same is true of the vast majority of Nietzsche's other allusions in *Zarathustra*. In the section "On Poets" (considered in detail below, demonstrating how Nietzsche uses allusion to reinforce his points), Nietzsche's criticism of the poetic tradition is evident even if one misses his playful and straightforward

127

allusions to Goethe and Shakespeare. As clear as Nietzsche's allusions usually are, the alert reader with working awareness of the West's classical texts should have no difficulty recognizing most of them; in any event, the overt argument of Zarathustra's speeches should keep the reader apprised of Nietzsche's basic aim in a passage. Readers are more likely to lose their orientation in the book by missing the text's basic sweep than by occasionally missing an allusion.

Difficult Sections

Two allusion-filled sections are more confusing than most. One is the section entitled "On Immaculate Perception." There Nietzsche suggests that a common perspective on life underlies the Christian suspicion of sexuality, the Kantian view that "pure" judgments of the beautiful must be detached, Schopenhauer's related view that a contemplative and will-less perspective on the rest of the world is the only genuinely ethical stance, and the cross-culturally common religious teaching that detachment from this world is essential to religiosity. The perspective implicit in all these views is a squeamish distaste for the nitty-gritty, physical, and passionate actuality of human existence—and this amounts, on Nietzsche's view, to an unhealthy opposition to the fundamental substance of life itself.

Nietzsche's strategy is to suggest the common denominator among the views just listed by making obvious references to them in the course of Zarathustra's speech in this section. The speech involves an imagistic attack on the lechery implicit in the doctrine of the "pure perceivers." Besides alluding in the title to the Christian perspective on sexuality implicit in the doctrine of the Immaculate Conception,[13] Nietzsche signals Christianity as a target when Zarathustra refers to "the monk in the moon" whose detachment is a form of voyeurism. "You lack all innocence

128

in your desire," says Zarathustra to such detached Christians, "and therefore you slander all desire."[14] The Kantian view is alluded to when Zarathustra recalls the time he once fancied "no better art" than that of the pure perceivers.[15] Schopenhauer, who urged absolute chastity as the proper lifestyle of the pure perceiver, is attacked when Zarathustra insists that the will to procreate is purer: "Where is innocence? Where there is a will to procreate. And he who wants to create beyond himself has the purest will."[16] The cross-cultural religious doctrine that detachment is the highest virtue is generally attacked in Zarathustra's parody of this doctrine's statements: "This would be the highest to my mind... to look at life without desire and not, like a dog, with my tongue hanging out.... This I should like best... to love the earth as the moon loves her, and to touch her beauty only with my eyes."[17]

The sustained metaphor of perverted and voyeuristic sexuality unifies the implicit attacks, but the section has been criticized for employing this device in an overly contrived way. "Labored sexual imagery," Kaufmann claims, "keeps this critique of detachment from becoming incisive. Not arid but, judged by high standards, a mismatch of message and metaphor."[18] I suspect that what is too contrived for Kaufmann's tastes may well be amusing to other readers. But the density of targets signaled by various allusions might make the passage difficult for unsuspecting readers to decipher, particularly because the sexual imagery is both consistent and dominant.

A second section in which multiple allusions may provoke confusion is the section entitled "On Great Events." In that section Zarathustra returns from a descent to hell, which is designed to remind the reader of the doctrine that Christ descended to hell during the interim between his death on the cross and his resurrection. The startling image that upsets the easy interpretation that Zarathustra is

129

attacking the Christian doctrine of hell is the firehound with whom Zarathustra claims he chatted. This image conflates the Greek myth of Hades, the gloomy realm of the dead that is guarded by the vicious, three-headed dog Cerebus, and the Christian doctrine of hell, which is conceived in popular imagination as an unquenchable fire in which sinners are eternally tortured. In belittling the firehound, a personification of these ugly visions of life after death, Zarathustra attacks what Nietzsche sees as their common hypocrisy of pretending to represent the truth of the life beyond. On his view, their real function is to torture the imaginations of the living and thereby to reinforce the power of the religious establishments that propagate these myths.

The allusion to both Christian and Greek myths of the afterlife does not, however, prove the crucial key to the meaning of the section. The section's title, "On Great Events," suggests that the section has something to do with political developments, and this is confirmed by Zarathustra's words to the firehound:

> Freedom is what all of you like best to bellow; but I have outgrown the belief in "great events" wherever there is much bellowing and smoke.
>
> Believe me, friend Hellishnoise: the greatest events—they are not our loudest but our stillest hours....
>
> ...And this word I shall add for those who overthrow statues: nothing is more foolish than casting salt into the sea and statues into the mud. The statue lay in the mud of your contempt; but precisely this is its law, that out of contempt life and living beauty come back to it. It rises again with more godlike features, seductive through suffering; and verily, it will yet thank you for having overthrown it, O you overthrowers....
>
> ...But be still, you hypocritical hound! You know your own kind best! Like you, the state is a hypocritical

hound; like you, it likes to talk with smoke and
bellowing.[19]

The firehound represents the spokesman for revolutionary
movements. The advocates of violent overthrow of political
structures and revolutionary changes are, like the most con-
servative religionists, captivated with grandiose external
images for their own inner violence. They impress themselves with imaginings spawned by their own hatred. Along
with religious preachers of hell and damnation, they are not
able to see that great changes in the human sphere are not
political or otherworldly, but a matter of inner, individual
transformation.

Zarathustra's attack on the firehound concludes with
reference to another firehound, an animal whose fire is the
fire of this-worldly passion and love of the earth. In this
remark Zarathustra is proposing a countermyth to the violent myths of suffering after death and political revolution.
His myth uses the image of fire as a symbol—not of suffering
or of bombings, but of passionate living that is rewarded by
its own vibrance. The fire that should concern the living is
the volcano-like fire of impassioned participation in this
life, a fire that wells up from the earthly substance of our
present existence.

EARLY DISSONANCE: ZARATHUSTRA
AS PROPHET

Especially in Part I, where Zarathustra seems a tireless
evangelist, Zarathustra's speeches may strike us as ex-
hausting. They may have sounded different to nineteenth-
century ears—if despite Nietzsche's doubts, there were contemporary ears to hear them. But to us in the latter half of
the twentieth century, the high biblical prose-style of Zarathustra's sermons can be grating. It is also apt to mislead

131

us. We associate this style with self-important preachers who present themselves as authorities on God's word. To those of us who are remotely sympathetic with Nietzsche's sensibilities regarding hypocritical uses of religion, such a style seems puffy, pompous, and reminiscent of those who veil ugly motives with apparent piety. But here is Nietzsche's prophet—his *alternative* to the preachers of Christianity—sounding as self-important as the worst of them and equally insistent on telling us what to do!

The dissonance between Nietzsche's antitraditional, individualistic message and the style of its harbinger seems ironic—and perhaps the irony is at Nietzsche's expense, at least in *Zarathustra*, Part I. He does seem to present Zarathustra as a serious preacher who has the answers in hand. But although Nietzsche may at this stage be somewhat taken in by his prophet (recall that Part I was written half a year before Part II), he himself is aware of the irony of his prophet's stance. He concludes Part I with the section already cited as the first major clue that Zarathustra has second thoughts about what he is doing. In a farewell speech that concludes some fifty pages of telling his disciples what to do, Zarathustra repudiates his stance as an authority figure. Oxymoronically, he tells his disciples to doubt every word he has said.

> Now I go alone, my disciples. You too go now, alone. Thus I want it. Verily, I counsel you: go away from me and resist Zarathustra. And even better: be ashamed of him! Perhaps he deceived you....
>
> You say you believe in Zarathustra? But what matters Zarathustra? You are my believers—but what matter all believers?...
>
> Now I bid you lose me and find yourselves; and only when you have denied me will I return to you.[20]

This passage indicates that Nietzche *intended* his reader to recognize that Zarathustra is not to be heard as an authority figure on the model of a traditional religious leader. Whether he succeeds in achieving a tone that supports this intention is debatable. Success in this matter may be accomplished less easily with us than with readers of his own era, however well contrived Nietzsche's literary strategy. The latter would have been more accustomed to diction that might strike our ears as absurdly lofty. And perhaps more important, the shock value of the statements made would undercut more strikingly the tendency to see Zarathustra as another pompous prophet when *Zarathustra* was new than it would for us, who probably know coincidentally that Nietzsche is a committed atheist and an opponent of Christian doctrine.

GROWING EVIDENCE OF ZARATHUSTRA'S AMBIVALENCE

Parts II and III reveal Nietzsche's considerable concern with the problem of Zarathustra's status as an authority figure. A recurrent theme throughout the rest of the book is that Zarathustra is frequently confused about his own perspective and that both he and his doctrine are continuously in the throes of growing pains. This theme is evident even in the opening of Part II. "Months and years" have elapsed since we have last seen Zarathustra,[21] and Part II opens with Zarathustra awakening from a dream and reflecting,

Why was I so startled in my dream that I awoke? Did not a child step up to me, carrying a mirror? "O Zarathustra," the child said to me, "look at yourself in the mirror." But when I looked into the mirror I cried out,

133

and my heart was shaken: for it was not myself I saw,
but a devil's grimace and scornful laughter. Verily, all-
too-well do I understand the sign and admonition of the
dream: my *teaching* is in danger; weeds pose as wheat.
My enemies have grown powerful and have distorted
my teaching till those dearest to me must be ashamed of
the gifts I gave them. I have lost my friends; the hour
has come to seek my lost ones.[22]

Zarathustra's dream interpretation is quick, and it
seems to be in keeping with the interpretation of the close
of Part I that sees Zarathustra's misgivings as doubt that
others have understood him. But on closer inspection this
dream interpretation suggests that Zarathustra is not so
clear in his own mind about what he really thinks of his
disciples. His interpretation passes a judgment on the disciples' doubts about him that goes contrary to what he indicated to them in his last sermon. The disciples have
evidently done what Zarathustra urged; they have pursued
their own route and become skeptical of Zarathustra. But
now, in his privacy, Zarathustra responds to his disciples'
apostasy with horror, and he snaps to the conclusion that
his "enemies" are responsible.

Zarathustra sets aside the obvious suggestion of the mirror as a dream symbol, the suggestion that the dream reflects
something about himself. The reflection that the dream
presents is not complimentary; it shows "a devil's grimace
and scornful laughter." Zarathustra's avoidance of the possibility that the dream reveals more about himself than
about his disciples indicates that he is deceiving himself.
And for the short run this self-deception seems successful.
Zarathustra acts on his dream interpretation and reengages
in his project of teaching. The next several sections of Part
II present speeches much on the order of those in Part I.

Only in the seventh section of Part II do we see Zarathustra slip out of the familiar mold of authoritative preacher to which he has quickly returned. In that section, entitled "On the Tarantula," he preaches a sermon on the ugly and pervasive undercurrent of revenge that lurks behind the modern doctrine that all men are created equal. *"That man be delivered from revenge,* that is for me the bridge to the highest hope, and a rainbow after long storms."[23] But at the end of the section, Zarathustra admits that he himself cannot completely adhere to his own doctrine. "Alas," says Zarathustra after his sermon has reached a cadence,

> then the tarantula, my old enemy bit me....
> Indeed, it has avenged itself. And alas, now it will make my soul, too, whirl with revenge. But to keep me from whirling, my friends, tie me tight to this column. Rather would I be a stylite even, than a whirl of revenge.
> Verily, Zarathustra is no cyclone or whirlwind; and if he is a dancer, he will never dance the tarantella.[24]

Zarathustra appears to take a courageous attitude toward his own weakness, vowing to resist it as much as he can. But the effect of Nietzsche's reference to Zarathustra's incapacity is contrary to that of Zarathustra's authoritative persona. The persona asserts the validity of Zarathustra's doctrine, but it tends to undercut the individualistic thrust of the doctrine. By contrast, reference to Zarathustra's inability to live up to his own teachings tends to undercut the convincingness of his doctrine as well as his stature in our eyes. And this might make us wonder whether Nietzsche is disavowing the positions that Zarathustra promoted earlier. Is Nietzsche attempting to compensate for one flaw in his presentation with another?

Nietzsche's project of presenting his hero's incapacities

seems too systematic to be *simply* an effort to compensate for a flaw in his earlier depiction of Zarathustra, although it is effectively that. The remainder of Part II reveals a pattern of increasingly pronounced dissonance between the confident tone of Zarathustra's teaching and his growing suspicion that they neither represent wisdom nor assure a sense of meaning in his life. Two sections after "On the Tarantula," Nietzsche presents the first of a series of three songs of Zarathustra. The first, "The Night Song," is a lament about the emotional strain of maintaining the stance of a teacher who appears to his disciples as a bottomless well of insight and generosity.[25] "The Dancing Song," which I discuss in greater detail shortly, is a song about life's evasive nonconformity to Zarathustra's insights; Zarathustra becomes depressed during the course of singing it. "The Tomb Song" is a lament about visions and insights of Zarathustra's youth that no longer remain alive for him. In this song he again refers to his "enemies," who he claims have poisoned the sweet vows of his immaturity by making them too difficult to keep. In these songs we are given a glimpse of the inner discontent that lies behind Zarathustra's public poise. It is significantly that in each of these cases Zarathustra's mood reflects a disturbance about the status of his teaching in the context of his own life.

Zarathustra's speeches resume after "The Tomb Song," but the reader has been made aware of his doubts about the value of his doctrine and his role as a teacher. These doubts become clearer to us when, after several speeches, Zarathustra has another nightmare. The details of this dream are more elaborate than those of the earlier dream, and I shall say more about them shortly. What is interesting in this context is that Zarathustra is no longer willing to analyze his nightmare in the glib manner that we observed in the first section of Part II. When one of Zarathustra's disciples proposes Zarathustra's own earlier interpretation—

that this never dream was also about his enemies—Zarathustra shakes his head.

Zarathustra continues teaching, and in the section "On Redemption" he reaches one of his most elegant summaries of his psychological interpretation of the quest for redemption to this point. (That section, which represents a crucial statement of Zarathustra's developing theory of time, is the focus of Chapter 6 and will be discussed there. My interest here is in the ending of "On Redemption.") The section does not end with a rhetorical flourish that is in keeping with the forceful clarity of Zarathustra's speech. Instead we see Zarathustra interrupting himself in the midst of a round of rhetorical questions that ask who has yet overcome the spirit of revenge:

> "And when will that happen? Has the will been unharnessed yet from his own folly? Has the will yet become his own redeemer and joy-bringer? Has he unlearned the spirit of revenge...?
>
> ... That will which is the will to power must will something higher than any reconciliation, but how shall this be brought about? Who could teach him also to will backwards?"
>
> At this point in his speech it happened that Zarathustra suddenly stopped and looked altogether like one who has received a severe shock. Appalled, he looked at his disciples; his eyes pierced their thoughts and the thoughts behind their thoughts as arrows.[26]

The implication, consonant with that made by the end of "On the Tarantula," is that Zarathustra himself has not achieved the goal he is preaching. Zarathustra tries to recover his stage image with an opaque comment: "It is difficult to live with people because silence is so difficult. Especially for one who is garrulous." Presumably Zarathustra means that he recognizes that he was saying more than he had warrant to say. But Zarathustra's attempt to recover grace is cut short by the hunchback who had urged him to speak in the first place. At the end of the section, the hunchback asks, "But why does Zarathustra speak otherwise to us than to his disciples?"

> Zarathustra answered: "What is surprising in that? With hunchbacks one may well speak in a hunchbacked way."
> "All right," said the hunchback; "and one may well tell pupils tales out of school. But why does Zarathustra speak otherwise to his pupils than to himself?"[27]

The hunchback resembles the child of the fairy tale who announces that the emperor has no clothes. He evidently gets to Zarathustra. The section ends with the hunchback's question, not with the recurrent refrain "Thus spoke Zarathustra." The hunchback has had the last word in the exchange. The only speech that Zarathustra makes in Part II after this encounter occurs in the following section, "On Human Prudence." In this section, Zarathustra defends his own strategy of being humanly prudent—prudent, in other words, because he recognizes his own and other's weaknesses and tries to work around them, for example:

> That is my first instance of my human prudence, that I let myself be deceived in order not to be on guard against deceivers....
> This, however, is the second instance of my human prudence: I spare the *vain* more than the proud. Is not hurt vanity the mother of all tragedies?[28]

The Crisis

The following section, "The Stillest Hour," concludes Part II. This section shows Zarathustra at an extreme point of self-doubt and confusion about his teaching vocation. He is confronted in his stillest hour, the point at which he is furthest from his teaching persona, by a "voiceless voice." Zarathustra reports the episode after the fact:

> Yesterday, in the stillest hour, the ground gave under me, the dream began. The hand moved, the clock of my life drew a breath; never had I heard such stillness around me: my heart took fright.
>
> Then it spoke to me without voice, "You know it, Zarathustra?" And I cried with fright at this whispering, and the blood left my fact; but I remained silent.[29]

The content of the silent dialogue between Zarathustra and the voiceless voice is difficult to follow because it is not articulated. But the issue between the parties to this odd conversation is essentially the question of whether Zarathustra is willing or able to say what he knows.

The voiceless voice answers itself: "You know it, Zarathustra, but you do not say it." Zarathustra maintains that he does not *want* to say what he knows, but the voice questions this. Zarathustra shifts his position, claiming that although he would like to he really lacks the strength to say it. The voiceless voice tells him that risk to himself is fine, that he should "speak his word and break." Zarathustra responds that it really is not *his* word that he wants to say and that therefore someone more appropriate should say it. And so on. Zarathustra shifts his position every time the voiceless voice attacks one of his alibis. Finally Zarathustra runs out of excuses and returns to his first excuse—that he simply does not want to say what he knows. The voiceless voice responds with laughter and tells Zarathustra, "O Zarathustra, your fruit is ripe, but you are not ripe for your fruit. Thus you must return to solitude again; for you must yet become mellow."[30] Zarathustra accepts the verdict of

139

the voiceless voice and mournfully bids farewell to his auditors. He seems confused as to whether he told them as much
as he could:

> Now you have heard all, and why I must return to my
> solitude. Nothing have I kept from you, my friends. But
> this too you have heard from me, who is still the most
> taciturn of all men—and wants to be. Alas, my friends, I
> could tell you something, I still could give you some-
> thing. Why do I not give it? Am I stingy?[31]

Walter Kaufmann interprets Zarathustra's claimed unwillingness in this passage as follows: "Zarathustra cannot
yet get himself to proclaim the eternal recurrence and hence
he must leave in order to 'ripen.' "[32] Eternal recurrence, the
book's central doctrine (which we will consider in the following chapter), does become articulate in Part III after
being only suggested in Part II. But Zarathustra's evasive-
ness in the passage seems to be a deeper spiritual crisis than
Kaufmann suggests. Kaufmann's interpretation suggests
that the doctrine of eternal recurrence is already fully articulate and that Zarathustra is stymied simply by a per-
versity that he is unable to overcome. But it appears to me
that the possibility of Zarathustra's being articulate is the
very matter at issue in the passage. The entire dialogue
between Zarathustra and the voiceless voice is inaudible—
Zarathustra refers to it, in fact, as a "dream."[33] The vague-
ness of the discussion suggests that what is being portrayed
is *inner conflict* much more than that Zarathustra is aware
of a specific content.

The account resembles accounts of the spiritual crises
frequently reported by mystics and labeled in the Christian
tradition as "Dark Night of the Soul."[34] Evelyn Underhill
describes Dark Night of the Soul as "a period of utter blank-
ness and stagnation," "a period of fatigue and lassitude fol-

lowing a period of sustained mystical activity."[35] This period is characterized by anguish and a sense of loss, which may focus on the loss of God or on loss of intellectual clarity.[36] Mystics consider the Dark Night of the Soul to be a stage that is preliminary to a state of greater union with God. It serves, in Underhill's description, as "the final purification of the will or stronghold of personality, that it may be merged without any reserve 'in God where it was first.'"[37]

Although Nietzsche may be describing Zarathustra in a fashion reminiscent of the self-description of Christian mystics who experience Dark Night of the Soul, he does not mean for us to adopt the transcendent interpretation of Christian mystics as a key to what Zarathustra's is experiencing.[38] But the parallel may help us to focus on the extremity of Zarathustra's confusion. It appears that Zarathustra, after the fashion of certain mystics, has lost intellectual clarity and is tormented by a sense of ineffable disorientation. He himself does not seem to know what is wrong, or if he does know he does not know how to explain it.

Inarticulate as the crux of Zarathustra's problem is, his crisis centers on his ability to teach, and more specifically on his ability to verbalize what he knows. To borrow Nietzsche's own vocabulary from an earlier work, we might say that Zarathustra lacks the Apollonian words that will enable him to fix his insights into an apprehensible formulation. We have heard a lot of words going by in Part II, but the suggestion in "The Stillest Hour" is that none of these words has expressed the heart of Zarathustra's insights.

On Nietzsche's account, Zarathustra's problem resembles the problem of those members of the tragic audience, who are not moved to the transformed spiritual state at which tragedy aims because they do not have the underlying faith—that life is wonderful despite suffering—which charges the images of the drama. At best such audience members can enjoy a tragedy as an aesthetic play of images. In a comparable fashion Zarathustra seems to lack the faith that is crucial to the integrity of his teaching. The internal dissonance he experiences in "The Stillest Hour" indicates that he sees his recent teaching as a mere play with images. He has evidently lost touch with the spirit that moved him when he first vowed to share his insight with others. The tone of the section, so reminiscent of descriptions in the Christian mystical tradition, is appropriate, for Zarathustra's crisis might be called "religious" in the same sense that one might apply the term to Greek tragedy.

The Nature of Zarathustra's Problem

Our recollection of Nietzsche's discussion in *The Birth of Tragedy* of the function of Apollonian images can give us insight into the character of the discrepancy between Zarathustra's teaching and his inner state. Zarathustra's project as a teacher has been to clothe his insights about the dynamic actuality of life in the fixed formulations of words. Nietzsche's earlier analysis suggests why this project is inherently doomed to some degree of failure. Words, images, and all conveyances for articulate communication falsify the chaotic, ever-changing reality of life. They attempt to contain the dynamic of life in static forms, but the volatile cannot be fixed.[39] The project of articulating insights about the nature of life attempts the impossible feat of inventing fixed images for what is constantly changing. Therefore, the project of a philosophical teacher like Zarathustra is inherently an impossible project. In a sense, the truth about life can never be spoken.

That this problem has been on Zarathustra's mind while the crisis of "The Stillest Hour" has been building is evident in "The Dancing Song." There Zarathustra sings of Life and his Wisdom, whom he casts as two women with whom he is in love. He addresses the song to Life, and he recalls a recent conversation that he had with her. In that conversation Life scoffed at the way men project their own intellectual constructs upon her: "What *they* do not fathom is unfathomable. But I am merely changeable and wild and a woman in every way, and not virtuous. . . . [Y]ou men always present us with your own virtues." Zarathustra reports this, but claims that he did not believe it: "I never believe her and her laughter when she speaks ill of herself."[40]

As the song continues it becomes evident that Zarathustra's Wisdom (whom he designates as "my wild wisdom") is jealous of Life, and that Life is jealous of Wisdom. Zarathustra claims that his heart belongs to Life alone, but that he is confused by his Wisdom's resemblance to Life: "But that I am well disposed toward wisdom, and often too well, that is because she reminds me so much of life. . . . Is it my fault that the two look so similar?"[41]

Zarathustra's confusion, as Life sees it, is deeper than he realizes. When Zarathustra describes his Wisdom as being "changeable and stubborn" and "perhaps evil and false and a female in every way"—using almost exactly the terms of Life's self-description—Life laughs sarcastically and says, "Of whom are you speaking? . . . No doubt of me." Accepting Zarathustra's characterizations as applying to herself, she acknowledges that he means nothing flattering by it: "Even if you are right—should *that* be said to my face? But now speak of your wisdom too." The song ends with Zarathustra describing how he then gazed into Life's eyes: "I seemed to myself to be sinking into the unfathomable."[42]

Zarathustra's song indicates metaphorically the confusing disparity between life, with its chaotic wildness, and the "wisdom" through which men attempt to describe life. Because such a disparity inevitably exists, Nietzsche suggests, one can easily become confused in any articulation of one's insight. Is one being faithful to life or being enthralled by one's own system of expression? This suggestion is, in Nietzsche's earlier vocabulary, a Dionysian insight about the nature of the relationship of life and thought, and Zarathustra expresses this insight in the paradigmatic Dionysian mode of expression, that of song.

When Zarathustra returns from his musical mood to his more usual condition of thought, he is deeply depressed. He seems to feel removed from the vibrant enthrallment with life of which he sang. "What? Are you still alive, Zarathustra?" he asks himself. "Why? What for? By what? Whither? Where? How? Is it not folly still to be alive?"[43] Suggestive as the song may be for indicating the necessary distance between life and wisdom, it also indicates that Zarathustra sees his wisdom as having grown away from the life that initially inspired it. At the end of "The Dancing Song," Zarathustra finds the growth of this disparity to be a ground for doubting the value of his life and work.

The section "On Poets" indicates that at least Zarathustra still recognizes that one can become more out of touch with life through intoxication with one's own words than he is. The primary target of the section is Socrates, whose mission was to convert his contemporaries to the belief that rational inquiry could plumb the depths of reality. In his effort to convert his contemporaries to the method of rational inquiry, the Socrates of Plato's dialogues depicts the banishment of poets as essential to the formation of his ideal society. Poets, according to Socrates, perniciously draw the attention of their auditors to the delightful appearances of the sensible world, distracting them from the realm of true being, which is immaterial and changeless. Poets do not even provide their auditors with knowledge about the sensible world, only with imitative images of what the world looks like before rational reflection. Because the passionate aspects of the soul are more easily imitated than the truths available to reason, the poet indulges the irrational nature, thus exerting a harmful influence even on the good, who attempt to guide their lives by reason.[44] By regaling their auditors with appeals to "the honeyed muse," the poets are harmful to the state; their appeals lead to the consequence that "not law and the reason of mankind . . . , but pleasure and pain will be the rulers of our State." For these reasons, Plato's Socrates asserts, "There is from of old a quarrel between philosophy and poetry."[45]

In *The Birth of Tragedy*, Nietzsche denies that even Socrates himself could maintain this split between philosophy and poetry. He argues that Socrates gained the confidence of Athenian youth not through a demonstration of the efficacy of his rational methods but through the arational art of making himself an erotic image. His disciples were drawn to his teaching because they admired him as a teacher, and not the other way around. Furthermore, Socrates' death indicates that Socrates was calculatingly aware of his irrational appeals, for he deliberately provoked his judges into making him a martyr. *"The dying Socrates,"* claims Nietzsche, "became the new ideal, never seen before, of noble Greek youth: above all, the typical Hellenic youth, Plato, prostrated himself before this image with all the ardent devotion of his enthusiastic soul."[46]

Despite his charge that Socrates is inconsistent, Nietzsche directly confronts the Socratic opposition of philosophy and poetry through Zarathustra's speech "On Poets." The section begins with a disciple asking Zarathustra why he has said in the past that "the poets lie too much." Zarathustra's earlier claim that the poets lie too much links him with Socrates, for that was precisely the claim that Socrates made to justify banishing the poets. But the section reveals Zarathustra in his role as parodic alternative to Socrates. He offers the very un-Socratic response to his disciple that he himself is a poet and that he does lie too much: "*We* do not lie too much. We also know too little and we are bad learners; so we simply have to lie."[47]

Zarathustra, then, admits what Socrates refused to admit about himself: that he himself is a poet, the inventor of poetic lies, and that this invention is necessary. Zarathustra suggests, too, that this necessity is experienced by poets not just because they are poets but instead because they are human beings. Human beings necessarily interpret their world creatively, through images that are not literally accurate, and such invented truth is the only truth human beings have.

The understanding of truth that Zarathustra presents opposes that of Plato's Socrates, who claims, "Of that place beyond the heavens none of our earthly poets has yet sung, and none shall sing worthily."[48] Zarathustra, on the contrary, observes, "Alas, there are so many things between heaven and earth of which only the poets have dreamed."[49] This comment is an allusion to *Hamlet*, where Hamlet tells his Stoic friend Hortio when they both see the ghost of Hamlet's father, "There are more things in heaven and earth, Horatio, / Than are dreamt of in your philosophy."[50] Nietzsche suggests with this allusion that a skeptical, rationalistic philosophy is an insufficient access to the fullness of human reality.

Zarathustra does express certain misgivings about poetry, however. He indicates, for instance, his belief that although any image of reality distorts our view of life's actuality, images can be better or worse at communicating something of value for a healthy orientation toward life. "Ah, how weary I am of all the imperfections which must at all costs become events," he sighs.[51] With this allusion to Goethe, he suggests that even the greatest of poets are in some way lacking. The allusion refers to the Chorus Mysticus, which concludes Goethe's *Faust*:

> What is destructible
> Is but a parable;
> What fails ineluctably,
> The undeclarable,
> Here it was seen,
> Here it was action;
> The Eternal Feminine
> Lures to perfection.[52]

Zarathustra's dissatisfaction with Goethe's poetic stance is even more evident in his statement that "All that is 'permanent' is also a mere parable."[53] The poets who, like Goethe, share Socrates' belief that the deepest reality is changeless lie perniciously, in Nietzsche's view. They interfere with the insight that is fundamental to our healthy satisfaction in life, the insight that life is a dynamic flux which is delightful and powerful because it is exactly that.

Zarathustra's statement about the permanent underscores the fact that his misgivings about poetry are not the same as those of Socrates. Zarathustra clearly rejects Socrates' view that poetry is harmful because it does not communicate the truth, which Socrates considers absolute and "permanent." Zarathustra objects not to the fact that the poets lie but to the shallowness of their lies.

> I have grown weary of the poets, the old and the new: superficial they all seem to me, and shallow seas. Their thoughts have not penetrated deeply enough; therefore their feelings did not touch bottom.
> Some lust and some boredom: that has so far been their best reflection. All their harp jingling is to me the breathing and flitting of ghosts; what have they ever known of the fervor of tones?
> Nor are they clean enough for me: they all muddy their waters to make them appear deep. And they like

to pose as reconcilers: but mediators and mixers they
remain for me, and half-and-half and unclean.[54]

The poets pretend to offer a synthesizing vision of the
world of human experience, but this pretense is dishonest.
They actually display fleeting glimpses of their own bore-
dom and occasional lusts, and mix together ghostly frag-
ments, allusions to some spiritual beyond of which they
have heard from their poetic and intellectual tradition. Zarathustra criticizes the poets for not having enough of the
irrational power that Socrates criticizes even while he employs it: the erotic power of love and desire. "What have
they ever known of the fervor of tones?" The poets have
not, thus far, been fervent enough in their desire to see very
deeply into the reality about which they spin myths. Even
Socrates offered a greater vision of reality than most poets
do, for although Socrates' own lies obscured the status of
his rational project, he himself was fervent in his desire to
penetrate the real. And this fervor gave him the erotic power
that gained him the influence that transformed the Western
world.

Zarathustra seeks a kind of poetry that is deeper than
that achieved by the traditional poets. He seeks a poetry
that will effect a worldview, a synthetic view of the whole,
instead of a poetry that remains "half-and-half." The poetry
that he advocates must achieve a synthesis of dream and
fervent desire, a synthesis of the Apollonian and the Dionysian. This poetry would present a vision of human reality
that "lies less" than either traditional poetry, which only
gestures toward the ground of human experience, or the
Socratic tradition of reliance on rationality, which offers a
distorted picture of the human being's relationship to the
world.

Although Zarathustra is unable to judge his own efforts

as having any value during the crisis of "The Stillest Hour," the problem does not appear to be confusion about the relationship between words and the spiritual import that they try to communicate. In a way this is precisely what the voiceless voice tells him; his lack of knowledge is not the problem here. The problem, on the contrary, appears to be that Zarathustra is no longer in contact with the Dionysian spirit that moved his initial descent from the mountain and informed the vision that he tried to speak. Zarathustra has become more adept as a speaker, and in this way he has gained an audience, but he has lost contact with the pulse of his original message.

The dream in "The Soothsayer" suggests the cause of Zarathustra's problem: he has lost touch with the ground of his insight because he has become too bound to the set of formulations that he has used to communicate. In the dream, Zarathustra has become "a night watchman and a guardian of tombs upon the lonely mountain castle of death." His environment is dusty and Zarathustra comments, "Sultry and dusty lay my soul." He has keys, "the rustiest of all keys," which he knows how to use "to open the most creaking of all gates."[55] The movement of Zarathustra's life seems to consist entirely of slowing moving gates that creak angrily. The dream portrays Zarathustra as one whose life has become depressing and stagnant because his work consists of guarding monuments to what is no longer alive and using "rusty keys" to attempt insight into what is virtually dead.

In contrast to Zarathustra's murky soul is "the brightness of midnight,"[56] the moment in which he finds himself. Midnight is symbolically the moment that is most full of the potency of the present. It is the moment in which life is immediately experienced, but at the same time it is the moment in which the past is surrendered for the sake of going forward toward the future of a new day.[57] Even though Zarathustra is living in this moment, he is spiritually asleep to it and its brightness.

He is awakened by three strokes that "struck at the gate like thunder." That Zarathustra has developed the habit of orienting himself to what is past and dead is evident from the cry with which he responds to the strokes at the gate: "Alpa! Who is carrying his ashes up the mountain? Alpa! Alpa! Who is carrying his ashes up the mountain?"[58] Zarathustra attempts to use one of his rusty keys to open the gate that has been struck, but his key will not budge it. What moves the gate is a roaring wind that tears it apart suddenly. The wind also blows a new black coffin into Zarathustra's vault. The coffin bursts open and reveals a chaotic cauldron of living and transient things, a "thousandfold laughter" and a "thousand grimaces of children, angels, owls, fools, and butterflies as big as children."[59]

The coffin's contents are all ephemeral. Zarathustra's response is to be very frightened. His horror cannot be a response to the contents themselves, which do not seem terrifying, although it may be a response to their mockery. Their mockery is of a piece with the implicit mockery of the entire dream. Zarathustra has become so absorbed in guarding his articulations of his insights—protecting his teachings from his "enemies"—that he has come to see his life itself as a kind of vault for their preservation. His thinking has become so divorced from the vibrant chaos of life that he dreams of it as an intrusion. In Zarathustra's dream, life spews out of a coffin because the coffin is the place into which Zarathustra has mentally and spiritually consigned it. Like the audience members who are closed to tragedy's intended effect, Zarathustra has lost touch with his Dionysian roots. And the Apollonian keys he retains have lost the power to facilitate his ability to experience life directly.

Zarathustra must wait for life to awaken him from his deadening dogmatic slumber.

MAKING PEACE WITH AMBIVALENCE

As in the dream, life does awaken Zarathustra from the stagnant state that precipitates the crisis of "The Stillest Hour." Part III chronicles the gradual reestablishment of harmony between Zarathustra's thinking (and consequently his doctrines) and the commotion-filled stream of life. This development is turbulent even from the beginning of Part III: Zarathustra wanders around consoling himself "with hard maxims," only to recognize that in his spiritual state of distance from the rest of reality he is vulnerable to foolish enthusiasms. "Love is the danger of the loneliest; love of everything if only it is alive. Laughable, verily, are my folly and my modesty in love."[60] This insight gives way to a recognition that indicates a step back from alienated thought and toward a renewed state of involvement with the rest of the living world around him. Zarathustra recognizes that he really does love. "But then he recalled his friends when he had left; and, as if he had wronged them with his thoughts, he was angry with himself for his thoughts. And soon it happened that he who had laughed wept: from wrath and longing Zarathustra wept bitterly."[61]

The resumption of a passional sense of immediacy in living is a painful process, and Zarathustra is often confused by his own emotional reactions.[62] Much of Part III is a meditation on time and change, and the second section of Part III, "On the Vision and the Riddle," is central to this theme. In that section Zarathustra describes a vision in which he encounters a dwarf, called "the spirit of gravity," who urges him to see time as a kind of straitjacket that sentences us in the future to consequences determined by the past. Zar-

151

athustra angrily rejects the dwarf's theory and proposes his own theory of time, which gives primacy to the present moment as the moment in which one lives and is free to express oneself. This theory of time, as a formulation of the doctrine of eternal recurrence, has an important and problematic function in *Zarathustra*, and it will be the focus of the next chapter. After the discussion of the next chapter, readers will be able to recognize the connections between many of the topics of Part III's sermons and Zarathustra's vision.

Zarathustra's doctrine of time as presented early in Part III demonstrates that Zarathustra has realized that interpreting the present from a perspective that gives primacy to the past is both psychologically devastating and unnecessary. In "The Vision and the Riddle," to his own surprise, Zarathustra announces a theory that focuses on the originality of the present moment. The perspective revealed in this theory is contrary to that implied in Zarathustra's dream in "The Soothsayer," and his articulate reply to the dwarf indicates that he has developed a response to the malaise that interrupted his teaching at the end of Part II. That this response is at first more theoretical than experiential is evident in the climax of Part III, the section entitled "The Convalescent," in which Zarathustra again experiences an emotional breakdown. Yet that section shows that Zarathustra's theoretically expressed sense that time should be viewed from a present-oriented perspective has become fully internalized, with the consequence that harmony between his inner orientation and his thought is again achieved.

For reasons that will be considered in the next chapter, Zarathustra expresses his theory of time with a model of time as cyclical instead of linear. The doctrine is called "eternal recurrence" because its claim is that all of time will repeat itself eternally and that every moment in time will recur to eternity, again and again and again. "The Convalescent" opens with Zarathustra in a mad fit prompted by his thinking about the doctrine. If everything recurs, then all petty people and their pettiness will recur; this is the "abysmal thought" that gags Zarathustra.[63] He reasons further that every person, even the greatest, is too petty to be willed to recur eternally. With this thought in mind, Zarathustra concludes that all life is pointless and disgusting. "Nausea, nausea, nausea," he moans." "Woe is me!"[64]

Zarathustra's animals, the eagle and the snake, do not find anything convincing in Zarathustra's thoughts, and they make Zarathustra aware that he has upset himself needlessly with thoughts that have become disconnected from life. They prod him to leave the diseased isolation of his reflections and to encounter the world directly. "Step out of your cave," they tell him. "The world awaits you like a garden. . . . Step out of your cave! All things would be your physicians."[65] Zarathustra's response indicates how much he is under an Apollonian spell, which presents words as the fundamental access to the world and portrays the individual as essentially separate from everything else. Says Zarathustra:

> To every soul there belongs another world; for every
> soul, every other soul is an afterworld. . . .
>   For me—how should there be any outside-myself?
> There is no outside. But all sounds make us forget this;
> how lovely it is that we forget. Have not names and
> sounds been given to things that man might find things
> refreshing? Speaking is a beautiful folly: with that man
> dances over all things. How lovely is all talking, and all
> the deception of sounds! With sounds our love dances
> on many-hued rainbows."[66]

His animals remind Zarathustra that despite his allusions to dancing, he has forgotten something far more fundamental than the insight that words effect illusions: "O Zarathustra, to those who think as we do, all things themselves are dancing: they come and offer their hands and laugh and flee—and come back. Everything goes, everything comes back; eternally rolls the wheel of being."[67] The animals proceed to elaborate a statement of Zarathustra's doctrine of eternal recurrence that makes it appear to describe time as the matrix in which dancing takes place. Time is continually in motion, continually a celebration, and the means for resurgent expression of life. Zarathustra makes a speech in response, explaining the thoughts that led to his fit of nausea. But his animals stop him: "Do not speak on, O convalescent!... but go out where the world awaits you like a garden. Go out to the roses and bees and dovecots. But especially to the songbirds, that you may learn from them how to sing! For singing is for the convalescent; the healthy can speak."[68]

The animals' advice is the advice of Dionysian insight. Zarathustra's words and thoughts have become a painful disease because they have become detached from the unruly immediacy of life. The cure for this cannot be achieved through further thought, but it can be achieved through encountering the world in immediacy and feeling one's own vital connection with it. Song is the mode of this kind of encounter. Only those who already feel their vital connection with the rest of life are healthy—they can speak with confidence that their words are healthy. Zarathustra's words, however, have become sick. He should silence his speaking voice and learn to sing instead.

Zarathustra admits that he has realized this himself: "That I must sing again, this comfort and convalescence I invented for myself." But his animals insist that he should not rest content with his realization. "Do not speak on!"[69] He should try to sing immediately. Only in this way can he accomplish his vocation of teaching eternal recurrence.

The doctrine's value depends on its being experientially understood, and Zarathustra can communicate its importance only if he experientially understands it. Zarathustra's animals are sympathetic about the danger to which Zarathustra's vocation of teacher exposes him, the danger that he will lose sight of the experiential grounding of his doctrine in his effort to refine his ability to articulate it in words. "That you as the first must teach this doctrine," the animals say, "—how could this great destiny not be your greatest danger and sickness too?"[70]

The animals make their point to Zarathustra. After they restate the doctrine of eternal recurrence, their advice that Zarathustra sing still resounding, Zarathustra is silent. We are told at the end of "The Convalescent" that Zarathustra is "conversing with his soul." And afterward we see that Zarathustra has stopped speaking. The remainder of Part III consists only of three exuberant songs. The first, "On the Great Longing," is a song that Zarathustra sings to his soul, reminding it of the steps toward greater freedom that he has shared with it and urging it to sing along with him.

"The Other Dancing Song" recalls the first dancing song, for it begins in the same way, with Zarathustra gazing into Life's eyes. But this time he describes their encounter as a dance in which they play at dominating each other. Zarathustra wins the game, and he and Life come to an understanding about their relationship to each other and to Wisdom. "If your wisdom ever ran away from you, then my love would quickly run away from you too," Life admits to him, revealing her awareness that his love affair with his Wisdom is an expression of love for her.

Life also claims to know that Zarathustra is thinking of leaving her soon, presumably to go back to his Wisdom. This infidelity is necessitated by the nature of thought. Thought cannot become isomorphic with life because life refuses to conform itself to thought's standards of order.

Zarathustra tries to reassure Life that his infidelities are innocent: "Yes, I answered hesitantly, 'but you also know'—and I whispered something into her ear, right through her tangled yellow foolish tresses." Life reminds him that any statement falls short of accurate reflection of dynamic reality. "You *know* that, O Zarathustra? Nobody knows that."[71] In this comment Life has the last word, and the scene ends with Zarathustra totally enamored: "But then life was dearer to me than all my wisdom ever was."[72] The conclusion of the section, which follows immediately, states amid bell-chimes the lines of the book's famous song that praises life as joyous despite all its woes:

> O men, take care!
> What does deep midnight declare?
> I was asleep—
> From a deep dream I woke and swear:
> The world is deep,
> Deeper than day had been aware.
> Deep is its woe;
> Joy—deeper yet than agony:
> Woe implores: Go!
> But all joy wants eternity—
> Wants deep, wants deep eternity.[73]

The final section of Part III, "The Seven Seals (Or: The Yes and Amen Song)," identifies Zarathustra as one who has experienced this joy that is greater than agony. It is Zarathustra's seven-stanza song of desire for eternity. Every stanza ends with this affirmation:

> Never yet have I found the woman from whom I wanted
> children, unless it be this woman whom I love: for I
> love you, O eternity.
> *For I love you, O eternity.*[74]

The Ambivalence of Zarathustra's Doctrine

By the end of Part III, Zarathustra's love of life has healed the dissonance between his teachings and his inner orientation. As we shall see in Chapter 7, Zarathustra has not reached a final stage in which life and thought will never fall out of harmony. He will lose his way again by attending so much to the letter of his doctrines that he forgets their spirit. But we shall also see that he will again restore his balance.

The fact that Zarathustra has not reached a stage of assured spiritual achievement at the end of Part III is consistent with Nietzsche's basic point about doctrine, which has been our focus for much of this chapter. Life, Nietzsche insists, will never fit itself to our expectations, no matter how perceptive and articulate those expectations are. Our philosophical doctrines are formulations of our most perceptive and articulate expectations. They can enhance our lives tremendously by bringing aspects to our situation (on any level) into manageable focus. But they can also mislead us by predisposing us to see only certain aspects of the situation to the exclusion of others, which may in certain contexts be more important. More perniciously, they can absorb our attention so much that we come to take them too seriously, forgetting that their value depends on their ability to help us make sense of our lives and that this ability can wax and wane with time. By showing Zarathustra in the painful process of forgetting this character of his doctrine, and then showing the process by which he comes to remember, Nietzsche attempts to remind us that theory should enhance life, and not the other way around.

I have suggested in this chapter that the basic world-orientation of *Zarathustra* is not only in keeping with that of *The Birth of Tragedy* but also directly a further amplification of it. In the following chapter I shall demonstrate that Nietzsche's most basic innovation in *Zarathustra*—the doctrine of eternal recurrence—furthers the case against

157

Christianity as an antitragic worldview. I shall argue, specifically, that Nietzsche presents eternal recurrence as a tragic alternative to the doctrine that he sees as the essence of Christianity, the doctrine of sin.

6   Eternal Recurrence Versus the Doctrine of Sin

Perhaps the whole of *Zarathustra* may be reckoned as music.[1]

ALTHOUGH *Thus Spoke Zarathustra* has not been among the favorite topics of Nietzsche scholars, the doctrine of eternal recurrence has. The reason for this is not difficult to ascertain: the doctrine—which asserts that the cycle of events in time repeats itself an infinite number of times—is not conceptually clear. According to some readings, it is not even internally coherent.[2] And even if one can see some sense in what the doctrine asserts, the significance of the doctrine is not obvious. Alexander Nehamas, beginning his account of eternal recurrence, expresses the sentiment of many who have attempted to make sense of the doctrine: "Whatever else we may be tempted to say of Nietzsche's ideas, it is unlikely that we shall describe many of them as *sensible.*"[3]

Yet Nietzsche describes his "discovery" of eternal recurrence in terms of glowing self-congratulations. The idea is the "highest formula of affirmation that is at all attainable" and the product of a state that he describes as "6000 feet beyond man and time." We may be dubious about such a frame of mind, but we cannot dismiss eternal recurrence if we want to make sense of *Zarathustra.* According to Nietzsche, eternal recurrence is "the fundamental conception of this work."[4]

In what follows I shall consider both the meaning and

the significance of the doctrine. I begin by indicating some of the alternative readings of the doctrine that have been proposed and then present an interpretation that follows the general lines of one of these readings: eternal recurrence, as the idea is presented in *Thus Spoke Zarathustra*, is the expression of a general attitude toward life, an attitude that contrasts with the past-obsessed perspective that Nietzsche believes goes hand-in-hand with the Christian moral worldview.

I shall go on to suggest an analogy for the kind of present-centered perspective that the doctrine expresses: the temporal orientation proposed by the doctrine of eternal recurrence is like the temporal orientation that we assume while listening to a piece of music.

Having made these suggestions about the meaning of the doctrine, I shall consider some of the reasons the doctrine is so significant to Nietzsche's project in *Zarathustra*. In *Zarathustra* the doctrine provides an intuitive basis for an understanding of human behavior that is not mediated by the conceptual apparatus involved in the Christian doctrine of sin. By "doctrine of sin," I mean the entire conceptual model that Christianity uses to evaluate human actions, a model in which the concept of "sin" is central. I shall go on to show how eternal recurrence integrates the themes of the tragic worldview and opposition to the Christian moral perspective, thereby suggesting an answer to those who have wondered how Nietzsche could have ever maintained that eternal recurrence was his most important idea.[5]

My discussion emphasizes the doctrinal character of eternal recurrence. I view the doctrine of eternal recurrence as an interpretive scheme, accepted on faith rather than proof, that elaborates the implications of a basic worldview with respect to a specific subject matter. The subject matter treated by the doctrine of eternal recurrence is not narrow, but it is specific. The doctrine is concerned with the *nature* of the temporal matrix in which the range of our actions occur.

As Zarathustra's central doctrine, eternal recurrence exhibits the characteristic ambivalence of Zarathustra's doctrines, which we considered in Chapter 5. I contend that eternal recurrence is particularly well constructed to reveal this ambivalence because its very point is to gesture toward a state of mind. My analysis of the doctrine's ambivalence should help solve the mystery of why, if eternal recurrence is a "formula of affirmation," Zarathustra sometimes responds to the idea of the doctrine with horror.

WHAT DOES ETERNAL RECURRENCE MEAN?

What kind of theory is eternal recurrence? This question has been the central issue in scholarly debate on the doctrine. The rival interpretations reveal radically different ways of understanding Nietzsche, and it is not surprising that the proponents of these rival positions disagree about which of the texts that discuss the doctrine should be taken as central.

Bernd Magnus indicates three general types of answers given to the question of what kind of theory Nietzsche means to advance.[6] Some interpreters argue that Nietzsche intended the doctrine as a cosmological theory about the way time is constructed; they usually conclude that the theory advanced is not very good.[7] A second group construes the doctrine as a kind of ethical injunction; on this reading, the doctrine of eternal recurrence is an exhortation for us to act *as if* its claim about time were true.[8] Such interpreters disagree among themselves as to what the effect of our following this injunction would be, but they agree that the doctrine offers guidance with respect to particular actions we are contemplating. The doctrine functions, according to this view, in a manner that is reminiscent of Kant's first formulation of the categorical imperative: "Act only according to that maxim whereby thou canst at the same time will that it should become a universal law."[9]

A third line of interpretation, the line proposed by Magnus himself, contends that the doctrine represents an "existential imperative," a heuristic tool that illustrates "a particular attitude toward life." Specifically, this attitude is "the expression of nihilism already overcome," the attitude that is the characteristic of the *Übermensch* (overman).[10] Nehamas has also recently proposed a reading of eternal recurrence which, despite its serious differences from Magnus, resembles the latter in interpreting the doctrine as an emblem for the fullest life-affirmation.[11] Unfortunately for any effort to establish a secure sense of what the doctrine means, these very different views of the doctrine's meaning can all turn to textual evidence for support.[12] This is true even if we limit ourselves to the passages that deal with eternal recurrence in *Zarathustra*.[13]

The various ways in which Nietzsche discusses eternal recurrence are confusing, and a comprehensive consideration of his reference to the doctrine is apt to leave one in a quandary. Perhaps Nietzsche meant eternal recurrence to mean all the different things that interpreters have suggested, but if so, how he could have failed to worry that certain of the doctrines' roles may not have been compatible with others? Magnus, for instance, argues that the normative version of eternal recurrence, interpreted literally, is not compatible with the cosmological version. The latter, if true, would render the former pointless: however we lived, we would be living "as-if" eternal recurrence were a true theory of the world, because it *would* be a true theory of the world.[14] More perniciously, the deterministic view implicit in the cosmological claim that this life has already recurred an infinite number of times and is therefore "settled" is incompatible with any kind of normative injunction, for normative injunctions presuppose that we have freedom to choose to behave otherwise.[15]

The reading of eternal recurrence that I suggest below follows the lines of interpretation of Magnus and Nehamas. I shall treat the doctrine as a kind of expression for a fundamental orientation toward one's life, rather than as a cosmological thesis or a practical imperative. This type of reading makes the most sense of the doctrine as it is described in *Thus Spoke Zarathustra*. The book is focused on basic existential issues, not on questions of cosmology. (I deal with the significance of the cosmological tone of certain passages in *Zarathustra* in my discussion of the doctrine's ambivalence.) And while some interpreters may read *Zarathustra* as a handbook of ethical injunctions, Chapter 5 of this book makes clear why I do not. However, some of Nietzsche's discussions of eternal recurrence in other contexts do seem to invite cosmological and normative readings. The range of accounts of the doctrine are mentioned here not to set the stage for a thorough treatment of them and their implications, but to indicate the controversial and limited nature of my interpretation at the outset.

WHAT WOULD ETERNAL RECURRENCE MATTER?

One perplexity regarding the doctrine of eternal recurrence is likely to cross most readers' minds as soon as they hear of the doctrine. What difference does the doctrine of eternal recurrence make? Even if the theory of time it proposes were true, nothing in our lives would be any different. Zarathustra may be right that time is cyclical, but if he is— so what?

The more one contemplates this question, the more it appears that the truth of the doctrine's proposition about time would make no real difference in our lives. If an *identical* series of moments recurs over and over again an in-

163

finite number of times, a recurrence of a moment could not involve our recollection that we have been this way before.[16] If we did have such recollection, then the moments that constituted a recurrence of the series would not be identical repetitions of the pattern as it occurred before. Eternal recurrence, then, would not alter our memories. In fact, it would not make our experiences perceptually different in any way from what they would be if the doctrine's proposition concerning time were not true.

This reasoning about eternal recurrence strikes me as correct, but it leaves us in a quandary. Nietzsche, after all, believes that the value of a theory lies in its ability to contribute something to our lives. How can he consistently hold this view and at the same time propose eternal recurrence, a doctrine whose truth seems to make no tangible difference in our lives? Does not debate about the truth of eternal recurrence resemble the proverbial debate about the number of angels that can dance on the head of a pin? In either case, it appears that the debate's solution would have no significant pragmatic consequences.

The answer to this perplexity is that Nietzsche does think that the acceptance of his doctrine would make a fundamental difference to our experience. It is our acceptance of the doctrine, and not the *truth* of the doctrine's propositional content, that has practical implications for our lives. This sounds puzzling until we recognize the kind of difference that accepting eternal recurrence would make. The difference Nietzsche expects his doctrine to make is not a difference between what the series of events in our lives would look like if the doctrine were true and what the series would look like if it were false. The difference is a matter of our sense of the *significance* of the series.

Nietzsche's view resembles the view Wittgenstein expresses in his comment "The world of the happy is quite another than that of the unhappy."[17] These worlds are different not because their *contents* are different. They differ with respect to the attitudinal component that is a fundamental constituent of the world *in which we live and experience.*[18] Similarly, according to Nietzsche's way of looking at it, the time of our experience is always attitudinally conditioned. There is no time in our experience in which some attitude on our part is absent. We have good times, bad times, indifferent times, but no time in which attitude does not contribute fundamentally to the substance of what we experience. What the doctrine of eternal recurrence affects in our experience is this attitudinal aspect.

Heidegger makes a similar point about the way attitude makes a fundamental contribution to the nature of all our experiences in time. Discussing the role of state of mind in constituting what it is to be a human being in the world (*Dasein's* Being-in-the-world), Heidegger observes that state of mind determines the way the individual understands the possibilities toward which he projects himself through time. "A state-of-mind always has its understanding, even if it merely keeps it suppressed. Understanding always has its mood.... As *existentialia* states-of-mind and understanding charaterize the primordial disclosedness of Being-in-the-world. By way of having a mood, *Dasein* 'sees' possibilities, in terms of which it is."[19] Heidegger sees the possibilities and goals toward which we project ourselves as basic to our present sense of ourselves. But even our sense of what those goals and possibilities are is dependent on state-of-mind, or attitude.

In Nietzsche's view, our thoughts about the way time moves forward exert a powerful influence on the attitude with which we pursue our goals in time. Like Heidegger, Nietzsche believes that a sense of striving toward some future possibility (or possibilities) is an essential component of healthy human living; we have already observed this perspective in the content of Zarathustra's discussions of the last man and the overman. However, the attitude with which goals are pursued is equally important to a healthy human life.

Implicit in eternal recurrence, as a way of looking at time, is an orientation on what it means to be in the process of pursuing one's goals. There are many different senses of time that can accompany one's projects. One can work on a project as if one had all the time in the world in which to pursue it, and this independently of whether one does. Or one can rush frenetically toward a goal, sensing time almost as a commodity of which one is running out. One can despair of one's projects amounting to much in the future because so much of one's life or work is already past. Or one can sense the outcomes of one's pursuits so eagerly that one almost seizes the future in the present.

The doctrine of eternal recurrence, for reasons that will become clear shortly, promotes an attitude toward time that focuses on the present. The fact that this is not the only possible orientation toward experiential time itself justifies the claim that acceptance of eternal recurrence makes a difference. This difference, moreover, is quite significant as Nietzsche sees it, for he sees a very different perspective on time to be dominant in his culture. This latter perspective is also deeply entrenched, for it is implicit in the view of human activity that is propagated by the Christian moral worldview. Central to this view is the Christian doctrine of sin.

THE DOCTRINE OF SIN AND OUR ATTITUDE TOWARD TIME

According to Nietzsche, the Christian doctrine of sin promotes a certain perspective on our activities in time. In order to see why Nietzsche links the doctrine of sin to a temporal attitude, we should recall what we discovered about his views on the doctrine in Chapter 3. There we saw that Nietzsche sees two attitudes that have bearing on our general perspective on our actions to be consequences of the doctrine. On the one hand, interpreting the world in terms of sin ensures a sense of personal inadequacy. On the other hand, this mode of interpreting the world ensures the development of a vindictive spirit in the believer.

A low sense of self-worth, Nietzsche argues, is a corollary of the Christian moral outlook. The believer is told that certain of his actions—those that are deemed sinful—indelibly mark him as one who deserves punishment. This is not the last word of the Christian doctrine—for God is willing, despite our sinfulness, to forgive us if we repent—but the implication is that except for God's mercy, the sins we commit would doom us to eternal torture in hell.

Belief in this arrangement is likely to instill a sense of personal unworth even without further reflection, but it is easy to see that among the actions that Christian teaching designates as sinful are many that a healthy person would find it almost impossible to avoid. Most individuals manage to avoid committing murder, but few can entirely avoid anger. Yet anger is deemed a sin. Lust is deemed sinful, greed is deemed sinful, and pride is considered the deadliest of sins. The Christian moral worldview tells us that, but for God's grace, we would be in a completely no-win situation. Leading a normal human life will virtually assure that we act sinfully, but our sinful behavior makes us deserving of eternal suffering and gives us no prospect for happiness.

The low sense of self-worth that is promoted by the Christian doctrine of human sinfulness inspires a desire for palliatives, Nietzsche argues. Among the many manifestations of this desire that are typical of Christians are (1) the desire for the absolute reassurance that one is saved from the consequences of one's sin and (2) the desire to avenge oneself for one's being unable to overcome a sinful nature. In more secular terms, Nietzsche would describe these as a desire for all-or-nothing solutions and a desire to revenge oneself for one's feelings of powerlessness.

Having stimulated these desires, Christianity offers a single package that will satisfy both. This is the myth of eternal salvation. One can be absolutely saved if God grants his forgiveness, so one's ultimate status in the world depends exclusively on one's status in God's eyes. The various Christian churches have different views about the route by which one can legitimately assure oneself that one has been forgiven by God, for instance, the Roman Catholic Church contends that a person can perform prescribed penances (prayers or actions) to be assured that God has granted forgiveness, while Luther argued to his followers that faith alone could lead to salvation. Despite such disagreements, Christian churches commonly promise to reveal the route to salvation, where "salvation" means unequivocal reassurance that one is spared from eternal damnation.

In order for the idea that one is saved to be fully effective as a means of banishing one's sense of inadequacy and worthlessness, the believer needs to believe as well that some people are not saved. The notion of one's sinfulness promotes dissatisfaction with self, but the Christian, according to Nietzsche, can soothe himself with a twofold reflection: (1) "God loves me and forgives me" and (2) "I'm a better person than some people I know."

The Christian gains a sense of security by believing that, despite his own sinfulness, others are greater sinners and more deserving of suffering than himself. The burden of one's sinfulness is lightened, and the prospect of God's forgiveness seems more likely, if there are other people around who should feel this burden more powerfully than one does oneself. And here is where the spirit of vindictiveness enters the picture. The evidence that others *are* more guilty than oneself is that one *sees* them as more guilty. And so the believer is inspired by the low self-image that Christian belief instills to do what he can to make sure that others look guilty. Punishing where one can, conspicuously or subtly, establishes one's sense of moral superiority and enhances one's ability to believe oneself among the saved. Nietzsche's image of the nun who looks with disdain on women who live otherwise exemplifies this phenomenon, which he believes is a natural response of Christians to their doctrine. In his secular analysis, Nietzsche sees disgust with oneself, the consequence of belief in the doctrine of sin, as motivating a quest for revenge. Revenge is sought as a means of assuaging self-contempt and fear of the future.

Having this analysis freshly in mind we can see why Nietzsche believes that the motivation for these attitudes of self-contempt and vindictiveness is essentially linked to a perspective on time that undermines the significance of the present. The Christian conception that we are sinful is focused on *past* actions, as is evident on even cursory reflection. We are sinful from birth because our first parents sinned originally—certainly a matter of past action. Moreover, the sin that demonstrates our personal guilt is always embedded in our personal past. We feel guilty because of what we *have* done. And on the Christian ledger, any human being's past affords grounds for feeling guilty. Recognition that one's past includes events that might inspire guilt is a precondition to adopting the Christian route to salvation, for it is a sense of guilt that leads one to seek salvation in the first place. If we accept the Christian doctrine that we are guilty of sin, then we are accepting it as a consequence of reflection on our past.

The Christian perspective in this matter builds firmly on human psychology. Any reflection on the past is likely to provoke in us some degree of disturbance. The past is disturbing because we cannot change it. In the section called

"On Redemption", Zarathustra observes that a sense of powerlessness in the face of the past is part of the human condition. Inevitably we feel powerless with respect to some facets of our temporal lives because, as Zarathustra puts it, "the will cannot will backwards."[20] We cannot, by willing in the present, make the past different from what it was.

One can, however, attempt to deceive oneself by making the past appear different. This, according to Nietzsche, is the strategy of vindictiveness. "This, indeed this alone, is what *revenge* is," says Zarathustra, "the will's ill will against time and its 'it was.' "[21] And the Christian orientation reflects precisely this vindictive strategy.

Revenge is always a matter of "proving something," of arranging one's present activity so that it will make the past appear to be other than it was. Obvious, overt acts of revenge attempt to disprove the ostensible past victories of an enemy or, to be more accurate, to demonstrate that such victories must now be reinterpreted as less significant than they seemed. The Christian doctrine of sin attempts a similar but more subtle reinterpretation of past events. it achieves revenge over those who gratify themselves in ways it disapproves of by redefining this gratification after the fact. What was gratifying action at the time it was performed is reinterpreted as sin. The apparent significance of the action is entirely transformed. What appeared an enviably satisfying action can, by the Christian reinterpretation, be seen as a catalyst to eternal suffering unless one adopts the church's route to redemption. The vindictive spirit fostered by the doctrine of sin expresses itself in this type of condemning reinterpretation of the behavior of others.

The consequence of gaining such interpretive revenge on the pasts of others is that one feels less powerless in the face of one's own past actions. The doctrine of sin, then, offers a kind of solution to the feeling of impotence with regard to the past that is a natural consequence of human temporal nature. Unfortunately, this solution reinforces the problem. The consolation about one's own failings that is gained through vindictive interpretations of others' actions requires obsessive focus on the past. Admittedly, this focus is supported by thoughts of the distant future, when the consequences of all previous actions will be established once and for all. But even in contemplating eventual salvation or damnation, one is focused on the metaphoric tally-sheet of the virtuous and sinful actions that one has performed so far. One's status with respect to the distant future is a function of one's past.

The Christian orientation toward one's actions is retrospective. "What have I done?" is its basic mode of soul-searching. In this respect, it is not present-centered. But Nietzsche does not believe merely that the Christian orientation neglects attention to the present. He believes that it positively denigrates the present. It does this by conceiving of our entire lives in time as a kind of punishment.

Our lives come to be seen as punishment because they involve pain and feelings of powerlessness. The Christian moral interpretation, however, trains believers to look for guilt. Where there is suffering, suffering is probably deserved. If we are pained in this world, we probably deserve it. But this amounts to saying that *this* life in which we experience pain is itself a punishing life. And the Christian conception of salvation from sin—a trauma-free afterlife that is outside our life in time—reflects this view. Zarathustra explains:

> The spirit of revenge, my friends, has so far been the subject of man's best reflection; and where there was suffering, one always wanted punishment too.
>
> For "punishment" is what revenge calls itself; with a hypocritical lie it creates a good conscience for itself.
>
> Because there is suffering in those who will, inas-

much as they cannot will backwards, willing itself and all life were supposed to be—a punishment. And now cloud upon cloud rolled over the spirit, until eventually madness preached, "everything passes away; therefore everything deserves to pass away. And this too is justice, this law of time that it must devour its children." Thus preached madness.

"Things are ordered morally according to justice and punishment. Alas, where is redemption from the flux of things and from the punishment called existence?" Thus preached madness.

"Can there be redemption if there is eternal justice? Alas, the stone *It was* cannot be moved: all punishments must be eternal too." Thus preached madness.

"No deed can be annihilated: how could it be undone by punishment? This, this is what is eternal in the punishment called existence, that existence must eternally become deed and guilt again...." But, my brothers, you know this fable of madness.[22]

On Zarathustra's view, and Nietzsche's, Christianity casts a depressing shadow on our understanding of our lives in time by conceiving our lives as a demonstration of our guilt. The idea that suffering proves one's guilt is, according to their view, a fundamental if unstated premise of Christianity. While tracing the development of Christianity in *The Antichrist*, Nietzsche concludes that the development of this premise was crucial to the development of its moral worldview.

> The concept of God becomes a tool in the hands of priestly agitators, who now interpret all happiness as a reward, all unhappiness as punishment for disobeying God, as "sin": that most mendacious device of interpretation, the alleged "moral world order," with which the natural concepts of cause and effect are turned upside down once and for all....

> What is Jewish, what is Christian morality? Chance
> done out of its innocence; misfortune besmirched with
> the concept of "sin"; well-being as a danger, a "tempta-
> tion"; physiological indisposition poisoned with the
> worm of conscience.[23]

If suffering proves guilt, our lives demonstrate our guilt,
for we cannot avoid suffering. If suffering is punishment for
guilt, our lives themselves are a form of punishment. But
this amounts to a denigration of the entirety of our lives in
the present. The past has the significance of determining
the fate that we deserve in the fuller life that we will experience in the future after our death. Our present life, however, is but a symptom of our guilty pasts. It amounts to a
"vale of tears."

Every suggestion that Christianity makes about temporality indicates the same denigration of the present. The
future after death, in which we are either saved or punished,
alone establishes the significance of our lives. The only
action that can have any ultimate positive significance on
this scheme is action that is conducive to one's reception
of God's grace. But this amounts to an essentially passive
stance in the present. One aims at being appropriately receptive, and the means by which one achieves this aim,
according to Christian doctrine, are themselves passive or
past-oriented. Christian virtue amounts to the passive state
of having successfully eliminated passion. The active re-
pudiation of one's past sin is admired by Christianity, but
the orientation that is involved in such "activity" does not
focus on present action but instead rivets attention on the
past.

The implications of Christian doctrine for a perspective
on time are to dwarf the significance of the present for what,
on Nietzsche's view, is a perverse teleology. In the Christian
model, one assumes a linear progression from past to future

and concludes that one's future fate after death will settle the single important question about how one lived one's life: did it win salvation or not? We can recall Nietzsche's comments in *The Antichrist* that the essence of the Christian "law of love" is that the Christian wants to be paid well.

In summary, Nietzsche argues that the moral perspective of Christianity denigrates the actuality of our lives. It does so in a variety of ways, but one of the most fundamental is evident in the doctrine of sin's implications regarding the proper view of our temporal nature. The doctrine of sin interprets the present, which is the temporal location of our entire lives, as relatively unimportant by comparison with the past, the location of the sin that establishes our guilt, and the distant future, the location of the reward or punishment that will indicate for all time whether or not we were saved. The whole temporal perspective of this doctrine casts an unhappy shadow over our lives, which are lived in the temporal moment that is viewed by the Christian scheme as least significant.

ETERNAL RECURRENCE AND OUR ATTITUDE TOWARD TIME

A Present-Centered Theory

I have asserted that the doctrine of eternal recurrence, by contrast with Christian moral doctrine, focuses on the significance of the present. But what sense does it make to say this? Does not every moment have essentially the same status on the model of eternal recurrence? After all, according to the doctrine every moment recurs eternally, and in this respect the present moment is no different from any other.

Zarathustra's model of recurring time does, however,

treat the present moment as unique. It is unique in this model because the past and future collapse into one another. The past is a more distant future from that usually designated by the term "future." Because time is eternally recurring, however, we have no ground for assuming that this is the first instance of the temporal sequence, but if this is not the first instance, then the future is already the past in the sense that it has happened during previous recurrences. "The past" and "the future" are only relative designations on Nietzsche's cyclical model, and ultimately they are not distinguishable from one another. The present moment is the only moment in time that stands out from the swirl of recurrence. Moreover, it is a moment of privileged significance because it is the only moment in which we are actively involved in time.

This present-orientation is evident in the version of eternal recurrence that Zarathustra presents in the section entitled, "On the Vision and the Riddle."[24] In a part of the vision reported there, Zarathustra confronts a dwarf, whom he calls "the spirit of gravity," at a crossroads. There they argue about the way time should be conceived. The argument at first appears odd, for the dwarf and Zarathustra each holds a version of a cyclical theory. But this apparent similarity of their views makes the passage important: the passage pinpoints what Nietzsche takes to be significant about his cyclical time theory. The dwarf is content with the view that "time itself is a circle," but Zarathustra objects to this statement, which approaches time with the detachment of a God who has synoptic vision and who is not himself involved in the temporal sequence. Zarathustra retorts "angrily": "You spirit of gravity, . . . do not make things too easy for yourself!" He goes on to tell the dwarf his own perspective on cyclical time, a perspective that focuses on the present as the temporal site of both all activity *and* the establishment of its significance:

175

Behold...this moment! From this gateway, Moment, a
long, eternal lane leads *backward*: behind us lies an
eternity. Must not whatever *can* walk have walked on
this lane before? Must not whatever *can* happen have
happened, have been done, have passed by before? And
if everything has been there before—what do you think,
dwarf, of this moment? Must not this gateway too have
been there before? And are not all things knotted together so firmly that this moment draws after it *all* that
is to come? Therefore—itself too? For whatever *can*
walk—in this long lane out *there* too, it *must* walk once
more.[25]

Robert Gooding-Williams' commentary offers a succinct
summary of the ways the passage indicates that the present
moment is the perspective from which the whole span of
time is to be understood and evaluated:

Unlike the dwarf, Zarathustra experiences the whole of
time from the standpoint of the moment. It is *in the moment* that the two paths come together; it is *from the
moment* that "a long eternal lane leads backward"; and
it is *the moment* that "draws after it all that is to
come." Zarathustra privileges the present and experiences it, not only as the time between past and future,
but as the point where the past *begins* and where the
future *begins to show itself* (the past leads backward
from the moment, and the moment *draws the future
after it*). Furthermore, Zarathustra's projections of the
past and future, in that they originate and occur *under
the gateway*, appear to be inner determinations of the
present moment. In short, Zarathustra's experience, as
well as what he says, intimates that the present moment
encompasses and gives birth to every other moment.[26]

The present moment, in the account that Zarathustra
gives of his doctrine, does not occur in a temporal vacuum.

It is causally connected to all other moments. It is the point at which the causal streams of past and present converge. But this causal relationship does not render the present moment impotent, as the doctrine that past sin permanently establishes our state of guilt implicitly does. On the contrary, the causal connectedness of past, present, and future is the precondition of the present moment's *potency* in the time series.

The Role of Causality: Nietzsche's Determinism

Before we leave our discussion of the present-centeredness of Zarathustra's theory, it is necessary to have a clear understanding of this nature of the causal connectedness of past, present, and future. Such an understanding will help us to see what Nietzsche is and is not attacking in his confrontation with the Christian temporal orientation. In his recurrent exhortations that we should eliminate the concept of sin from our perspective on human behavior, Nietzsche is sometimes misunderstood to be claiming that we have no grounds for feeling guilty and that we should not give our past acts of inhumanity and cruelty a second thought. Such a reading sees Nietzsche as a kind of coach for our rationalizations. "There's no point in feeling guilty, since the past is all behind me," this interpretation reads into Nietzsche. "Today is all that matters."

Zarathustra's caricature of the last man, quoted in Chapter 4, should be sufficient to quash this kind of reading. That sketch reveals Nietzsche's aversion to an unreflective sense of "living in the present." His doctrine of eternal recurrence, however, does provide a theoretical basis for a certain sense of "living in the present."

How are past, present, and future conjoined in Zarathustra's time theory? They are conjoined by causality. Nietzsche believes that causal currents already in motion determine the shape of the present moment, and in this respect he is a determinist. His is not, however, a determinism of the classical, or "hard," variety. This type of determinism holds that all events are caused by other events and denies that human choice is free. Nietzsche's determinism, by contrast, resembles that of Spinoza, with whom he compares himself. On this view all events, including human choices, are casual resultants of other events. But this amounts to saying that the world operates in an orderly, as opposed to chaotic, fashion. Nietzsche does not deny that human desires and other dynamic mental states can have causal efficacy, but he asserts that these states themselves have causes, often stemming from the unconscious part of the mind.[27] Human beings can often act freely, in the sense of acting on their desires without interference or acting in a way that expresses character. But desires and character are themselves determined and conditioned by casual factors (sometimes genetic ones). When one acts "freely," on desire, one's actions nonetheless have causes, and these causes themselves are causally determined. The alternative, in Nietzsche's view, would amount to saying that free actions could be given no explanation whatsoever. Nietzsche finds this view unpalatable.[28]

Even this brief account of Nietzsche's determinism should make it clear why he believes that his sense of causality differs from the causality asserted by the Christian doctrine of sin. Nietzsche does not disagree with the Christian account's contention that the past has consequences that should be taken seriously in the present. He contends that the past *supplies the matter* with which one deals in the present moment. The individual, in fact, is the person he or she is in the present in part as a consequence of past experiences. To the extent that Christian doctrine sees the past as something to be taken seriously in the present, Nietzsche does not disagree.

What Nietzsche objects to is not the view that past

events have consequences, but the view that past *sins* determine our final condition and that this is the most important causal relationship for our lives. According to Nietzsche, the causal relationships between sin and ultimate damnation, and the relationship between the influx of God's grace and ultimate salvation, are relationships between fictional concepts. While sharing the temporal shape of meaningful causal accounts, these causal accounts are bogus; their terms are entirely imaginery. Furthermore, even if the terms of these accounts were nonfictional, they would still be too simplistic to provide a causal explanation for human action. No causal account whatever is offered for an action labeled "sin"; such action is simply seen as a choice of "free will." And the further effects of such actions in the temporal world, while perhaps mentioned in sermons, are de-emphasized. Attention is focused on the imaginary effect of "leading to eternal damnation."

Christianity, for all its absorption with guilt, does not take the past seriously enough as the source of causal currents that shape the reality of the present. It rivets itself on the past, not as a key for illuminating the present but as evidence that one should heed its threats of a dire future in a realm that Nietzsche sees as unreal. Nietzsche finds his own perspective far more serious with respect to the real significance of the past and causality. The past *as it pertains to us*, he contends, is not the temporal location of indelible proof that we are guilty. Instead, it is the background of causal forces that influence us right now.

THE ATTITUDE PROMOTED BY ETERNAL RECURRENCE: AN ANALOGY

I have suggested that Nietzsche is using the doctrine of eternal recurrence to give us an intuitive sense of human action as it would appear if we eliminated the concept of sin from our interpretation. But how would human action look according to the model of Nietzsche's temporal theory?

The negative accomplishment of the doctrine is clear. Let us focus on the present, as the theory does. If we adopt the doctrine of eternal recurrence as the basis of our temporal orientation, there are a number of typical perspectives on our actions that we cannot consistently adopt. We cannot view our actions, for instance, as a means of "settling things" for all time, of putting matters into some permanent order. Nor can we view our actions as steps to a firmly established state of security. We cannot view them as having meaning only insofar as they are the means of unquestionable progress toward some end. And we certainly cannot view them as the means of getting to heaven. Because past and future collapse into each other, the doctrine undercuts any view that finds the meaning of the present in its function as the means to a permanently secure future position.

But what, then, is the doctrine's positive attitudinal accomplishment? What alternative does it propose to a teleological apprehension of the present, a perspective on the present, that is, which sees it as the means toward securing one's goals? In answering this question, I will pursue Nietzsche's clue that the whole of *Zarathustra* might be reckoned as music and explore the analogy between the present-centeredness of musical experience and the present-orientation implicit in the doctrine of eternal recurrence. My pursuit of this analogy may at first appear digressive, but I am convinced that the music analogy will convey an impression of the attitude toward action that Nietzsche's doctrine encourages much more clearly than further conceptual comment.

In his book *Sound and Symbol: Music and the External World*, Victor Zuckerkandl discusses the temporal structure of music. He observes several features of the temporality of music that are reminiscent of the theory of time expressed by the doctrine of eternal recurrence. Most generally, the temporality of music resembles that described by Nietzsche's doctrine in being present-oriented and in seeing past and future in terms of their contribution to the immediate experience of the present. For these reasons Zuckerkandl's analysis will assist my analogy.

The Temporality of Music

The musical meaning of the individual musical tone is perceived, on Zuckerkandl's analysis, as involving the "promise of the whole" of the work.[29] The tone's meaning is established by its pointing to other tones, but this meaning "lies not in what it points to but *in the pointing* itself. ...[W]hat the tone means is actually and fully contained in the tone itself."[30] The individual tone and its relation to the whole parallels the relationship of the individual moment and the whole of time, particularly because the individual tone is itself a musical "moment" which appears and is replaced in time.

Our perception of the musical present, however, is not divorced from a sense of what precedes it. Zuckerkandl says:

> We count one-*two*, and not one-*one*. Here "two" does not mean simply "beat number 2," but "away from." The entire process is therefore an "away from—back to," not a flux but...a constantly repeated cycle, for the "one" that closes one cycle simultaneously begins another.[31]

Although our experience of the musical present is conditioned by the musical past of the work, we do not experience the beat through the mediation of memory:

> When we identify the beat, the part of a measure upon which a particular tone falls, we do not do so because we had secretly counted along, or reckoned up in mem-

ory, but because the characteristic direction of the wave phase upon which the tone falls ... can be heard in and from the tone directly.[32]

The individual tone or chord of tones that is heard at any particular moment, though related to both the past and future of the musical work, is experienced only in the present. To deal with the present-tense of musical articulation as though it were understandable only with reference to memory would be musical bad faith. In fact, the attempt to contain the flux of music by the imposition of memory is impossible; music itself is lost in such an endeavor:

> Let anyone who is capable of it call to mind the imme-
> diately preceding tone of a melody that he is hearing.
> *The instant he does so, he will have lost the thread of
> the melody.* ... Any turning back of consciousness for
> the purpose of making past tones present immediately
> annuls the possibility of musical hearing.[33]

Music resists any attempt to deny its immediacy and to wed it to the past. Music is never past-oriented, nor does it even suggest permanence. The musical tone, nevertheless, stands in intimate relationship with what has gone before. The earlier links in the temporal chain are not obliterated, but are preserved as active forces in the successive present links.[34] Music is also linked to the future, says Zuckerlandl, for every tone carries with it an expectation. But

> the expectation that I feel upon hearing a tone in a mel-
> ody is not directed toward any *event* ... ; it is directed
> toward futurity, toward what can never become present.
> ... Without leaving the present behind me, I experience
> futurity as that toward which the present is directed
> and always remains directed.[35]

The past and the future are both connected with the awareness of the present tone, but not as specific past and future events. The past is preserved in forces that shape the present moment, and the future is present as a sense of direction. Particularity is to be experienced only in the present. A simultaneous awareness of past and future is part of what is experienced in the present; but correctly viewed, this awareness is only a sense of a whole in which the present moment is the immediately experienced part.

Musical Temporality and Eternal Recurrence

Our musical awareness of time resembles the perspective on time that Nietzsche suggested by the doctrine of eternal recurrence. The temporal perspective of each acknowledges the significance of past and future, but focuses on the vitality of the present moment as the central element in our experience of temporality. Music is related to eternal recurrence through the particularity of the individual tone. Though related to the temporal totality of the musical work, the musical tone is nevertheless experienced as an immediately present *moment* in which a reflection of the temporal whole is contained. In this respect it is like the present moment as described by the doctrine of eternal recurrence.

With his doctrine of eternal recurrence, Nietzsche is urging us to approach our experiences with an attitudinal perspective that resembles our attitude in musical listening. This perspective is present-centered, but its present-centeredness does not involve the loss of awareness of future goals. The temporal perspective of eternal recurrence does not involve drowning ourselves in the present. Instead this perspective conceives of our goals as something like dynamic forces operative in the present. This is the same kind of goal-orientation as that evident in Zarathustra's early admonitions that we should be "arrows of longing for the overman." These are not exhortations to see the present merely as a means to a future end. Instead, they represent a call for us to recognize that a sense of future ends is part of what constitutes a meaningful sense of the present.[36]

Our attitude in musical listening is not fully characterized by the expression "present-oriented," however elaborate our analysis of what this expression means. Our attitude in musical listening is an attitude of *delight* in the present. Our delight, like our musical concentration, is not contingent on our sense that some clear progress is being made. On the contrary, we enjoy great music because of its circuitousness, its ingenuity at taking devious paths toward its evident aims, its instinct for moving in ways contrary to precedent, its unmitigated sense of life.[37] We enjoy the fullness of the present musical moment, even if it is dissonant, not for its efficiency in moving toward the evident musical goal, but for its own surprising presence.[38]

Eternal recurrence promotes a similar attitude toward the contents of our experience of time. The attitude of highest affirmation is not mere acceptance, but positive delight in whatever is before one. In this respect eternal recurrence is in accord with Nietzsche's doctrine of *amor fati* (love of fate), the doctrine that the best way to live is to love every moment of life for exactly what it is. "My formula for greatness in a human being is *amor fati:* that one wants nothing to be different, not forward, not backward, not in all eternity. Not merely bear what is necessary, still less conceal it ... but love it."[39] Loving the entire shape of one's life in every moment is Nietzsche's ideal for living, and this ideal perspective toward the moment is the orientation toward time indicated by the doctrine of eternal recurrence.

WHY IS ETERNAL RECURRENCE SO SIGNIFICANT?

Further Implications for the Christian Moral Worldview

Referring to *Zarathustra*, Nietzsche writes to Overbeck: "There has not been since Voltaire such an outrageous attack on Christianity—and to tell the truth, even Voltaire had no idea that one could attack it in *this* way."[40] This description of *Zarathustra*'s attack on Christianity applies particularly to his development of the doctrine of eternal recurrence. On surface inspection, who would think that a simple theory about the structure of time could amount to an attack on Christian doctrine? And yet this doctrine functions to disrupt basic premises of the Christian moral doctrine at their roots.

The doctrine of eternal recurrence undercuts the linear model of time that is essential for the Christian moral worldview to make sense. Belief in future punishment or reward for past action depends on a linear theory of time; past causes determine future effects that are permanent and represent an end point to which the flow of time leads. The doctrine of eternal recurrence challenges the familiar view of time, and in so doing it rejects the view that future reward for past action could plausibly be construed as the key to the significance of human life through time. In order to see why this is so, we need to remember what the "future" amounts to in Nietzsche's theory. The concept "future," on Nietzsche's cyclical model of time, does not designate a stable temporal location. If everything recurs, then points of our past are points of a more distant future than the time that we think of as not yet having arrived.

The concept of a future reward that definitively establishes the significance of every action makes no sense on this model of time, for nothing that happens in the future can establish the significance of anything once and for all. The past will return. Furthermore, even if sinful action did consistently result in future punishment, this would only temporarily affect the apparent significance of past actions that were "immorally" gratifying. It would not establish their significance for all time. "Sinful" action could not be analyzed as intrinsically deserving of suffering. The recurrence of gratification would recurrently call into question the negative judgment that the Christian perspective passes on these actions. On their recurrence those actions would produce their initially gratifying effects again.

The force of the Christian concepts of heaven and hell would be undercut by Nietzsche's theory of time. Their function in grounding permanently valid judgments on actions would be eliminated because all permanence would be eliminated. On a linear model, time can have an end point in a realm in which permanence reigns. On a cyclical model it cannot.

By rendering meaningless the concept of a permanently valid judgment of any action, the doctrine of eternal recurrence undercuts a further implication of the doctrine of sin that Nietzsche finds especially insidious. This implication follows from the Christian view that the human being stands in need of redemption. The sinister insinuation, on Nietzsche's understanding, is that past guilt is indelible and constitutive of one's present being.

The Christian conception of redemption from sin posits that we can be spared from the consequences that stem from our sinfulness. God may forgive us and allow us to escape the fires of hell. On this view, however, we remain sinful creatures, and we have no power to undo that fact. The past remains proof of our guiltiness, and we remain powerless in the face of it. Not our power, but only God's, can be effective in undoing the deserved consequences of our past sinful actions.

Nietzsche, by contrast, emphasizes our power to make ourselves what we are in the present. He denies that our present essence is constituted in part by past guilt. And the perspective on the present that is offered by the doctrine of eternal recurrence is fundamental to his argument. On this model of time, the self of the present, far from being constituted by the past, has a kind of power over it. The present self, in acting, can modify the significance of what the self in the past has been. Our wills are not capriciously free to abolish the forces that lead into the present, or to make ourselves into different persons on whom the past has had no real influence. Our wills are able to reformulate the spectrum of materials that our past bequeaths us by focusing them into patterns of aspiration. Zarathustra's sermon "On Redemption" summarizes this view concisely:

> I walk among men as among fragments of the future—
> that future which I envisage. And this is all my creating
> and striving, that I create and carry together into One
> what is fragment and riddle and dreadful accident. And
> how could I bear to be a man if man were not also a
> creator and guesser of riddles and redeemer of
> accidents?
>   To redeem those who lived in the past and to recreate
> all "it was" into a "thus I will it"—that alone should I
> call redemption. Will—that is the name of the liberator
> and joy-bringer; thus I taught you, my friends.[41]

This potential of the will allows the will to "redeem" its past—and the historical past that influences it. Redemption, understood in this way, involves converting the materials of the past into constructions that the presently active individual views as valuable. The materials of the past are redeemed, on Nietzsche's model, by actually being reconstructed along lines suggested by our aspirations. The Christian "redemption," by contrast, reinforces a guilt-ridden fixation on the facts of our past actions. In so doing, it reinforces a denigration of the present and denies our power to reconstitute ourselves continually. Nietzsche repudiates both these aspects of the Christian model of redemption, and he uses the doctrine of eternal recurrence in developing his own alternative model.

Nietzsche's Central Themes and Eternal Recurrence

Having observed various ways in which the doctrine of eternal recurrence opposes Christian doctrine, we are in a position to see how a number of Nietzsche's big themes come together in Zarathustra's doctrine. Moreover, our recognition that several important themes converge in the doctrine of eternal recurrence should help us understand why Nietzsche sees the doctrine as so significant. The doctrine is the central thought of *Zarathustra* because it carries with it currents from several of Nietzsche's central thoughts.

The subtly anti-Christian moves that Nietzsche makes in proposing the doctrine are the negative side of the doctrine's story. We have also seen that the same doctrine plays an affirmative role in developing our sense of the alternative perspective on life that Nietzsche described in *The Birth of Tragedy* as "Dionysian." The positive vocation of the doctrine of eternal recurrence is to suggest the temporal orientation of the tragic worldview that has been fundamental to Nietzsche's thought since his earliest writings.

The tragic worldview does not pass negative judgment on the meaning of the present on the basis of past misfortune, error, or catastrophe, even when the past is so recent that it touches the present. When we adopt the tragic worldview, we remember the traumatic character of some of our past situations and we recognize our susceptibility to future trauma. But more directly, we have a joyful response toward life; we sense that the present, where we experience the convergence of vital energies, is, beyond any other attribute, wondrous.

This perspective on what is important and valuable in life has a markedly temporal dimension. In the doctrine of eternal recurrence, Nietzsche attempts to summarize the temporal aspects of this perspective. Perhaps the doctrine represents too cryptic a mode of shorthand for most of us to easily see the full-blown tragic worldview behind the formulation that time infinitely recurs. But our discussion of the temporal perspective of eternal recurrence and its similarity to that involved in listening to music should enable us to appreciate a more accessible statement of Nietzsche's entire worldview: "Dionysus vs. the Crucified"[42] With this summary statement, Nietzsche opposes the tragic to the Christian worldview. By considering the relationship between this summary and Nietzsche's temporal views, we can observe the important threads that Nietzsche's theory of time connects.

Nietzsche uses the formula "Dionysus vs. the Crucified" to close *Ecce Homo*, the last work he completed before his madness. "Have I been understood?" he asks, "—*Dionysus vs. the Crucified.*"[43] I quote here one of Nietzsche's notes of the same era, where he develops the formula at some length, and then amplify on the temporal nature of the views expressed in light of our analysis of the doctrine of eternal recurrence.

> Dionysus versus the "Crucified": there you have the antithesis. It is *not* a difference in regard to their martyrdom—it is a difference in the meaning of it. Life itself, its eternal fruitfulness and recurrence, creates torment, destruction, the will to annihilation. In the other case, suffering—the "Crucified as the innocent one"—counts as an objection to this life, as a formula for its condemnation.—One will see that the problem is that of the meaning of suffering: whether a Christian meaning or a

tragic meaning. In the former case, it is supposed to be the path to a holy existence; in the latter case, being is counted as *holy enough* to justify even a monstrous amount of suffering. The tragic man affirms even the harshest suffering: he is sufficiently strong, rich, and capable of deifying to do so. The Christian denies even the happiest lot on earth: he is sufficiently weak, poor, disinherited to suffer from life in whatever form he meets it. The god on the cross is a curse on life, a signpost to seek redemption from life; Dionysus cut to pieces is a *promise* of life: it will be eternally reborn and return again from destruction.[44]

The Christian image of the crucifixion is an emblem of the ugliest consequences of action that a teleological (and therefore linear) theory of time can envisage. As a consequence of our guilt—the millstone of the past that we drag around with us—a completely innocent and perfectly good human being is tortured to death. If we take this image to heart, we will most likely become increasingly transfixed by the indelible character of the worst events in our past, in the process deadening our ability to take an innocent approach to anything.

The image of Dionysus, by contrast, is an emblem of the vitality of life as we experience it in music. When we listen to music we approach the present innocently. No matter how many times we have listened to a great work of music, we hear it as fresh; our educated expectations regarding how the music will unfold do not interfere with the immediacy of our hearing.

Nietzsche's doctrine of eternal recurrence is designed to recall us to the Dionysian character of temporality. It reminds us that the present moment—the moment in which our entire lives are lived—has the greatest value to us when we approach it as we approach the present of music. On this model, the present is not divorced from our awareness of past and future. But it is the focus of the perspective on life that Nietzsche has consistently seen as the worldview that will answer our doubts about life's meaning. The present moment is valued not because it serves as a means to an ultimate assured gratification, but because it is an immediate source of joy in itself.

THE AMBIVALENCE OF ETERNAL RECURRENCE AS A DOCTRINE

The doctrine of eternal recurrence is a doctrine in a full sense. Accepted on faith, it is not a conclusion of logic, but an expression of the implications of a fundamental worldview for a particular aspect of human experience. The doctrine of eternal recurrence, specifically, expresses the implications of a worldview of tragic life-affirmation with respect to the temporal aspect of human experience.

But is this, the reader might ask, really so clear? Does not eternal recurrence assume a number of guises, some not affirmative at all? As we have seen in Chapter 5, Zarathustra seemed anything but thrilled with life in "The Stillest Hour," which Kaufmann and others have read as the dawn of the doctrine. And he was horrified when, in "The Convalescent," he realized that the doctrine promised the return of everything, even the petty people and petty behavior that he so despises. A well-known statement of the doctrine in *The Gay Science* supports the view that eternal recurrence can as easily be considered horrifying as life-affirming.

> *The greatest weight.* — What, if some day or night a demon were to steal after you into your loneliest loneliness and say to you: "This life as you now live it and have lived it, you will have to live once more and innu-

merable times more; and there will be nothing new in it, but every pain and every joy and every thought and sigh and everything unutterably small or great in your life will have to return to you, all in the same succession and sequence.... "

Would you not throw yourself down and gnash your teeth and curse the demon who spoke thus? Or have you once experienced a tremendous moment when you would have answered him: "You are a god and never have I heard anything more divine." If this thought gained possession of you, it would change you as you are or perhaps crush you.[45]

Not only do these textual passages suggest that the worldview indicated by eternal recurrence is not a rosy one. The conceptual content of the doctrine is difficult to reconcile with a vision of life as all-embraceable. If each and every moment of life recurs, that means that every hideous event of world history will recur over and over and over again. But who could love such a world? Wouldn't such a world be infinitely less lovable than a world in which each atrocity happens once? But if that is a reasonable conclusion to draw, then the doctrine of eternal recurrence would seem to be much less capable of supporting an attitude of love of life than the linear model of time that Nietzsche rejects. How can our interpretation of Zarathustra's doctrine stand in the face of such textual and logical considerations?

My answer to these disturbing considerations is that the doctrine of eternal recurrence *is* an ambivalent doctrine and that it does admit of darker readings than the one that I have suggested. The fact that multiple, attitudinally disparate readings would be consistent with the letter of the doctrine's claims does not imply, however, that all are equally valid ways of interpreting what Nietzsche means by it. I believe that the darker, "abysmal" reading of eternal recurrence is inconsistent with what Nietzsche means by the doctrine, even though Zarathustra himself sometimes falls into this interpretation. In order to explain why, I return to my analysis of doctrines from Chapter 5.

All Zarathustra's doctrines—eternal recurrence included—perform an ambivalent role in Zarathustra's experience. A doctrine's positive function is to articulate an insight whose value to the future conduct of one's life lies in its ability to bring a certain aspect of life into manageable focus. To the extent, however, that one takes a doctrine to be unswervingly relevant to all of one's life situations, it ceases to perform a positive role. Instead, it tends to blind one to other aspects of one's situation besides the one that it brings into relief. The result is that it becomes a distraction from one's ability to understand and evaluate one's situation responsively.

As I have analyzed the doctrine of eternal recurrence, it performs the positive function of intimating an outlook on the temporal sweep of our lives that reflects insight into its dynamism and openness toward the possibilities that temporality entails. The doctrine, on this reading, provides a kind of education for our intuitions by means of a model. What the doctrine is not is an unswervingly true description of human reality. On the contrary, it is presented much more as a heuristic image of temporality than as a propositional thesis.

An alternative interpretation that the letter of the doctrine could support might see it as a factual description of human reality. The doctrine, on this reading, would be articulating an unchangingly true thesis about the nature of human life. Such an account might seem most plausible, particularly to those who are approaching the doctrine from the background of philosophical training that teaches them to isolate the propositional content of any argument.

But this reading would be inconsistent with the thrust of *Zarathustra* as I have analyzed it thus far. The frequently observable ironic distance between articulations of Zarathustra's insights and his fluctuating attitudinal orientation has a function. This function is to indicate that there is always a disparity between the rigid letter of an expressed doctrine and the vital, inner orientation that provoked it. A spiritual, experiential state is a component of any insight, whereas a doctrine is, as the passage cited in Chapter 1 puts it, a "transposition of a spiritual state." A doctrine represents a kind of transcription that cannot fully notate the inner state behind it. At best, it can provoke a memory of the state after it has fled.

One implication of this interpretation of doctrines is that it is possible to remember the verbal formulation one has used to articulate insight without remembering its internal correlative. One can, in other words, remember the words but not the spirit.[46] In my understanding, this is the situation in which Zarathustra appears at a number of points in the book. Among these points are those in which Zarathustra responds to the thought of eternal recurrence with horror and nausea. The fact that he at times is horrified by the thought of his own doctrine indicates that he is not always in a spiritual state that accords with the powerful and jubilant frame of mind that Nietzsche insists the doctrine expresses.

The Causes of Zarathustra's Negative Reactions

Horror at the doctrine's implications is not always the same response when it is reported in *Zarathustra*. In "The Stillest Hour," for instance, there appears to be no particular concern about what sorts of things will recur. Indeed, the doctrine is not yet articulated. Zarathustra's negative feeling here might be seen as a response to implications of the doctrine that are evident when it becomes formulated, but the relevant implications seem to be those that regard the efficacy of one's will in the present.

Zarathustra is told in this passage that he has a potency he is not utilizing. His negative response is to feel incapacitated. Zarathustra is afraid that he is simply not strong enough for the implications of his own insight; therefore he simply refuses to look at them. This response is consistent with implications of the doctrine in its later, articulate form. Heidegger analyzes the existential burden of the doctrine's present-orientation:

> The Moment ... [is] the center of the striving; what recurs—if it is to recur—is decided by the Moment and by the force with which the Moment can cope with whatever in it is repelled by such striving. That is what is peculiar to, and hardest to bear in, the doctrine of eternal return—to wit, that eternity *is* in the Moment, that the Moment is not the fleeting "now," not an instant of time whizzing by a spectator, but the collision of future and past. Here the Moment comes to itself. It determines how everything recurs.[47]

The doctrine, whether one takes it to be in its nascent stage in "The Stillest Hour" or considers its more fully developed form, suggests that Zarathustra has more possibilities than he has yet acknowledged. In Sartrean terms, Zarathustra is in bad faith in "The Stillest Hour," and his motivation is straightforwardly the desire to avoid the burden of his own freedom. The distance between Zarathustra's inner state and the state essential to the insight of eternal recurrence is a function of his unwillingness to follow his thought through to its existential implications. The painful feelings he experiences result from the growing sense that the doctrinal teaching at which he has become adept to this point is divorced from the insight that is growing within him. He resists confronting this pain and what it indicates.

The negative feeling that arises in response to the as yet inarticulate thought that is developing within stems from this resistance, not from the intrinsically horrifying character of the thought itself. The burdensome nature of the thought's content may also be dimly evident to Zarathustra even before he can articulate it, but to judge the thought as burdensome is already to impose an interpretation on it, not simply to see the thought for what it is. This whole passage has little to do with the negativity we might see implicit in the doctrine. The disturbance Zarathustra feels here has less to do with what the doctrine states than with his relationship to himself.

The climax of Zarathustra's negative response to eternal recurrence, by contrast, is directly relevant to the question of whether the doctrine implies something hideous about the world. This climax occurs in "The Convalescent." If eternal recurrence is true, Zarathustra realizes there, even "the smallest" will recur. The eternal claim of the pettiest to exist along with the greatest strikes him as reason for despair.

But how is Zarathustra understanding his doctrine at this point? He is looking to the doctrine for a factual statement about human reality. If he finds such a statement, he, like those who accept the Christian worldview, will have a formula that resolves the experiential tensions of life into some complete picture. Zarathustra evidently believes that the doctrine of eternal recurrence offers a story about life's meaning. His problem is that he has come to look at it as a final solution to the problem of meaning. And now, looking at it this way, he finds that he is appalled by the final solution, since the picture of life that it paints enshrines the petty with all the rest. (We might add that it enshrines moral monsters and atrocities as well, a matter about which I shall have more to say.)

But Zarathustra has gone astray in seeing his doctrine in this way, for the very point that the doctrine was formulated to express is that there is no final solution to life's tensions. There is no timeless state of bliss, and there is no ultimate "true story" about life and meaning.

Eternal recurrence, of all Zarathustra's doctrines, indicates the ambivalent character of doctrines. It denies the validity of any rigid interpretation of a doctrine, and yet its formulations admit of exactly such a misguided approach. Zarathustra's horror over the recurrence of the smallest stems from his having slipped into a rigid way of thinking about its message. As we noted Chapter 5, he has become entranced by Apollonian constructions and forgotten the Dionysian, musical insight that spawned his doctrine. The insight of his doctrine refutes the possibility of any "true picture" of life, whether horrible or idyllic. The positive side of this denial, however, is the doctrine's affirmation of life as an ongoing adventure in which one can always take a fresh approach to the tensions one confronts.

Must We Love Atrocities?

This account still does not address what is perhaps the most important aspect of Zarathustra's malaise. Are not some of the features of life that the doctrine would affirm actually abhorrent? Does not the doctrine urge love of life even in cases in which love would be a genuinely sick response? This seems to be the implication, especially if the doctrine of eternal recurrence is seen as converging with the doctrine of *amor fati*. Nietzsche's formulations of the doctrine that emphasize the recurrence of each and every moment invite these concerns. In *Zarathustra*'s "Drunken Song" we find such a formulation:

Have you ever said Yes to a single joy? O my friends, then you said Yes too to *all* woe. All things are entangled, ensnared, enamored; if ever you wanted one thing twice, if ever you said, "You please me, happiness! Abide, moment!" then you wanted *all* back. All anew,

all eternally, all entangled, ensnared, enamored—oh,
then you *loved* the world. Eternal ones, love it eternally
and evermore.[48]

Does this not mean that Zarathustra is exhorting us to love
moral atrocities if we have ever loved anything?

I begin my response with a question: What does
Nietzsche mean by making such a formulation a part of
"The Drunken Song"? Does not this context suggest that
Zarathustra is doing something other than sermonizing,
something other than giving us propositional formulations
of the truth? Does not the title of this context call to mind
the Dionysian, the tragic, the love of life despite the tragic?
Zarathustra here is not reminding his disciples "Don't you
know that your ever having been ecstatically happy logi-
cally entails that you affirm all the dark aspects of life?"
He is not lecturing that hurtful events are in themselves
good. Instead he is singing, and to our ears, the song he sings
is not far from the blues.

What do I mean by this image of Zarathustra as blues
singer? Let us return to the distinction that Nietzsche
makes between tragic and Christian perspectives on the
horrible and tragic elements of life. The Christian worldview responds to these elements with the myth of eternal
salvation, which provides so thorough a redemption that
the worst atrocity can be given a good face. Nietzsche sees
the longing for this kind of redemption as understandable,
so much so that certain of Zarathustra's comments and
meditations reflect such a longing. But although he sees the
quest for this kind of redemption as understandable,
Nietzsche sees the goal as unattainable and the addiction
to this quest as psychologically disastrous. This is one of
the central points about Nietzsche's thought that we considered in Chapter 2.

It would be inconsistent for Nietzsche to be offering redemption on the Christian model with the doctrine of eternal recurrence, but the doctrine of eternal recurrence, like the Christian worldview, does offer a kind of theodicy. Like the Christian theodicy, the doctrine provides a framework in which tragic events and moral atrocities take their place beside life's lighter contents, a framework in which the overall significance of such horrors can be assessed. But Nietzsche is not attempting with this framework to whitewash what is negative in life into something positive. The doctrine of eternal recurrence does involve a modified version of the Christian point that pain is often a precondition to what is pleasurable or in some other way valuable; in this regard it suggests that what is painful need not be seen as absolutely negative. But the binding together of all things that Nietzsche announces through Zarathustra's doctrine of eternal recurrence suggests something different. It suggests that the whole may be valuable even if some of the parts in their own right are horrible or tragic, and that if we love life as a whole we cannot edit out the vulnerability to the tragic that is an inescapable condition of our existence. I used the image of the blues to represent this perspective because an acceptance of the way things are resounds from blues music, despite the lyrics' account of the bad things that are happening.

The doctrine of eternal recurrence directs us to the tragic interpretation of life. This interpretation holds that despite the horrors and evils that life inevitably involves, life is autotelically valuable. Put more concretely, Nietzsche's tragic perspective entails that a person who has cancer, for instance, may deeply feel that being alive is wonderful, although his present experiences are all conditioned by his having cancer. The tragic does not necessarily rob any particular moment of its value. Each moment is involved in the vibrant movement of life, and Nietzsche's point is that participation in this movement is fundamentally gratifying in itself.

One need not love what is horrible or morally atrocious in order to "love life despite its horrors."[49] But one must accept the stance of vulnerability to such horrors if one is to assume the attitude of loving life expressed by the doctrine of eternal recurrence. This is the sense in which Nietzsche believes that we must embrace what strikes us as unpalatable in life. Embracing life in all its details amounts to confronting the whole of it from a position of vulnerability.

There is another side to Zarathustra's musings about "each and every moment." Given Zarathustra's predisposition to replace what he no longer finds in Christianity with some other kind of answer, it is not at all surprising that he would seek some formula that would make "each and every moment" of his life meaningful. This is because Zarathustra, the man who suddenly realizes that he has no God, realizes almost simultaneously that he is alone in a nearly devastating sense. His experiences, across the span of "each and every moment" occur without the audience his forebears found in God.[50]

With the liberation he feels from a God who saw everything, Zarathustra at times feels virtual paralysis at the thought that his actions have an audience only if he can find one, and that many of his actions, for lack of an audience, might well signify nothing. So desire to find a key that will give meaning to "each and every moment" arises in the context of his quest to overcome nihilism in the wake of God's death. The doctrine of eternal recurrence, construed as performing the positive function that Nietzsche intends, does not provide the kind of reassurance that Zarathustra, "the loneliest," seeks. But his search for this kind of reassurance is an inevitable part of the psychological adventure that Nietzsche is recounting.[51] This does much to explain why Nietzsche sometimes emphasizes the recurrence of each and every moment, even though he ultimately endorses an interpretation of the doctrine that focuses on the dynamic of the life that is loved, and not on life's atomistic components.

At certain points in Zarathustra's chronicle, we see him embracing the dynamic sweep of time with a tragic, vulnerable outlook. This is the outlook that pervades his "Drunken Song." But the dynamic nature of his life itself makes it possible for him to lose sight of the worldview that he sometimes embodies so joyously. Nietzsche's humorous parable on this matter, *Zarathustra*, Part IV, will be the focus of the following chapter.

7 Where Zarathustra Ends Up

Free *from* what? As if that mattered to Zarathustra! But
your eyes should tell me brightly: free *for* what?[1]

THE FOURTH and last part of Nietzsche's *Thus
Spoke Zarathustra* is stylistically dissimilar to Parts I
through III, and this has not always met with admiration
from the book's readers.[2] For instance, R.J. Hollingdale
writes:

> The fourth part, written in the autumn and winter of
> 1884–85, was intended as the first of a second group of
> three parts. It is markedly inferior in style and content
> and contains no new ideas, and Nietzsche was wise to
> call a halt to the work: the glowing conclusion of the
> third part is the book's true climax, and the seal upon
> what was by then a completed philosophical outlook on
> the world.[3]

The points of contrast between *Zarathustra*, Part IV, and
what precedes it are numerous both in style and in content.[4]
While certain sections in Parts I through III have internal story
lines, a continuous plot does not bind the sections together.
Part IV, by contrast, is a sustained narrative in which the plot
of each section is more or less subordinate to the story line of
the whole. Parts I through III are also similar to one another in
their relative seriousness of tone compared with Part IV. Zarathustra laughs at himself and others on occasion in the earlier

three parts, but one comes away from these parts with the sense that seriousness, more than laughter, has been promoted. Often the tone in these parts is somber or in some other way dark. Part IV, by contrast, tells a story that is not only funny but often raucous. Burlesque, which would be out of place in the earlier parts, easily takes its place in the narrative of Part IV.[5]

The details of Part IV's construction also contrast with the earlier parts. Part IV is told in a narrative voice that is unprecedentedly strong; it makes ironic asides about the story being told and makes comments that suggest it speaks from a perspective that is temporally removed from the events it describes.[6] Part IV is also unique among the parts of the book in granting significant roles to other human characters besides Zarathustra. Once introduced, these characters remain on stage through Part IV, and we are also told something about the events in their lives hitherto. This concern with other characters as more than mere occasions for Zarathustra's remarks finds no precedent in the earlier parts of the book. Furthermore, the parodies supplied by the narrative of Part IV are more brazen than those involved in any of the previous three parts. For instance, the biblical Last Supper and Plato's *Symposium* are wildly satirized in Zarathustra's "Last Supper."

The significance of the changes in Nietzsche's authorial policy in Part IV is not immediately obvious. It is clear that Nietzsche himself felt that Part IV was a different sort of work from Parts I–III, for he insisted on keeping Part IV in a private production to be shared only with his closest friends. He had only forty copies printed, he distributed only seven, and he told some of the recipients to keep Part IV quiet. To Overbeck he wrote: "I have sent no copy to Burckhardt or to anyone in Basel. Please let us remain silent about the existence of a fourth part."[7] And to Carl von Gersdorff he wrote: "There is a fourth (last) part to *Zarathustra*, a sort of sublime finale, which is not intended for the public.... But this part should and must now be printed—20 copies, for me and for distribution among my friends, and with every discretion."[8]

Nietzsche's bombastic remarks about secretiveness during this period are not exclusively connected to *Zarathustra*, Part IV; he wrote to Overbeck, for instance, of his desire to withdraw Parts I–III from circulation.[9] But this attitude is particularly pronounced in the case of *Zarathustra*, Part IV. Nietzsche eventually wrote to Peter Gast that he wanted to recall the few copies of Part IV he had distributed to friends, remarking, "I read it these past few days and almost died of emotion." He adds, "If I publish it later, after a few decades of world crisis—wars!—then that will be the proper time"[10] The megalomania of this remark was characteristic of Nietzsche at the time he wrote this letter—less than a month before his mental breakdown. But it is clear that he viewed Part IV as a work in its own right, with a life separate from that of the first three parts.

One might conclude that Nietzsche is certainly right that Part IV is a production unto itself, but question whether it is really a part of the larger Zarathustra production at all, apart from its main character. The received view, in fact, concurs with Hollingdale that Part IV is relatively unimportant and that it contributes nothing new to the work. The view that Parts I through III are really the basic work is facilitated by the interpretation of Part IV that focuses on the higher men as parodies of Nietzsche's estranged friends and acquaintances. Ronald Hayman, for instance, comments on the "fairly crude" satire of Part IV, whose caricatures may be referring to such notable figures in Nietzsche's life as Wagner, Liszt, Rohde, and/or Overbeck. He concludes that Nietzsche's secretiveness about Part IV was an indication that he was "nervous that his friends would recognize themselves" in it.[11]

My plan in this chapter is to attack the received view. Nietzsche's own attitude toward Part IV is ground enough for reconsidering it. Although he sees the part, as well as the entire book, as highly personal,[12] he considers Zarathustra "the most profound book" that mankind possesses and Part IV the "sublime finale."[13] His own satisfaction in Part IV, which he voices in correspondence to Overbeck,[14] is more objectively indicated by his conclusion after writing it that Part IV would be the final part of Zarathustra despite his earlier plans to write several more parts.[15] The prima facie evidence of Nietzsche's own opinion of the importance of Part IV suggests that it deserves more critical attention than it has been given, both as a self-contained entity in its own right and as a culminating conclusion to Thus Spoke Zarathustra as a whole.

The basis on which I defend the significance of Zarathustra, Part IV, is, to my knowledge, novel. I shall propose that Part IV has structural aims that are different from what has gone before it. Specifically, I contend that Part IV is a satire constructed on the model of Apuleius' Golden Ass. I conclude that the parallels between The Golden Ass and Zarathustra, Part IV, indicate that Part IV is Menippean satire and that the significance of Part IV turns on the question of how Nietzsche's satirical intent is to be taken. The Golden Ass,, I ultimately argue, provides us with important hints as to how that question should be answered.

MENIPPEAN SATIRE

Nietzsche's Knowledge of the Menippean Tradition

Nietzsche was both a student and a professor of classical philology, so it is hardly surprising that he was aware of Menippean satire. A more interesting point, which is revealed by Nietzsche's correspondence, is that he also admired this literary form. Writing to his friend Erwin Rohde during his final year of schooling, Nietzsche describes the presentation he made to the Classical Society at Leipzig.

The topic was Menippean satire (which he names with its less-common label "Varronian satire"), and he expresses his thrill at the success of the talk with the retrospectively ironic comment "It will be all right in this academic career." That he feels the tone of Menippean satire somehow pleasantly aligned with his own experience is suggested by his allusion to Menippus, the Greek cynic who allegedly invented this genre, in the next paragraph.[16] There he tells Rohde of his plans for graduation and the complex emotional reaction that they arouse: "Ah, dear friend, it will feel like being a bridgegroom, joy and vexation mingled, humor, γενοζ σπονδεγₑλοιογ, Menippus!"[17]

That Nietzsche was familiar with the Menippean ass stories is at least suggested by his choice of the genre of Menippean satire as his topic, although a text of his talk does not exist.[18] A text that we do possess, "Beiträge zur Quellen kunde und Kritik des Laertius Diogenes," suggests even more strongly that Nietzsche was interested in this topic. In a section of that essay entitled "Der Cyinker Menippus," he discusses the relationship between Menippean satire and the genre employed by the later figure Varro.[19] But his praise of Rohde's work of the period indicates conclusively that Nietzsche knew of both Lucian's and Apuleius' versions of the ass story; Rohde had written a work on Lucian's *The Ass* which considered Apuleius' version as well: "ΛΟΤΚΙΟΣ Η ΟΝΟΣ und ihr Verhältnis zu Lucius von Patrae und den Metamorphosen des Apuleius." In a postscript to the cited letter, Nietzsche comments that Rohde should have the manuscript recalled from the publisher of *Rheinisches Museum*, who had informed him that another paper on the topic had been selected for publication. Nietzsche was, in fact, instrumental in having Rohde's paper published in Leipzig in early 1869.[20]

The evidence of the letter to Rohde is that Nietzsche, long before writing *Zarathustra*, was cognizant of the generic features of Menippean satire. A consideration of these features will put us in a position to see that Nietzsche was not only familiar with the basic formula but also appears to have employed it.

Generic Features of Menippean Satire

Northup Frye offers a detailed description of the Menippean satire in his *Anatomy of Criticism*. This form, according to Frye, "deals less with people as such than with mental attitudes," and these attitudes frequently stem from a particular character's occupational orientation toward life. The Menippean satire is characteristically abstract in its depictions of the human beings it makes fun of. It "resembles the confession in its ability to handle abstract ideas and theories, and differs from the novel in its characterization, which is stylized rather than naturalistic, and presents people as mouthpieces of the ideas they represent."[21] A stock character is the *philosophus gloriosus*, whose pedantic stance is ridiculed. Says Frye, "The novelist sees evil and folly as social diseases, but the Menippean satirist sees them as diseases of the intellect, as a kind of maddened pedantry which the *philosophus gloriosus* at once symbolizes and defines."[22] By the standards of the novel, the Menippean satire presents a "loose-jointed" narrative. The story it may tell of "the exploits of heroes" is subordinate to "the free play of intellectual fancy and the kind of humorous observation that produces caricature."

> At its most concentrated the Menippean satire presents us with a vision of the world in terms of a single intellectual pattern. The intellectual structure built up from the story makes for violent dislocations in the customary logic of narrative, though the appearance of carelessness that results reflects only the carelessness of the reader or his tendency to judge by a novel-centered conception of fiction.[23]

The setting of the Menippean satire, at least in its short form, is "usually a dialogue or colloquy, in which the dramatic interest is in a conflict of ideas rather than of character."[24] One of the satirist's tactics for dealing with intellectual matters is to show "his exuberance in intellectual ways, by piling up an enormous mass of erudition about his theme or in overwhelming his pedantic targets with an avalanche of their own jargon." As an instance of the use of this tactic, Frye cites Macrobius' *Saturnalia*, "where people sit at a banquet and pour out a vast mass of erudition on every subject that might conceivably come up in a conversation."[25] Frye observes that Plato is "a strong influence" on this type of Menippean satire.[26]

Menippean Satire and Zarathustra, Part IV

Our consideration of Frye's characterization of Menippean satire puts us in a position to see numerous points of similarity between the genre's formulaic features and the features of *Zarathustra*, Part IV. The treatment of characters in Part IV, to begin with, is in accord with the stylized caricatures of Menippean satire. Although much of Part IV is devoted to our making the acquaintance of the higher man, these characters function as "mouthpieces" for mental attitudes that bear some distorted relationship to those that Zarathustra has promoted. They are presented in a stylized fashion that comes off as caricature. Their very presence, as erring students influenced by Zarathustra, effects a kind of ridicule of Zarathustra as a *philosophus gloriosus*, a philosophical teacher whose previous pedagogical poses have failed to effect genuine communication.

Zarathustra is also ridiculed as someone who is sometimes out of touch with the rest of the world by the narrative voice that drops in and out of Part IV. Zarathustra imagines himself to be sleeping for a long time when he pauses to rest under a tree at noon, but the narrative voice corrects his faulty impression. When Zarathustra gets up from his resting place, says the narrator, "the sun stood still straight over his head. But from this one might justly conclude that Zarathustra had not slept long."[27] The recurrent distancing of Part IV's narrating voice from the impressions of Zarathustra suggests something not even hinted at in the earlier parts: Zarathustra can be wrong about things.

Despite the presence of the distinct narrating voice, which does lend Part IV a sense of closure that had been absent since the Prologue, the story told is nonetheless a "loose-jointed narrative." The encounters with the higher men are interspersed with tales of their experiences (however ideational), and the movement of the story is interrupted several times by songs sung by the Magician, the Shadow, and even Zarathustra himself. The activities of Zarathustra may be more consistently narrated than in the other parts of the book, but the emphasis on what is said remains much stronger than the emphasis on what is done. Conflict between characters, when it occurs, is a conflict of ideas, as is the case when the Conscientious in Spirit objects to the Magician's seductive disconcern with truth.[28]

One feature that unifies Part IV despite the vagaries of the narrative is the motif of the dinner party. This motif serves the obvious function of parodying Scripture and Plato. But in addition it makes the setting of Part IV typical of many Menippean satires, which themselves draw on Plato's *Symposium* as a model.

The basic characteristics that Frye associates with Menippean satire, then, all seem to match the broad outline of *Zarathustra*, Part IV. This fact in itself supports the claim that Part IV is written in the manner of a Menippean satire. But stronger support comes from a more detailed analysis of the text. The text features an ass, whose presence is noted recurrently but whose function is not at all clear. This ass will prove an important clue to Nietzsche's purpose in writing Part IV.

THE STORY OF THE ASS

The ass slips into Part IV of *Zarathustra* without much pomp and circumstance. He is the beast of burden for two kings who are fleeing the false pomposity that kingship has become. Their tale of this flight quickly overshadows interest in their laden beast, and yet Zarathustra has made note of the animal. "Strange! Stange!" he commented when he first caught sight of its owners. "How does this fit together? Two kings I see—and only one ass!"[29] The ass, too, soon has his moment for a comment. Zarathustra announces that he will make a rhyme which is not fit for everybody's ears and that he has "long become unaccustomed to any consideration for long ears," and at this point the ass is said to "get in a word." The ass, the narrator tells us, "said clearly and with evil intent, Yeah-Yuh."[30]

The comment of the ass is certainly opaque, and his further contributions to Zarathustra's convocation of the higher men are described in the same unclear way. The ass responds "Yeah-Yuh," again with evil intent, when one of the kings flatters Zarathustra with the maxim "And verily, he is the strangest sage who is also clever and no ass."[31] The ass's vocabulary becomes no wider through the rest of the book. It is his "Yeah-Yuh" that seems to blend, in Zarathustra's hearing, with the gay noise that the higher men are making inside the cave at one point.[32] And when the higher men invent the ass festival and sing a litany in his honor, the ass punctuates every stanza with his bray, "Yeah-Yuh."[33]

By contrast with the ass in either Lucian's *Story of the Ass*[34] or Apuleius' *Golden Ass*[35] the ass of Part IV has a relatively uninteresting role. The only hint we have as to his inner experience is the recurrent suggestion that his intent is evil. While Lucian's and Apuleius' asses are really human beings, the ass in *Zarathustra* is evidently supposed to be genuinely an ass, albeit with some limited personality; and the higher men's worship of the ass as a god is presumably to be viewed as benign folly at best.

The obvious contrast between Zarathustra's ass and the man-turned-ass of Apuleius and Lucian should not, however, obscure the prevalence of allusions in Part IV to the earlier works. In order to make the presence of these allusions evident, I shall summarize the details of the ass stories of Lucian and Apuleius. Both versions draw on the same model, an earlier Greek original, which is lost except in truncated form.[36] Until the end of their accounts, Lucian and Apuleius tell essentially the same story; but Apuleius' story is much more elaborate and includes many additional stories, most notably "Cupid and Psyche," a romantic tale that contrasts with the consistently burlesque tone of Lucian's *Story of the Ass*.

The common plot of Lucian and Apuleius consists of the narrator's tale of a trip he made to Thessaly, where he stayed in the home of a wealthy friend of a friend. His host's wife is well known for her magical powers. In the story recounted, Lucius, the narrator, takes the maid of the household as a lover, and the early part of the narrative consists largely of lascivious accounts of their exploits. Lucius, however, is avidly curious about magic, and eventually he persuades the maid to let him spy on her mistress while the latter is casting a spell. Lucius sees the mistress transform herself into a bird with an ointment, and after she has flown away he insists that the maid rub him with the ointment, so that he too can gain a bird's perspective on the world. The maid attempts to comply with his demand, but she grabs the wrong ointment jar and transforms her lover not into a bird but into an ass.[37] She tells him that the antidote is simple: he only has to eat roses in order to become a human being again. But the rest of the tale demonstrates how difficult this antidote is to secure. Lucius the ass has a lengthy series of misadventures in which he is shuffled from one owner to another, sometimes stolen, almost always treated cruelly, and continuously occupying a good vantage point for observing human behavior.

Lucius' fortune throughout the majority of the tale is dismal, but it begins to turn when he is caught stealing food from his final master and his master's brother, both of whom are cooks for a wealthy gentleman who is fond of grand entertainments. The cooks find the gourmet thievery of the ass so amusing that they give him wine as well as food, and later they have him trained to do tricks for public entertainment. Lucius makes such a hit as an entertainer, and his repertoire becomes so large, that he is eventually scheduled to perform an act of copulation in the amphitheater with a woman sentenced to death. He manages to eat some roses after arriving at the amphitheater and returns to human form before the performance begins. The versions of Lucian and Apuleius diverge at this point. In Lucian's tale, Lucius the man is shunned by a woman who had regularly paid for the erotic favors of Lucius the ass, and the story ends with Lucius sailing for home and then sacrificing to the gods.

In Apuleius' version, Lucius has a vision of the goddess Isis the night before his scheduled theater performance, a vision in which she predicts the appearance of the roses. After his transformation into human shape, Lucius is initiated into the Mysteries of Isis. The ending of the book drops the satiric tone of what precedes it and reveals Apuleius as a serious evangelist for the Isiac religion.[38]

The ending of *Zarathustra*, Part IV, which stands in similar contrast to the tone of the rest of the narrative,

213

shows Zarathustra in something resembling a mystical vision from which he recovers in a mood of spiritual rejuvenation. The significance of "The Sign," the final section of the book, is problematic,[39] but for purposes of comparison, *Zarathustra*, Part IV, appears to correspond more closely to Apuleius' version of the ass story than to Lucian's. For this reason I refer primarily to *The Golden Ass* in what follows, although most of *Zarathustra's* specific points of similarity with Apuleius' tale correspond to elements that occur in Lucian's ass story as well.[40]

The plot summary just presented is detailed enough to reveal resonances between *The Golden Ass* and details of *Zarathustra*, Part IV. Zarathustra resembles Lucius in having a position that allows him to encounter a wide range of characters who reveal their stories to him. He resembles Lucius, also, in being mistaken, in a sense, for someone other than who he is, for each of the higher men sees Zarathustra as the patron of some doctrine to which he has subscribed, although Zarathustra sees each of these doctrines as a misunderstanding of his views. We are evidently supposed to see Zarathustra as the human being with the clearest perspective in Part IV, flawed though it proves to be, and in this he ironically resembles Apuleius' long-eared ass, who is somewhat consoled by his ability to see and hear more as a consequence of his asinine position.[41] Zarathustra also resembles Apuleius' ass with respect to where their stories end, for both, after straying far from their original position, ultimately regain their previous perspective, now enlarged by their experiences. (I shall have more to say about the significance of this "Fall and Redemption" motif in Zarathustra's story.)

Roses provide a further common feature of the two works, and they appear as a symbol of redemption in *Zarathustra* as in *The Golden Ass*. Zarathustra throws roses when he wants to cure the Conscientious Man of the view he is proselytizing, the view that fear is the basic emotion and that security is to be valued, whether in science or in the gospel of Zarathustra. Roses are a repeated but unexplained image, too, in Zarathustra's speech on the higher man. He says, for instance, "This crown of him who laughs, this rose-wreath crown: I myself have put on this crown, I myself have pronounced my laughter holy."[42] And he repeats this image at the end of the speech:

> What does it matter that you are failures? How much is
> still possible! so *learn* to laugh away over yourselves!
> Lift up your hearts, you good dancers, high, higher!
> And do not forget good laughter. The crown of him who
> laughs, this rose-wreath crown: to you, my brothers, I
> throw this crown. Laughter I have pronounced holy;
> you higher men, *learn* to laugh![43]

The significance of Zarathustra's association of a rose-wreath, laughter, and the overcoming of failure is worth probing, and I shall discuss it shortly. For now, it is worth observing that the roses through which Apuleius' ass finds redemption appear in the form of a garland.[44]

An additional detail from the basic outline of the ass story that appears in *Zarathustra* is the ass drinking wine. The Ugliest Man offers the ass wine to drink at the ass festival,[45] and this detail is emphasized by the narrator in one of his strange outbursts, this one occurring in "The Drunken Song":

> There are even some who relate that the ass danced too,
> and that it had not been for nothing that the ugliest man
> had given him wine to drink before. Now it may have
> been so or otherwise; and if the ass really did not dance
> that night, yet greater and stranger wonders occurred
> than the dancing of an ass would have been. In short,

as the proverb of Zarathustra says: "What does it
matter?"[46]

These reminders of the ass story are striking for the
peculiarity of their insertion into the narrative of *Zarathustra*, Part IV. The point of these parallels has yet to be
considered, but their existence can hardly be doubted when
more of the details of *The Golden Ass* are compared with
Part IV of *Zarathustra*.

I shall trace several more points of this comparison,
which should further corroborate my claim that there is a
connection between the works. Ultimately they will help
us understand the point of this connection.

The Golden Ass begins with a tale told about Socrates,
who is depicted as a tattered old man brought to ruin by
the seduction of a witch. This is certainly a burlesque re-
versal of the traditional Platonic portrait of Socrates. In this
it parallels Nietzsche's consistent, if quieter, parody of Socrates in the character of Zarathustra, who reverses both the
doctrine and the concept of wisdom that are part of the
Socratic tradition. Accordingly, Part IV begins with a reference to the Myth of the Cave, but this reference quickly
gives way to a burlesque portrait of Zarathustra that is
kindred in tone to Apuleius' sketch of Socrates. Zarathustra's animals ask him why he has become such a mess;[47]
Apuleius' Socrates, similarly, is asked, "Why are you sitting
here in such a frightful state?"[48] Even if the similarity of
phrasing and positioning in the cases of these comments is
coincidental, Socrates is clearly a satiric target in both texts.

Mistaken identity is thematic in Apuleius even before
Lucius is transformed into an ass, and it is similarly thematic in *Zarathustra*. A striking case of such confusion
occurs when Lucius believes that he has stabbed three bandits to death, while actually he merely gored some wineskins with his sword. This particular bit of folly is greeted

with laughter everywhere. In fact, the incident takes on a festive quality because Lucius' mistake has coincided with the Festival of Laughter celebrated each year by the town he is visiting.[49] Not only does the praise of laughter implied by this event resemble the point of Zarathustra's paean in the speech to the higher men; the confusion of wineskins with bandits, Lucius with an ordinary ass, and other confusions of this sort are similar to Zarathustra's mistaken but ultimately vindicated belief that everyone he meets is the source of the cry of distress that he hears.[50]

The Festival of Laughter is not, however, the only festive event mentioned in *The Golden Ass*. After being transformed into an ass, Lucius is taken by bandits to a mountain cave where a kidnapped girl begs him to help her escape. She promises that if he does her parents will honor him in gratitude—and what she describes, if not exactly an ass festival, at least demonstrates a similar spirit:

> I'll have a memorial set up at home, a carved plaque picturing our flight, and I'll get some clever author to write the story out in a book for future generations to read. The title will be, let me see: "Flight on Ass-back; or, How a Young Lady of Royal Blood Escaped from Captivity." It's not a very learned subject, of course, but you'll have your niche in history: you'll be a modern instance to strengthen people's belief in mythology.[51]

This ass memorial, which is to be constructed in a spirit of gratitude and to confirm people's faith in religion, is akin to *Zarathustra*'s ass festival. The latter appalls Zarathustra because of its fortification of religious belief, but he concludes that it is a hopeful sign because it was born in a spirit of gratitude.

Thematic and stylistic elements of *The Golden Ass* also concur with features of Part IV of *Zarathustra*. The long tale of Cupid and Psyche emphasizes one of *Zarathustra*'s central themes: pity. Psyche, who has lost happiness because of her sacrilegious curiosity, is able to regain it by performing a series of tasks in which she withstands the temptation to become distracted by pity.[52] The concept of pity is invoked recurrently throughout the rest of the book as well, often in improbable contexts. The kidnapped girl believes an old woman who lives with the bandits to be not "incapable of pity" because she has white hair.[53] In another vignette, a manservant who has allowed his master to be cuckolded is manacled; he weeps and howls while being escorted down the street, "trying to excite the pity of passersby," although the ass comments, "What good that would have done, I'm sure I don't know."[54] Pity is also invoked as a term of sexual persuasion by Lucius himself in his human form. His initial sexual encounter with the maid, Fotis, is precipitated by his cry "Oh, Fotis, this is killing me! Unless you take pity on me I'm as good as dead."[55] And pity is also the term used to describe the cuckold's wife's spirit when accepting a suitor to her bed.[56] It is significant that the human response of pity is consistently linked with disaster in *The Golden Ass*, as it is in Zarathustra's case, although Apuleius does present the divine pity of Isis in a favorable light.[57]

Several comments made by Apuleius' ass invite speculation regarding the extent to which Nietzsche is intentionally pushing his allusion to *The Golden Ass*. *Zarathustra*'s ass is praised in the ass-festival litany as affirming everything with his "Yea-Yuh."[58] This is clearly a travesty of God's pronouncements on the goodness of creation in Genesis. Perhaps more strikingly in the context, however, it indicates the higher men's absorption of Zarathustra's doctrine without genuine spiritual comprehension, for they recite the expressions of life-affirmation that Zarathustra has advocated without indicating the vitality that would make these words meaningful. Nevertheless, "Yea-Yuh" might also remind the reader of Apuleius of the equally absurd, if more negative, braying of his ass. In trying to defend himself justly against accusations that he stole from the man who had been his host as a human being, Apuleius' ass screams, "Non-non,"[59] and when attempting to stop the ravishment of an unsuspecting dinner guest by wicked "priestesses" who live with one of the owners, the ass gets out "He-whore! He-whore!"[60] Another detail of Apuleius' story that is at least amusing when juxtaposed with *Zarathustra* is the abrupt outburst of the ass to the reader about the depravity of the legal profession, which in his view is demonstrated by the conviction of Socrates. As in the case of the outbursts of the narrator in *Zarathustra*, Part IV, this outbursts ends as abruptly as it begins. But this ending is particularly comical in its self-ironical reminder to the reader of who is doing the talking: "Forgive this outburst! I can hear my readers protesting: "Hey, what's all this about! Are we going to let an ass lecture us in philosophy?' "[61]

This remark may not have been anywhere in Nietzsche's mind when he composed *Zarathustra*, Part IV, but the range of resonances between Part IV of *Zarathustra* and *The Golden Ass* suggests that Nietzsche used the latter to some extent as a model. M. M. Bakhtin's analysis of *The Golden Ass*, to which I now turn, suggests some general reasons why Nietzsche might have found an amenable model in Apuleius' work. Among the structural features of *The Golden Ass* that Bakhtin observes are many that help to focus the reader's attention on individual experience in time.

BAKHTIN'S ANALYSIS

Bakhtin analyzes *The Golden Ass* not as a satire per se but as a particular type of ancient novel. Specifically, he characterizes this type as an "adventure novel of everyday life." The most striking peculiarity of this form is its "mix of adventure-time with everyday time." Accordingly, Bakhtin emphasizes the temporal dimension of Apuleius' story as well as its focus on individual experience. His analysis is of use to us because these central features of *The Golden Ass* find parallels in *Zarathustra*, Part IV.[62]

Temporality

The basic theme of *The Golden Ass*, Bakhtin tells us, is the theme of development. Through time the sudden transformations of Lucius into an ass and back into human form may appear to defy the concept of development, for they happen in an instant. But even these instantaneous metamorphoses recall the mythological idea lurking behind all ancient images of metamorphosis. This is "the idea of development—but one that unfolds not so much in a straight line as spasmodically, a line with 'knots' in it, one that therefore constitutes a distinctive type of *temporal sequence*."[63] Metamorphosis is a matter of development that unfolds visibly; development is conspicuous because distinct forms are assumed over the course of time. Although the mythological motif of metamorphosis was applied to "the entire human world, and to nature," it is intimately linked with "concern for the individual."[64]

The ancient concept of metamorphosis underwent considerable development before Apuleius. Only in a late stage of its development was the emphasis on "the private metamorphosis of individual, isolated beings." Apuleius took this emphasis further than any of his literary ancestors known to us. The scope of metamorphosis, no longer "the cosmic and historical whole," became in his work "the entire life-long destiny of a man, at all its critical turning points."[65]

Already in observing this characteristic of *The Golden Ass*, we can recognize its affinity with *Zarathustra*—in Part IV and in its other parts as well. In discussing the *Bildungs-*

roman character of *Zarathustra,* we observed that the work recounts a tale of Zarathustra's development over time as a particular individual. Moreover, the kinds of events that Nietzsche reports indicate his concern with critical turning points in life development. We do not read a continuous biographical account—Zarathustra is off stage between the book's parts and sections for periods of unspecified length. Zarathustra's chronicle, like Apuleius' novel,

> does not, strictly speaking, unfold in *biographical time.* It depicts only the *exceptional,* utterly *unusual* moments of a man's life, moments that are very short compared to the whole length of a human life. But these moments shape *the definitive image of the man, his essence, as well as the nature of his entire subsequent life.*[66]

In the sense of depicting Zarathustra's most significant and transformative moments, all of *Zarathustra* resembles *The Golden Ass.* But *The Golden Ass* tells a story that has a much stronger element of closure than Zarathustra as a whole. And although the conclusion of *The Golden Ass* is rather open-ended, it provides a kind of end-point toward which the movement of the story was aiming throughout. In these respects, *Zarathustra,* Part IV, much more strongly resembles *The Golden Ass* than does the book as a whole. These considerations justify my focusing, for the remainder of my discussion of Bakhtin, on the relevance of his analysis to *Zarathustra,* Part IV.

The Golden Ass, Bakhtin tells us, is an adventure novel. But the developmental structure that he observes is not specifically dictated by the work's adventure-story character. Along with the adventure sequence is another that "interprets it:" "guilt—punishment—redemption—blessedness."[67] The novel tells a story of Fall and Redemption. The structure of Zarathustra's story, on examination, proves similar. The plot of Part IV involves Zarathustra's movement from a position of distress literally downward into the "sin" of pity. The adventurous consequences of his sin comprise the body of Part IV, but they build to a moment of eventual redemption through insight, a matter about which I shall have much more to say.

The pattern of the story of the Fall creates a sense of closure and directionality in the tale recounted. Bakhtin stresses this character of temporality in Apuleius by contrast with the mythical character of time in Greek adventure stories.

> Here time is not merely technical, not a mere distribution of days, hours, moments that are reversible, transposable, unlimited internally, along a straight line; here the temporal sequence is an integrated and *irreversible whole*. And as a consequence, the abstractness so characteristic of Greek adventure time falls away. Quite the contrary, this new temporal sequence demands precisely concreteness of expression.[68]

Individual, Private Experience

The irreversibility of the temporal dimension that we find in *The Golden Ass*—and in *Zarathustra*, Part IV—is important, Bakhtin tells us, for it is the proper literary sense of time for the telling of a personal story. The life of nature involves a different sense of time, that of endless repetition and renewal, but an individual's life is monodirectional and finite. The story of such a life must therefore be an account of development toward an end.

The temporal dimension of *The Golden Ass* is not its only structural component that suits it to the telling of an individual story. The individual's life is also well emblemized by the motif of venturing forth along roads, Bakhtin observes. The actual spatial movement coincides with and reminds us of the more metaphoric "course" of a person's life. An adventure story is thus an appropriate form for a personal life history. It is worth noting that this symbolic strategy is utilized in both *The Golden Ass* and *Zarathustra,* Part IV. The hero of each ventures forth from home and travels proverbial highways and byways.[69]

The character of this traveling in an adventure novel of everyday life is distinctive. The hero is not really a part of the world he passes through, nor are his life's significant turning points. For precisely this reason, however, he has a privileged perspective on it. As we have observed, this position in the world is common to both Lucius the ass and Zarathustra. Bakhtin, however, analyzes the importance of this characteristic in Apuleius' novel as a means of revealing what is private and personal.

> The everyday life that Lucius observes and studies is an *exclusively personal and private life.* By its very nature there can be nothing *public* about it. All its events are the personal affairs of isolated people: they could not occur "in the eyes of the world," publicly, in the presence of a *chorus.* These events are not liable to public reckoning on the open square.[70]

Bakhtin goes on to analyze the literary strategy of depicting eavesdropping and snooping as a means of resolving the paradox between communication and the private:

> When the private individual and private life entered literature (in the Hellenistic era)... problems inevitably were bound to arise. *A contradiction developed between the public nature of the literary form and the private nature of its content....* The quintessentially private life that entered the novel at this time was, by its very nature and as opposed to public life, *closed.* In

223

essence one could only *spy* and *eavesdrop* on it. The literature of private life is essentially a literature of snooping about, of overhearing "how others live."[71]

The literary function of such out-of-place heroes as Lucius the ass and Zarathustra is to reveal a side of life that is not susceptible to direct observation. We do not have access to what is private in the lives of others. Our own roles with respect to those we observe always condition the way they reveal themselves. We cannot see what they are like independent of the motivations inherent to social intercourse.

The fictional role of the sort played by Lucius or Zarathustra has the function of conveying what individuals are like outside the constraints of social interaction. Zarathustra and Lucius do not affect the behavior of others as we affect it in our social world for they are portrayed as being essentially outsiders. They embody what Bakhtin calls "the philosophy of the third person in private life":

> This is the philosophy of a person who knows only private life and craves it alone, but who does not participate in it, who has no place in it—and therefore sees it in sharp focus, as a whole, in all its nakedness, playing out all its roles but not fusing his identity with any one of them.[72]

We can snoop on individuals in intimacy when we read the stories of Lucius and Zarathustra because their position is essentially that of a spy on the rest of the world.

It is significant that the temporality of everyday life is incoherent compared with that of the developing hero in *The Golden Ass*, and this point applies as well to *Zarathustra*, Part IV. The very day in both is a "maelstrom of personal life" in which time is "chopped up into separate segments, each encompassing a separate episode... The

224

everyday world is scattered, fragmented, deprived of essential connections"[73] The contrast between the potpourri of everyday life and the directional sequence of the stories of Lucius and Zarathustra underscores the importance of temporal structure for meaningful individuality. The lifestyles of Lucius and Zarathustra are characterized by detachment and episodic distress. But the structure of their stories urges us to see their lives as desirably significant compared with life in the random flux of the everyday.

The structural aspects of *The Golden Ass* that Bakhtin illuminates suggest general reasons why Nietzsche might have seen it as a likely model for *Zarathustra* Part IV. Intending to write a tale of Zarathustra's fall from and return to insight, the Fall story motif of *The Golden Ass* is apt. The ribald nature of Apuleius' tale, too, would make it a more welcome model on which to focus than the traditional scriptural saga. Moreover, when we consider the structural devices of *The Golden Ass*, we see techniques that emphasize experienced, goal-directed temporality and the individual, private character of human experience. Because these are central concerns evident in the whole *Zarathustra* project, it is easy to understand why Nietzsche might have wanted to experiment with Apuleius' successful techniques.

Reflection on the multiple parallels between *The Golden Ass* and *Zarathustra* suggests that Nietzsche is deliberately alluding to the earlier work and using it as a type of model. But what is the significance of this relationship? Even if Zarathustra's ass is a deliberate reminder of the Menippean ass of Apuleius, we might ask, so what? Has this association clarified anything about what Nietzsche is doing in Part IV of his book? Or are we left with no more than the basic impression we have on reading *Thus Spoke Zarathustra* alone, the impression that someone is being called an ass?

THE SATIRE OF *ZARATHUSTRA*, PART IV

We can now see that Nietzsche's allusions to *The Golden Ass* in *Zarathustra* provide strong suggestions about how the raucous satire of Part IV is to be taken. In particular, they provide hints as to (1) who is being called an ass, (2) what being called an ass means in the context; and (3) the significance of the peculiar final section of the book, "The Sign."

Who Is The Ass?

Perhaps we do not need to compare *Zarathustra* to the work of Apuleius in order to see that Zarathustra is being called an ass in a certain sense. This suggestion is made by the simple inclusion of the king's comment about the sage who is no ass. The king means to compliment Zarathustra, but we know that the king, like all the higher men, is duped as to who Zarathustra really is. And we see Zarathustra himself taken in again and again; in other words, he is made an ass. He takes each of the higher men to be the source of the cry of distress; because this is in some sense true he is deceived again when he decides he was wrong; the Magician's seductive powers sway Zarathustra half the time; and in the end Zarathustra concludes that he was always deceived in thinking that the higher men were his proper companions.

In a sense Zarathustra's various double-takes of the higher men suggest that *they* are asses, as does their acquiescence in the nonsense of the ass festival itself. But even then they expose Zarathustra's own folly, which had almost been buried in his speech that commented on theirs. Each has had something to say in defense of the ass festival that makes some sense to Zarathustra, often to the latter's edification. The Conscientious Man makes the point about Zarathustra's folly directly:

> And whoever has too much spirit might well grow fool-
> ishly fond of stupidity and folly itself. Think about
> yourself, O Zarathustra! You yourself—verily, over-
> abundance and wisdom could easily turn you too into
> an ass. Is not the perfect sage fond of walking on the
> most crooked ways? The evidence shows this, O Zara-
> thustra—and you are the evidence.[74]

The Ugliest Man is less direct, but implicitly he contributes
to the thrust of this criticism when he responds to Zarathustra's accusation that he has revived God.

> O Zarathustra, ... "you are a rogue! Whether that one
> *still* lives or lives again or is thoroughly dead—which of
> the two of us knows that best? I ask you. But one thing I
> do know; it was from you yourself that I learned it
> once, O Zarathustra: whoever would kill most thor-
> oughly, *laughs*".[75]

The text of Part IV itself, therefore provides evidence
for the view that Zarathustra is presented as some kind of
ass. The allusions to *The Golden Ass* only reinforce this
suggestion because Apuleius' ass is like Zarathustra in being
the central character of the narrative and the person with
whose perspective we are most likely to empathize.

The Significance of The Ass

The value of the connection of *The Golden Ass* and
Zarathustra for our interpretation of Part IV becomes evident when we move to consideration of what it means to
see Part IV's Zarathustra as a kind of ass. This is an important question for the status of Nietzsche's *Zarathustra*
project as a whole, for we might otherwise conclude that
Nietzsche is closing his book by ridiculing its hitherto serious protaganist out of existence. In this interpretation *Zarathustra*, Part IV, would offer a seriously problematic

gesture, for it would force us to question whether Nietzsche intended to stand behind the previous "doctrinal" parts of the book at all.[76]Nietzsche's own comments undercut this interpretation. But the buffoonish figure that Zarathustra cuts in his own eyes as well as those of the higher men represents on the surface an *ad hominem* argument against Zarathustra's statements so far. And if Nietzsche intends such an *ad hominem* argument by portraying Zarathustra as an ass, we seem to be given a paltry and not sublime finale to the book purportedly concerned with what Zarathustra spoke.

As I shall explain shortly, "The Sign" complicates Part IV too much for us to pass this depressing judgment on the force of the book's ending quickly, but consideration of the allusion to *The Golden Ass* spares *Zarathustra* this fate even before "The Sign" is discussed. The point of Apuleius' work is seriously evangelical and the evangelistic point is, in blasphemous summation, that there is spirtual value in being an ass.

On one view, Lucius the ass has had a meaningless time of it by the end of *The Golden Ass;* he has confronted one near disaster after another, all as a consequence of indulging his curiosity. The obsessive quality of this characteristic is clearly condemned by Apuleius' fable.[77] One might conclude that Apuleius is preaching that one is better off without curiosity in the first place.

But curiosity is not only an ambivalent vice[78]; it is also a paradigmatic characteristic of a philosopher, a vocation that Apuleius himself was eager to claim.[79] Apuleius' ultimate moral is not that curiosity should be squelched in its nascent stages, but that it must be accompanied by developing spiritual maturity if it is not to be disastrous. The tale of Lucius is a story of spiritual development that follows the model of "the human soul" being "alienated from the true reality, yet searching unceasingly for it and being eventually admitted to it by initiation into the mysteries."[80] The point of the story, which is a strikingly un-Christian treatment of the topic of sin and the suffering it causes,[81] is that sin is error that can be redeemed.

And the redemption that the story recommends is achieved by growing through misadventures that can eventually be laughed at. This is the serious point of Apuleius' burlesque, and it may be Nietzsche's point in *Zarathustra*, Part IV, as well. The fact that we do the laughing at Lucius, while Zarathustra urges the higher men to laugh at themselves, does not undercut the parallel. The higher men and Zarathustra himself achieve the self-irony almost as little as does Lucius while trapped in the ass's body. But the self-ironical distance from one's own folly that laughter demonstrates is the achievement that redeems Lucius' hilarious tribulations and the attainment that ultimately separates Zarathustra from the higher men in "The Sign," as we shall see below. The redemption of folly—for "sin" in Nietzsche's view is a meaningful concept only to the extent that it can be diagnosed as error or folly in some human context—is not the conversion of folly into something sensible; it is growth beyond folly to a perspective from which it is laughable.

If this is the case, folly need not be seen as a completely negative component of a life that could be meaningful only if folly did not disrupt its coherence. Folly can be the means of achieving insight that can open up a new and more valuable dimension of meaning. Lucius, more or less a typical human being, understood his experience as a quest for "coupling and guzzling"[82] until his experiences as an eavesdropping ass altered his perspective on what is valuable in human life.[83] Error and its unfortunate consequences serve the positive function of expediting insight that makes a new level of maturity possible.

The same phenomenon is visible in Zarathustra. He

confronts his own folly at the ass festival. His own error, which has contributed to the pitiable condition of the higher men, is the error of having held his own doctrine, at times, as rigidly as they have interpreted it. The ass festival disturbs him because he is viewing his doctrine of the death of God as a value to preserve, when honesty forces him to acknowledge, at least to himself, that the Ugliest Man is right, that no one does know how dead God is, and that if God is really dead no ass festival can represent a spiritual or cultural danger. Zarathustra absorbs this lesson, and after rebuking the irreverent observations of the higher men about himself, he makes a remarkable about-face and praises the ass festival in a playfully blasphemous tone:

> Do not forget this night and this ass festival, you higher men. *This* you invented when you were with me and I take that for a good sign: such things are invented only by convalescents.
>   And when you celebrate it again, this ass festival, do it for your own sakes, and also do it for my sake. And in remembrance of me.[84]

The Book's Mystical Ending

Zarathustra's willingness to confront the edifying insinuations of the higher men about his own folly puts him in a frame of mind to have the mystical experience recounted in "The Sign." What Zarathustra has there is not far removed from the mystical experience that Lucius encounters when he is initiated into the Mysteries of Isis at the end of *The Golden Ass*, even though there is the significant difference that Zarathustra receives only a sign, not a complete spiritual reorientation. This difference is consonant with a highly significant difference between Apuleius and Nietzsche: Apuleius is proselytizing his beliefs in the Isiac religion and neo-Platonism,[85] while Nietzsche is promulgating a spiritual vision that maintains firm ties with earthly, apparent reality. The intrusion of another dimension of reality is far more welcome in Apuleius' story than it is in Nietzsche's. The fact that mystical experience occurs in any form at the finale of Nietzsche's story is therefore quite significant. It provides a concession on Nietzsche's part, as on Zarathustra's, that the death of God does not resolve or even address all problems of religion and spirituality, and that the atheist prophet Zarathustra is as much engaged in a quest for answers as anyone else.

Zarathustra's quest, however, is portrayed as ongoing. Like Apuleius' hero, Zarathustra does not reach a final state of wisdom. While recalling Apuleius' conclusion, Zarathustra's mystical experience is more in keeping with the momentum of the story that precedes it.[86] No matter how profound the insight that Zarathustra experiences in "The Sign," we are reminded that the value of insight is never definitively established. Instead, it must be dynamically and continuously reformulated through further experience.[87]

By the end of the book, Zarathustra has acquired greater sophistication in recognizing his own mistakes than he has possessed previously, and this, the final paragraph suggests, provides him with renewed strength to continue with the work in which he is involved. The insight Zarathustra has achieved is important, but it does not grant him a resting place. This point is reinforced when he speaks of the nearness of his children—the progeny of attained maturity—although the children are not yet present. What Zarathustra does have is a vision of a laughing lion.

The imagistic sketch of the stages of spiritual development that Zarathustra recounted in his early speech on "The Three Metamorphoses" portrayed the lion as representing the intermediate stage of the soul; at the lion stage the previously embraced inheritance of tradition is rejected. The next stage, that of the child, is the stage of the soul's maturity, which is characterized by the activity of playful arrangement and rearrangement of contents provided by one's life in the world. Laughing lions, it would seem, represent the soul in the last part of the second stage, where emphatic rejection of previous error (which nonetheless retains a kind of value) gives way to laughter, a benign embracing of what error still has to offer.

Zarathustra's spiritual stage when he departs from our view is, in essence, similar to that of Lucius at the end of *The Golden Ass*. Both works end with a description of their hero on the verge of spiritual maturity, a precipice surmounted by learning from misadventure. In both cases this learning is painful, but it is embraced as well as what is painful can be embraced—embraced, then, through laughter. Such embracing does more than grant comfortable continuity, and thus a kind of meaning, to an otherwise fragmentary existence. It opens the possibility that one's perspective on meaning can be significantly transformed. One might come to see even folly that instigates disaster as valuable for its instructive incitement to wisdom.

Conclusion:
Taking It Seriously

A man's maturity—consists in having found again the seriousness one had as a child, at play.[1]

WE last see Zarathustra at an odd juncture of triumph. "Am I concerned with *happiness?* I am concerned with my *work,*" Zarathustra announces at the close of his chronicle[2] He has made peace with his own failures and feels ready to return to his work as a teacher. As he steps out of our range, he steps down once again from the heights of his mountain cave to his mission of teaching below.

Part IV has shown us a certain kind of sense underlying Zarathustra's nonsense, and now it seems that he has recovered from his confusion. Perhaps Part IV's hilarity has been essentially a means to a very serious end—to show us that maturity can emerge unexpectedly and spare us from folly in the future. Zarathustra, after all, seems convinced that *now* he knows what he should have known all along and that *now* he can find the right ears for his gospel.

The context of the entire book, however, should suggest that this interpretation is questionable. Folly and nonsense have been Zarathustra's constant companions throughout the book, particularly at the moments when he takes himself and his work most seriously. His final words take both so seriously that we ought to be suspicious. And the words themselves are dramatically ironic. Overflowing happiness was the original motivation of Zarathustra's work; what sense does it make for him now to claim that work still

233

matters but happiness does not? And how can he claim that happiness does not matter? His consistent message has been that the quality of our existence here and now is all-important to the meaning of our lives. Most ironic of all, we have no reason to think that these serious words herald an unprecedented period of success in Zarathustra's work. Why should we think that he won't become addled again by a sense of self-importance, or that now, despite his failures in the past, he is really on the brink of finding his ideal students?

The end of *Zarathustra*, then, involves a mixed message. Zarathustra's final words show that in a sense he *has* learned his own lesson. His concern with his work reveals his recognition that the value of his present activity does not derive from the eventual "happiness" it may produce, but instead is a quality of the activity itself. To this extent, he succeeds in living out the tragic worldview. But all the same, we have no reason to expect this recognition to be any more a bastion against future failure than any of Zarathustra's other insights. After all his maturing experiences and his genuine development as a thinker and teacher, Zarathustra remains prone to folly and mishap.

The mixed signals of the book's finale are not new. The book's full title is already a beacon of mixed messages, and the ironic discrepancy between Zarathustra's overt message and his varying states of mind is integral to the book's structure. I want to suggest that the ending, with its tensions, alludes imagistically to the difficult balance involved in living tragically, a balance that must take even life's nonsense into account.

We have seen that Nietzsche's tragic worldview differs from nontragic worldviews, including that of Christianity, by not taking successful achievement of some final goal to be the determinant of value for the activity that precedes it. The value of activity is imminent, and although valuable activity is projective and partially constituted by the aims that direct it, its present being is self-justifying.

From the tragic point of view, the end of *Zarathustra* makes sense. Zarathustra has regained his understanding of what his work is all about. He has been reminded that the work itself is something he values. He does not value the work because he is sure it will succeed. His "Sign" is the only indication he has that his efforts are not entirely misguided, and even this reassurance is a matter of his own needy interpretation. The narrator reminds us that Zarathustra's vision is more a reflection of his inner state than a depiction that is objectively real: "All this lasted a long time, or a short time: for properly speaking there is *no* time on earth for such things." And Zarathustra himself asks, when his vision recedes, "What happened to me just now?"[3] Zarathustra does not value his work because it will clearly produce results; he values it because it strikes him as a good thing to be doing.[4]

ZARATHUSTRA'S IRONIC SIN

Zarathustra's apparently harsh words at the end of the book make sense in this context too, although they also reflect Nietzsche's elitism. The passage leading up to the exclamation quoted above deserves comment, for after Zarathustra's seeming appreciation of the higher men through much of Part IV, he speaks of them disparagingly at the book's close.

> "O you higher men, it was *your* distress that this old soothsayer prophesied to me yesterday morning; to your distress he wanted to seduce and tempt me. O Zarathustra, he said to me, I come to seduce you to your final sin.
>
> "To my final sin?" shouted Zarathustra, and he

laughed angrily at his own words; *"what* was it that
was saved up for me as my final sin?"

And once more Zarathustra became absorbed in himself, and he sat down again on the big stone and reflected. Suddenly he jumped up. "Pity! Pity for the
higher man!" he cried out, and his face changed to
bronze. "Well, then, *that* has had its time! My suffering
and my pity for suffering—what does it matter? Am I
concerned with *happiness?* I am concerned with my
work."[5]

Zarathustra rejects his pity for the higher man as his
"final sin." "Sin" in his mouth must be spoken ironically,
because "sin" is the central term in a moral worldview he
has abandoned. Doubly ironically, the "sin" he confesses
to himself is paradigmatically opposite to what that worldview would take to be a sin. "Pity" (in German, *Mitleid*,
which, we noted, can also be translated as "compassion")
is upheld by the Christian worldview as the essence of virtue, while Zarathustra's stony-hearted exit would by its
standards be judged quintessentially unadmirable.

Why does Zarathustra see his pity as a "sin," as a temptation he should not have given in to? His compassion for
the higher men has led to failure. At least, it has had no
positive impact. Zarathustra gave his insights the most apt
expression they could have when he taught them musically
in "The Drunken Song" the night before. If the higher men
had really understood his message, they would be awake
and bounding with *joie de vivre.* But instead, in mimicry
of Socrates' disciples after the *Symposium*, they sleep away
the exuberance of the previous night.

From a realistic standpoint, Zarathustra's response that
they are not *his* disciples seems hasty. But in the stylized
fashion of the *Symposium,* their sleep reflects the fact that
they are not ultimately open to their teachers' insights as
much as does the sleep of Socrates' disciples. That upon

waking they respond with fright to the sign that cheerfully fortifies Zarathustra's worldview—the laughing lion—only reinforces his realization that they are not kindred spirits.

But if they are not kindred spirits, if they are closed to the buoyant attitude of Zarathustra's gospel despite their articulate recitations of his doctrines, then Zarathustra has been wasting his time with them. He realizes that clearly now. And he asks himself *why* he wasted his time. His answer is easy—he was moved by pity.

Pity is rejected at the end of Part IV, not because it is antithetical to Zarathustra's spiritual states, but because it is one of them, and one that has dangers. Zarathustra has fallen into a natural inclination of his character, one that we have seen since his intervention in the dying moments of the addled tightrope walker. In that case, his pity led him to propagate his gospel to a man whose death was eased by it. Zarathustra himself lost nothing. In Part IV, however, Zarathustra's pity has been a distraction from his real mission: he has been barking up the wrong tree.

But this does not yet explain the irony involved in Zarathustra's seeing his pity as a "final sin." Cynically, we could concede that it is "final" in that Nietzsche does not show us any more of Zarathustra's adventures, foible-filled or otherwise. But as we have observed, we have no reason to think that Zarathustra is putting folly behind him forever. The thrust of the entire book is against this. And the dramatic momentum of Part IV offers us little ground for reading "The Sign" as an ultimately transformative climax. After all, Zarathustra's "Sign" does not change *his* perspective on anything—even on his relationship to the "higher men," whom he has already disavowed.

What does Zarathustra realize when he calls his pity his "final sin"? He realizes that he has fallen into the kind of thinking that judges acts to be sinful. This thinking evaluates past acts with respect to ultimate goals and responds to those that it deems obstructive with guilt. Zarathustra's pity strikes him as sinful because, like all sins, it has interfered with success in his effort to communicate his insight. He responds with a moment of distraught analysis of his immediate past: What has happened? How has he failed? In essence, he has a Christian-style examination of conscience.

But Zarathustra's "sin" is also his *final* sin. It is final in the sense that he has seen *through* his own thinking and recognized that he has slipped into the orientation of the Christian worldview he rejects. Examining himself, he finds that he feels "sinful" for his failure to adhere to his own gospel, and he regrets having acted in a manner counterproductive to his goal.

From the standpoint of Zarathustra's anti-Christian gospel, his pity has been a "sin," but for Zarathustra to look at his pity this way is to forget what his gospel is about. His parting shot involves his remembering. Zarathustra makes his pity a *final* sin by actively breaking with the mentality that sees any act as sinful. He puts "sin" as a concept behind him and ends his saga in the spirit of his doctrine, going forward openly into the future. The "harsh" words previously quoted are a performative statement of Zarathustra's break with his own sense of sinning.

> "Well then, *that* has had its time. My suffering and my pity for suffering—what does it matter? Am I concerned with *happiness*? I am concerned with my *work*.
>
> "Well then! The lion came, my children are near, Zarathustra has ripened, my hour has come; this is *my* morning, *my* day is breaking: *rise now, rise, thou great noon!*"
>
> Thus spoke Zarathustra, and he left his cave, glowing and strong as a morning sun that comes out of dark mountains.[6]

THE GOSPEL OF LOVING LIFE

Zarathustra's perspective at the end of the book represents Nietzsche's view of what it is to be serious about life. To be serious about life is not to commit oneself to a goal or an abstract ideal and to be concerned obsessively with its successful realization. Instead, it is to be fully engaged in one's present. Full engagement in the present, while it involves recognition of the ends toward which immediate activities are directed, involves appreciation of the immediate contents of the present as well. The present moment, at any point in time, however distant from the attainment of some projected goal, affords an experiential richness that itself makes life meaningful. To be aware of this richness throughout the moments of one's life is to be serious about life in all its parts. It is, to mutate a Kantian formulation, to treat living as an end in itself, not as a mere means, or, in one of Nietzsche's own formulas, it is to treat living as play.

Taking life seriously in the way that Nietzsche suggests does not mean ignoring the fact that the contents of life are often disappointing or silly, especially when judged in relation to the goals that are our guiding projects. Zarathustra is sometimes portrayed as a buffoon, and this is deliberate on Nietzsche's part. To make the effort to engage oneself in one's present is to expose oneself to strange, even ridiculous experiences. Nietzsche underscores this point by showing us many such experiences in his hero's life: the circus accident, the tarantula bite, the chance overhearing of a soothsayer whose words make an inappropriately depressing mark, the ass festival conducted by Zarathustra's guests in his own home, and so forth.

Events such as these might be seen as distractions from one's serious business in living, because in context they may seem to be distractions from the point of the book. But

239

in Nietzsche's tragic worldview they are part of the serious business *of* living. Of course, in experiencing the oddities and accidents of which life is full, we respond emotionally to what we take to be their role in facilitating or hindering our larger projects. But we can simultaneously enjoy them immediately, in a manner not dictated by our recognition of their facilitative or obstructive function. We are capable of taking a complex attitude toward the experiences of our lives, and by doing so in the manner that *Zarathustra* suggests, we can pursue our goals without giving up the wild magic of living.

The recurrent image of Zarathustra's love affair with life suggests the complexity of the attitude with which, in Nietzsche's view, the events of our lives can most valuably be experienced. In a love affair, every event that touches on one's relationship with the other person is rich and meaningful. This is true even of those events that are dissonant with or obstructive to one's goals in the relationship. Nietzsche's consistent suggestion regarding the meaning of life—whether expressed in terms of tragedy, eternal recurrence, or stories about events in Zarathustra's life—is that every moment of life can be full of significance for us, just as every moment in a love affair is full.

Our lives are meaningful when we love our lives. This deceptively simple statement summarizes the insight behind Nietzsche's tragic worldview. In *Zarathustra*, as in many of his other works, Nietzsche attempts to make suggestions as to how, in living, we can come to love living. The suggestions he makes are open-ended, but this open-endedness is in keeping with his view that meaning in life, like love, is a volatile commodity, something that can grow or dissipate and something that can only be learned over time. Nietzsche's remarks in *The Gay Science*, section 334, on the way that we learn to love can illuminate the developmental structure that he sees as intrinsic to finding meaning in our lives. It is significant that Nietzsche uses a musical model in this discussion to explicate how we come to love anything, including ourselves. Our love of anything, Nietzsche begins, depends first on our attending to it.

> *One must learn to love.*—This is what happens to us in music: First one has to *learn to hear* a figure and melody at all, to detect and distinguish it, to isolate it and delimit it as a separate life. Then it requires some exertion and good will to *tolerate* it in spite of its strangeness, to be patient with its appearance and expression, and kindhearted about its oddity. Finally there comes a moment when we are *used* to it, when we wait for it, when we sense that we should miss it if it were missing; and now it continues to compel and enchant us relentlessly until we have become its humble and enraptured lovers who desire nothing better from the world that it and only it.
>
> But that is what happens to us not only in music. That is how we have *learned to love* all things that we now love. In the end we are always rewarded for our good will, our patience, fairmindedness, and gentleness with what is strange; gradually, it sheds its veil and turns out to be a new and indescribable beauty. That is its *thanks* for our hospitality. Even those who love themselves will have learned it in this way; for there is no other way. Love, too, has to be learned.[7]

The central, "tragic" message of *Zarathustra* is that meaning in life is to be found in simply loving life for its own sake. The meaning we can find in this way is not a secure possession. It is a dynamic matter of attitude, intuition, and subtlety—of the elusive thing named by the word "balance." *Thus Spoke Zarathustra* is largely concerned with the question of what constitutes a satisfying condition of balance in an individual's life. In treating this question, the book reminds us that balance is fragile, if always reattainable. The book speaks to us by making suggestions, through Zarathustra's experiences, about how to gain balance in our own lives. In general, *Zarathustra* suggests, we would be far more likely to love our lives, and thereby create in them a meaningful kind of balance, if we allowed ourselves to be moved more often by what is immediately before us. The implication is not that we should abandon the goals that currently preoccupy us, but only that we should shift the emphasis of our attention and concern to the immediate. "For, as Zarathustra's proverb says, one thing is more necessary than another."[8]

Abbreviations

The following abbreviations are used for frequently cited editions and collections of works by Friedrich Nietzsche.

A   *The Antichrist.* Translated by Walter Kaufmann. In *The Portable Nietzsche,* edited by Walter Kaufmann. New York: Viking Press, 1968.

ADV   *On the Advantage and Disadvantage of History for Life.* Translated by Peter Preuss. Indianapolis: Hackett Publishing, 1980.

BGE   *Beyond Good and Evil.* Translated by Walter Kaufmann. New York: Random House, 1966.

BT   *The Birth of Tragedy.* (together with *The Case of Wagner*). Translated by Walter Kaufmann. New York: Random House, 1967.

CW   *The Case of Wagner* (together with *The Birth of Tragedy*). Translated by Walter Kaufmann. New York: Random House, 1967.

D   *Daybreak.* Translated by R. J. Hollingdale. Cambridge, Eng.: Cambridge University Press, 1982.

EH   *Ecce Homo* (together with *On the Genealogy of Morals*). Translated by Walter Kaufmann. New York: Random House, 1969.

GM   *On the Genealogy of Morals* (together with *Ecce Homo.*) Translated by Walter Kaufmann and R. J. Hollingdale. New York: Random House, 1969.

GS   *The Gay Science.* Translated by Walter Kaufmann. New York: Random House, 1974.

HATH I   *Human, All Too Human: A Book for Free Spirits.* Translated by Marion Faber, with Stephen Leh-

243

	mann. Lincoln: University of Nebraska Press, 1984.
HATH II	*Human, All Too Human,* Vol II. Volume VII of *The Complete Works of Friedrich Nietzsche.* Edited by Oscar Levy. 18 vols. London: George Allen & Unwin, 1911.
KGB	*Kritische Gesamtausgabe Briefwechsel.* Edited by G. Colli and M. Montinari. 24 vols. in 4 parts. Berlin: Walter de Gruyter, 1975ff.
KGW	*Kritische Gesamtausgabe Werke.* Edited by G. Colli and M. Montinari. 30 vols. in 8 parts. Berlin: Walter de Gruyter, 1967ff.
Middleton	*Selected Letters of Friedrich Nietzsche.* Edited and translated by Christopher Middleton. Chicago: University of Chicago Press, 1969.
Schlechta	*Werke in Drei Baenden.* 3 vols. Edited by Karl Schlechta. 3rd ed. Munich: Carl Hansers, 1965.
TI	*Twilight of the Idols.* Translated by Walter Kaufmann. In *The Portable Nietzsche,* edited by Walter Kaufmann. New York: Viking Press, 1968.
TSZ	*Thus Spoke Zarathustra.* Translated by Walter Kaufmann. In *The Portable Nietzsche,* edited by Walter Kaufmann. New York: Viking Press, 1968.
WP	*The Will to Power.* Translated by Walter Kaufmann and R. J. Hollingdale, edited by Walter Kaufmann. New York: Random House, 1967.

Notes

Preface

1. *EH*, p. 246; Schelechta, II, p. 1089; *KGW*, VI/3, p. 255. Full data for abbreviated forms of primary sources in the notes are given in the list of abbreviation on p.000.

2. R. J. Hollingdale, *Nietzsche* (Boston: Routledge & Kegan Paul, 1973), p. 73.

3. Brand Blanshard, *On Philosophical Style* (Manchester: Manchester University Press, 1954), pp. 14–15.

4. Hollingdale (1973), p. 73.

5. Crane Brinton, *Nietzsche* (New York: Harper & Row, 1941), pp. 61, 220–221.

6. F. D. Luke, "Nietzsche and the Imagery of Height," *Nietzsche's Imagery and Thought: A Collection of Essays*, ed. Malcolm Pasley (London: Methuen, 1978), p. 104.

7. See J. P. Stern, *A Study of Nietzsche* (Cambridge: Cambridge University Press, 1979), p. 157.

8. Stern, p. 158.

9. Hans-Georg Gadamer, "Das Drama Zarathustras," trans. Zygmunt Adamczewski, in David Goicoechea, ed., *The Great Year Zarathustra (1881–1981)* (New York: Lanham, 1983), p. 341.

10. Martin Heidegger, *Nietzsche*, Volume II: *The Eternal Recurrence of the Same*, trans. David Farrell Krell (San Francisco: Harper & Row, 1984), pp. 35–36.

11. Richard Schacht, *Nietzsche* (London: Routledge & Kegan Paul, 1983), pp. xiii–xiv.

12. Gadamer, p. 347.

13. Harold Alderman, *Nietzsche's Gift* (Athens: Ohio University Press, 1977).

14. Anke Bennholdt-Thomsen, *Nietzsches "Also Sprach Zarathustra" als literarisches Phaenomen*, Eine Revision (Frankfurt: Athenaeum, 1974).

15. Alexander Nehamas, *Nietzsche: Life as Literature* (Cambridge, Mass: Harvard University Press, 1985), p. 18.

16. Arthur C. Danto, *Nietzsche as Philosopher: An Original Study* (New York: Columbia University Press, 1965), pp. 19–20.

17. Hollingdale (1973) p. 73.

18. Martin Heidegger is most notorious for treating Nietzsche's *Nachlass* (unpublished materials) on a par with published texts. See, for example, Martin Heidegger, *Nietzsche*, Vol. I: *The Will to Power as Art*, translated by David Farrell Krell (New York: Harper & Row, 1979), pp. 3–11. For the case against this strategy, see Bernd Magnus, "Nietzsche's Philosophy in 1888: *The Will to Power* and the *Übermensch*," *Journal of the History of Philosophy*, XXIV, No 1: 79–99.

Chapter 1

1. *TSZ*, p. 152; Schlechta, II, p. 305; *KGW*, VI/1, p. 44.

2. *BGE*, Sec. 6, p. 13; Schlechta, II, p. 571; KGW, VI/2, pp. 13–14.

3. *BGE*, Sec. 5, p. 12, Schlechta, II, p. 570; *KGW*, V1/2, p. 13.

4. *BGE*, sec. 6, p. 14; Schlechta, II, p. 572; *KGW*, VI/2, p. 14.

5. See *BGE*, sec. 6, p. 14; Schlechta, II, p. 572; *KGW*, VI/2, p. 14.

6. See *GS*, Preface to 2nd ed., p. 35; Schlechta, II, p. 12; *KGW*, V/2, p. 17.

7. *GS*, preface to 2nd ed., p. 33; Schlechta, II, p. 10; *KGW*, V/2, p. 15.

8. *GS*, preface to 2nd ed., p. 35; Schlechta, II, p. 12; KGW, V/2, p. 17.

9. *BT*, p. 20; Schlechta, I, p. 12; *KGW*, III/1, p. 9.

10. Letter to Lou Salomé, probably September 16, 1882, in Schlechta, III, p. 1189; *KGB*, III/1, p. 259.

11. *EH*, p. 266; Schlechta, II, p. 1104; *KGW*, VI/3, p. 303.

12. *BGE*, Sec. 22, p. 30; Schlechta, II, p. 586; *KGW*, VI/2, p. 31.

13. *BT*, p. 20; Schlechta, I, p. 12; *KGW*, III/1, p. 9.

14. *BGE*, sec. 226, p. 154; Schlechta, II, p. 690; *KGW*, VI/2, p. 168.

15. *EH*, p. 217; Schlechta, II, p. 1065; *KGW*, VI/3, p. 256.

16. See, e.g., *BGE*, sec. 61, p. 72; Schlechta, II, p. 621; *KGW*, VI/2, p. 77.

17. See *BGE*, sec. 241, p. 174; Schlechta, II, p. 706; *KGW*, VI/2, p. 188.

18. See letter to Malwida von Meysenbug, end of March 1883, in Middleton, p. 211; Schlechta, III, p. 1205; *KGB*, III/1, p. 357.

19. See Middleton, pp. 184–185n; see also letter to Overbeck, December 25, 1882, in Middleton, pp. 198–199; Schlechta, III, pp. 1198–1199; *KGB*, III/1, pp. 311–312.

20. See Middleton p. 208n.

21. Letter to Overbeck, December 25, 1882, in Middleton, p. 199; Schlechta, III, p. 1198; *KGB*, III/1, p. 312.

22. Letter to Gast, February 19, 1883, in Middleton p. 207; Schlechta, III, p. 1201; *KGB*, III/1, p. 333.

23. Letter to Rohde, February 22, 1884, in Middleton, p. 221; Schlechta, III, p. 1216; *KGB*, III/1, pp. 479–480.

24. Letter to Overbeck, received May 2, 1884, in Middleton, p. 223; Schlechta, III, p. 1218; *KGB*, III/1, p. 497.

25. Letter to Elisabeth Nietzsche, May 20, 1884, in Middleton, p. 241.

26. See letter to Peter Gast, April 6, 1883, in Middleton, p. 211; *KGB*, III/1, pp. 357–358.

27. Letter to Overbeck, December 25, 1882, in Middleton, p. 199; Schlechta, III, p. 1198; *KGB*, III/1, p. 312.

28. Letter to Gast, February 2, 1883, in Middleton, p. 207; Schlechta, III, p. 1201; *KGB*, III/1, p. 333.

29. Letter to Heinrich von Stein, beginning December 1882, in Middleton, pp. 197–198; Schlechta, III, p. 1196; *KGB*, III/1, p. 288.

30. Letter to Overbeck, September 1882, in Middleton p. 193; Schlechta, III, p. 1191; *KGB*, III/1, p. 255.

31. Letter to Malwida von Meysenbug, August 1883, in Middleton, p. 216; Schlechta, III, p. 1211; *KGB*, III/1, p. 404.

32. *TSZ*, p. 209; Schlechta, II, pp. 354–356; *KGW*, VI/1, p. 121.
33. Letter to Gast, April 6, 1883, in Middleton, p. 211; *KGB*, III/1, pp. 357–358.
34 Letter to Heinrich von Stein, beginning December 1882, in Middleton, pp. 197–198; Schlechta, III, pp. 1195–1196; *KGB*, III/1, pp. 287–288.
35. Letter to Overbeck, February 11, 1883, in Middleton, p. 206; Schlechta, III, p. 1200; *KGB*, III/1, p. 326.
36. See J. P. Stern, *Friedrich Nietzsche* (New York: Penguin Books, 1978), pp. 95–104, 121–122. See also H. F. Peters, *My Sister My Spouse: A Biography of Lou Andreas-Salomé* (New York: Norton, 1962), p. 123, where Peters cites Lou's comment that she and Nietzsche shared a common religious trait in their characters.
37. See Paul Tillich, *Dynamics of Faith* (New York: Harper & Bros., 1957), pp. 1–4.
38. Letter to Gast, February 19, 1883, in Middleton, p. 207; Schlechta, III, p. 1201; *KGB*, III/1, p. 333.
39. Letter to Carl von Gersdorff, June 28, 1883, in Middleton, p. 213; Schlechta, III, p. 1208; *KGB*, III/1, pp. 386–387.
40. Letter to Overbeck, Summer 1883, in Middleton, p. 214; Schlechta, III, p. 1209; *KGB*, III/1, p. 427.
41. Letter to Overbeck, February 11, 1883, in Middleton, p. 207; Schlechta, III, p. 1200; *KGB*, III/1, p. 326.

Chapter 2

1. Friedrich Nietzsche, "Wir Philologen," Sec. 7, included in part in "Nietzsche on Classics and Classicists," selected and translated by William Arrowsmith, *Arion*, II, No. 1 (Spring 1963): 10–11; Schlechta, III, p. 325; *KGW*, IV/1, no. 3 (62), p. 107.
2. See photo insert between pp. 152 and 153 in Peters, *My Sister My Spouse*. A picture of Nietzsche, reprinted there, was sent by Nietzsche to Lou with the inscription "Friedrich Nietzsche, formerly a professor, now a roaming fugitive."
3. See M.S. Silk and J.P. Stern, *Nietzsche on Tragedy* (Cambridge: Cambridge University Press, 1981), p. 97.
4. See *TI*, pp. 473–479, 556–563; Schlechta, II, pp. 951–956, 1027–1032; *KGW*, VI/3, pp. 61–67, 148–154. These sections are

not only significant portions of the book; in a sense they also provide the book's frame. "The Problem of Socrates" is the first full section of the book after a preface and a series of aphorisms, and "What I Owe to the Ancients" is the last full section, followed only by a brief repetition of a part of *Thus Spoke Zarathustra*.

5. *BT*, p. 33; Schlechta, I, p. 21; *KGW*, III/1, p. 22.

6. Nietzsche had received the unusual honor of being appointed to a chair in philology at Basel without having completed his dissertation; therefore his first book had been anticipated with considerable interest. See Ronald Hayman, *Nietzsche: A Critical Life* (New York: Oxford University Press, 1980), pp. 101–105. For an account of the various immediate responses to *The Birth of Tragedy* by classicists, and also by Wagner, see Silk and Stern, pp. 90–107.

7. Silk and Stern, p. 96. For recent discussions of the debate between Wilamowitz and Nietzsche, see W.M. Calder, III, "The Wilamowitz-Nietzsche Struggle: New Documents and a Reappraisal," *Nietzsche-Studien*, XII (1983): 214–254; and Jaap Mansfeld, "The Wilamowitz-Nietzsche Struggle: Another New Document and Some Further Comments," *Nietzsche-Studien*, XV (1986): 41–58.

8. Nietzsche's account of tragedy is not without its critics. For a critical view of his comments, see Gerald F. Else, *The Origin and Early Form of Greek Tragedy* (Cambridge, Mass.: Harvard University Press, 1965), esp. pp. 9-10, p. 30. See also Walter Kaufmann, *Tragedy and Philosophy* (Princeton: Princeton University Press, 1968), pp. 191–227.

9. *BT*, p. 19; Schlechta, I, p. 11; *KGW*, III/1, p. 8.

10. Granted, this is an interpretation of Nietzsche's formula rather than a paraphrase. It is, however, an interpretation that is grounded in Nietzsche's text. See *BT*, pp. 95–96; Schlecta, I, pp. 84–85; *KGW*, III/1, p. 95, where Nietzsche claims that science inevitably approaches its limits "at which it must turn into *art*." One may argue that Nietzsche is mistaken in his quasi-argument that accompanies this claim, in which he derives this association of science and art from Kant's claims about reason inevitably moving toward its own limits. See *BT*, pp. 98, 112, 120–121; Schlechta, I, pp. 86–87, 101, and 110; *KGW*, III/1, pp. 97, 114,

124. Nonetheless, it is clear that Nietzsche is convinced that science inevitably reaches limits at which art becomes necessary. It is also clear that Nietzsche sees art as a healing *ancilla* of life, which sustains human existence. See *BT*, p. 59; Schlechta, I, p. 48; *KGW*, III/1, p. 52, e.g., "Art saves him, and through art—life."

11. See e.g., *ADV*, p. 14; Schlechta, I, p. 218; *KGW*, III/1, pp. 252–253: "May our estimation of the historical be but an occidental prejudice; as long as, within these prejudices, we make progress and do not stand still! As long as we constantly learn to improve our ability to do history for the sake of *life*." He also cites several respects in which history can be dangerous to nations, culture, and individuals. See *ADV*, p. 28; Schlechta, I, p. 237; *KGW*, III/1, p. 275.

12. See Arthur Schopenhauer, *The World as Will and Representation*, 2 vols., trans E. F. J. Payne (New York: Dover Publications, 1969 [Vol. I] and 1958 [Vol. II], Vol. I, pp. 252–255.

13. Schopenhauer, I, p. 252.

14. *BT*, p. 42; Schlechta, I, pp. 29–30; *KGW*, III/1, p. 31.

15. Schopenhauer's metaphysics owes much to Kant's, a fact that Schopenhauer acknowledges. See Schopenhauer, I, pp. 170–174.

16. See *BT*, p. 42; Schlechta, I, p. 30; *KGW*, III/1, pp. 31–32.

17. *BT*, p. 34; Schlechta, I, p. 22; *KGW*, III/1, p. 22.

18. *BT*, p. 35; Schlechta, I, pp. 22–23; *KGW*, III/1, p. 23.

19. The visual arts were almost exclusively representational during the era in which Nietzsche wrote *The Birth of Tragedy*, and it is clear that he saw painting and sculpture as inherently representational.

20. Not all music is Dionysian, according to Nietzsche. He acknowledges the existence of a kind of Apollonian music that involved the striking of tones in accordance with the wave beat of rhythm. See *BT*, p. 40; Schlechta, I, p. 28; *KGW*, III/1, p. 29.

21. *BT*, p. 40; Schlechta, I, p. 28; *KGW*, III/1, pp. 29–30.

22. *BT*, p. 52; Schlechta, I, p. 40; *KGW*, III/1, p. 43.

23. See, for example, Saint Augustine, *The City of God*, in *Basic Writings of Saint Augustine*, ed. Whitney J. Oates, 2 vols. (New York: Random House, 1948), Vol. II, Book XIV, chap. 11, pp. 255–256.

24. *BT*, p. 23; Schlechta, I, p. 15; *KGW*, III/1, pp. 12–13.

25. *BT*, p. 59; Schlechta, I, p. 47; *KGW*, III/1, p. 52.

26. *BT*, p. 39; Schlechta, I, p. 27; *KGW*, III/1, p. 28.

27. I have attempted, where possible, to avoid sexist constructions in my use of personal pronouns. In some cases, such as this, I have opted for masculine personal pronouns because the alternative proved too unwieldy. In such cases I am not using masculine terms in the restrictive sense, but in the generic sense to refer to all individuals.

28. *BT*, p. 61; Schlechta, I, p. 49; *KGW*, III/1, p. 54

29. *BT*, p. 59; Schlechta, I, p. 47; *KGW*, III/1, pp. 51–52.

30. *BT*, p. 64; Schlechta, I, p. 52; *KGW*, III/1, p. 57.

31. *BT*, p. 62; Schlechta, I, p. 50; *KGW*, III/1, p. 55.

32. *BT*, p. 64; Schlechta, I, p. 52; *KGW*, III/1, p. 57.

33. *BT*, p. 73; Schlechta, I, p. 61; *KGW*, III/1, p. 68.

34. Nietzsche does not think that the tragic effect is often actually achieved. See *BT*, p. 132; Schlechta, I, p. 122; *KGW*, III/1, p. 138.

Chapter 3

1. Nietzsche, letter to Overbeck, April 7, 1884, in Middleton p. 223; Schlechta, III, p. 1218; *KGB*, III/1, p. 496.

2. Nehamas argues that Nietzsche's efforts to move his readers to his position is consistent with his perspectivism. See Nehamas, *Nietzsche*, pp. 36–39, 64–73. Nehamas argues that Nietzsche's use of changing genres and styles is part of Nietzsche's effort to be consistent on this matter.

3. See *D*, sec. 3, p. 9; Schlechta, I, p. 1017; *KGW*, V/1, pp. 15–16.

4. See *D*, sec. 16, p. 15; Schlechta, I, p. 1025; *KGW*, V/1, p. 25.

5. *D*, sec. 11, pp. 12–13; Schlechta, I, pp. 1021–1022; *KGW*, V/1 p. 21.

6. See *D*, sec. 9, pp. 10–12; Schlechta, I, pp. 1019–1021; *KGW*, V/1, pp. 17–20.

7. See *D*, sec. 34, p. 36; Schlechta, I, p. 1037; *KGW*, V/1, p.

39, where Nietzsche discusses the way morality is learned by imitation.

8. *D*, sec. 19, p. 18; Schlechta, I, p. 1028; *KGW*, V/1, p. 28.

9 This attempt is not only basic to Nietzsche's general ambition in his writing. See *EH*, p. 265; Schlechta II, p. 1104; *KGW*, VI/3, p. 302.

10. *D*, sec. 103, p. 60; Schlechta, I, p. 1077; *KGW*, V/1, p. 90.

11. *D*, sec. 33, pp. 24–25; Schlechta, I, p. 1036; *KGW*, V/1, pp. 38–39.

12. *D*, sec. 81, p. 48; Schlechta, I, p. 1066; *KGW*, V/1, p. 74.

13. *D*, sec. 94, p. 54; Schlechta, I, p. 1073; *KGW*, V/1, p. 82.

14. *D*, sec. 78, p. 48; Schlechta, I, p. 1065; *KGW*, V/1, p. 73.

15. *D*, sec. 103, p. 60; Schlechta, I, pp. 1076–1077; *KGW*, V/1, p. 89.

16. *D*, sec. 62, p. 37–38; Schlechta, I, p. 1053; *KGW*, V/1, p. 58.

17. *D*, sec. 66, p. 39; Schlechta, I, p. 1054; *KGW*, V/1, p. 60.

18. *D*, sec. 71, p. 43; Schlechta, I, p. 1059; *KGW*, V/1, p. 65.

19. *D*, sec. 90, p. 52; Schlechta, I, p. 1071; *KGW*, V/1 pp. 79–80.

20. *D*, sec. 77, pp. 46–47; Schlechta, I, p. 1064; *KGW*, V/1, p. 71.

21. *A*, pp. 581–582; Schlechta, II, p. 1175; *KGW*, VI/3, p. 179.

22. *A*, p. 582; Schlechta, II, p. 1175; *KGW*, *VI/3*, p. 180.

23. *D*, sec. 61, p. 37; Schlechta, I, p. 1052; *KGW*, V/1, pp. 57–58.

24. *D*, sec. 102, p. 59; Schlechta, I, p. 1076; *KGW*, V/1, p. 88.

25 *D*, sec. 549, p. 221; Schlechta, I, p. 1269; *KGW*, V/1, p. 323.

26. *D*, sec. 59, p. 36; Schlechta, I, p. 1051; *KGW*, V/1, pp. 55–56.

27. Matthew 19:24.

28. Nietzsche makes note, several times, of the fear-inspiring rhetoric of Lenten preachers. See *D*, sec. 53, p. 34; Schlechta, I, p. 1048; *KGW*, V/1, p. 52. See also *D* sec. 77, p. 47; Schlechta, I, p. 1064; *KGW*, V/1, p. 71.

29. *D*, sec. 57, p. 35; Schlechta, I, p. 1050; *KGW*, V/1, p. 55.

30. *D*, sec. 87, p. 50–51; Schlechta, I, p. 1069; *KGW*, V/1, p. 77.

31. *D*, sec. 215, pp. 134–135; Schlechta, I, pp. 1163–1164; *KGW*, V/1, pp. 193–194.

32. *D*, sec. 211, p. 133; Schlechta, I, p. 1162; *KGW*, V/1, p. 192.

33. *D*, sec. 132, p. 82; Schlechta, I, p. 1103; *KGW*, V/1, p. 121.

34. *D*, sec. 494, pp. 201–202; Schlechta, I, p. 1245; *KGW*, V/1, p. 295.

35. For an account of the most extreme doctrine of the human being's inability to do anything to ensure salvation, see Loraine Boettner, *The Reformed Doctrine of Predestination* (Grand Rapids, Mich.: William B. Eerdmans 1932). On p. 61, Boettner quotes the Westminster Confession, chap. 9, sec. 3: "Man by his fall into a state of sin, hath wholly lost all ability of will to any spiritual good accompanying salvation; so as a natural man, being altogether averse from good, and dead in sin, is not able, by his own strength, to convert himself, or to prepare himself thereunto."

36. *D*, sec. 140, p. 88; Schlechta, I, p. 1110; *KGW*, V/1. pp. 129–130.

37. *D*, sec. 30, p. 23; Schlechta, I, p. 1034; *KGW*, V/1, p. 36.

38. *D*, sec. 202, p. 121; Schlechta, I, p. 1150; *KGW*, V/1, p. 177.

39. *D*, sec. 252, p. 143; Schlechta, I, p. 1175; *KGW*, V/1, p. 207.

40. See *D*, sec. 236, p. 139; Schlechta, I, p. 1169; *KGW*, V/1, p. 201.

41. See *D*, sec. 366, p. 168; Schlechta, I, p. 1207; *KGW*, V/1, p. 245.

42. *D*, sec. 13, p. 13; Schlechta, I, p. 1022; *KGW*, V/1, p. 22.

43. *D*, sec. 78, p. 47; Schlechta, I, p. 1065; *KGW*, V/1, p. 72.

44. For Nietzsche's analysis of the timid spirit encouraged by conventional morality, see *BGE*, secs. 197, 198, 201, pp. 108–110, 112–114; Schlechta, II, pp. 653–654, 657–659; *KGW*, VI/2, pp. 119–121, 123–125. Bergmann discusses the mediocrity of the virtuous in Nietzsche's account in "After Morality, or Preliminary to Nietzsche" (Paper delivered at "Reading Nietzsche," a symposium of American Nietzsche scholars, University of Texas at Austin, February 1985), pp. 45–48, to be published in a revised version

in *Reading Nietzsche,* ed. Robert C. Solomon and Kathleen Higgins.

45. *D*, sec. 174, pp. 105–106; Schlechta, I, p. 1130; *KGW*, V/1, p. 154.

46. *D*, sec. 133, pp. 83–84; Schlechta, I, p. 1105; *KGW*, V/1, pp. 123–124.

47. Nietzsche's objection to the Christian worldview is not primarily directed at the falsehood of its claims—nor should it be, in light of comments to the effect that "Truth is the kind of error without which a certain species of life could not live" (WP, sec. 493, p. 272; Schlechta, III, p. 844; *KGW*, VII/3, sec. 34 [253], p. 226. See also *GS*, sec. 265, p. 219; Schlechta, II, p. 159; *KGW*, V/2, p. 1961). Nietzsche's objection to Christian doctrine is primarily based on his view that it has unhealthful consequences.

48. *D*, sec. 87, p. 51; Schlechta, I, p. 1069; *KGW*, V/1, p. 77.

49. *D*, sec. 559, p. 225; Schlechta, I, pp. 1274–1275; *KGW*, V/1, pp. 329–330.

50. For a discussion of Luther's claim that "faith alone justifies," see Martin Luther, "Martin Luther's Treatise on Christian Liberty (The Freedom of a Christian)," in *Luther's Works,* ed. Helmut T. Lehmann, Vol. XXXI, *Career of the Reformer: I,* ed. Harold J. Grimm (Philadelphia: Fortress Press, 1957), pp. 343–377.

51. *D*, sec. 29, p. 22; Schlechta, I, p. 1034; *KGW*, V/1, p. 35.

52. See *D*, sec. 70, p. 42; Schlechta, I, p. 1058; *KGW*, V/1, p. 64.

53. See *D*, sec. 73, p. 44; Schlechta, I, p. 1061; *KGW*, V/1, p. 68.

54. Matt. 6:33. See *D*, sec. 456, p. 191; Schlechta, I, p. 1232; *KGW*, V/1, p. 279.

55. See *D*, sec. 26, pp. 20–21; Schlechta, I, pp. 1031–1032; *KGW*, V/1, pp. 32–33.

56. *D*, sec. 76, p. 45; Schlechta, I, p. 1062; *KGW*, V/1, p. 69.

57. *TI*, p. 562; Schlechta, II, p. 1032; *KGW*, VI/3, p. 154.

58. *D*, sec. 148, pp. 93–94; Schlechta, I, p. 1117; *KGW*, V/1, p. 138.

59. *D*, sec. 108, p. 63; Schlechta, I, p. 1080; *KGW*, V/1, p. 93.

60. See *D*, sec. 9, pp. 10–11; Schlechta, I, pp. 1019–1021; *KGW*, V/1, pp. 17–20.

61. See *D*, sec. 496, p. 202; Schlechta, I, p. 1246; *KGW*, V/1, p. 295.

62. *D*, sec. 132, p. 83; Schlechta, I, p. 1104; *KGW*, V/1, p. 122.

63. See *D*, sec. 500, pp. 203–204; Schlechta, I, p. 1248; *KGW*, V/1, p. 298.

64. See *D*, sec. 529, pp. 209–210; Schlechta, I, pp. 1255–1256; *KGW*, V/1, p. 307.

65. Martin Luther, "A Mighty Fortress Is Our God."

66. See, e.g., *D*, sec. 436, p. 186; Schlechta, I, p. 1226; *KGW*, V/1, pp. 271–272.

67. See *D*, sec. 560, p. 225; Schlechta, I, p. 1275; *KGW*, V/1, p. 330, where Nietzsche discusses the range of things we are at liberty to do with our passions.

68. *D*, sec. 563, p. 226; Schlechta, I, p. 1276; *KGW*, V/1, p. 332.

Chapter 4

1. *TSZ*, p. 329; Schlechta, II, p. 463; KGW, VI/1, p. 268.

2. Alderman, *Nietzsche's Gift*, p. 37.

3. *TSZ*, p. 439; Schlechta, II, p. 561; *KGW*, VI/1, p. 404.

4. See *TSZ*, pp. 264–267; Schlechta, II, pp. 403–406; *KGW*, VI/1, pp. 189–192 ("Der Wanderer"). See also *TSZ*, pp. 333–336; Schlechta, II, pp. 467–469; *KGW*, VI/1, pp. 274–277 ("Von der grossen Sehnsucht"). Not all of Zarathustra's private thoughts are recorded, however. Sometimes Zarathustra is portrayed as lapsing into silent meditation with his soul (see *TSZ*, p. 248; Schlechta, II, p. 391; *KGW*, VI/1, p. 171). Zarthustra is also told by one of his auditors that he speaks to himself differently from the way he speaks to his disciples, and Zarathustra admits that he speaks differently to different audiences (*TSZ*, p. 254; Schlechta, II, p. 396; *KGW*, VI/1, p. 178). This suggests that Zarathustra calculates the effects his words will have on his students and chooses his words accordingly.

5. *TSZ*, p. 122; Schlecta, II, p. 277; *KGW*, VI/1, p. 5.

6. *TSZ*, p. 122; Schlechta, II, p. 277; *KGW*, VI/1, p. 6.

7. See *BT*, pp. 82–93; Schlechta, I, pp. 71–82; *KGW*, III/1, pp. 79–92. It would not be difficult to construct a case supporting the

view that Nietzsche's picture of Socrates is something of a caricature.

8. *BT*, p. 96; Schlechta, I, p. 85; *KGW*, III/1, p. 96.

9. *BT*, pp. 92–93; Schlechta, I, p. 82; *KGW*, III/1, p. 92.

10. Plato, *Phaedo*, trans. Hugh Tredennick, *The Collected Dialogues of Plato, Including the Letters*, ed. Edith Hamilton and Huntington Cairns, Bollingen Series LXXI (Princeton: Princeton University Press, 1961), lines 61a-b, pp. 43–44.

11. Silk and Stern aptly note that with the image of the Socrates who practices music, Nietzsche is concerned not solely with the art of music but with art in general. They observe too that "the paradox, Socratic *mousike*, points to a mode of artistic discourse for which *The Birth of Tragedy* is the original, perhaps imperfect, prototype" (see Silk and Stern, p. 194). Nietzsche clearly believes that his style of writing warrants the term "music" in some instances (see *EH*, p. 295; Schlechta, II, p. 1128; *KGW*, VI/3, p. 333). But his focus on the Dionysian art of music shows that he intends his writing to call to mind the Dionysian ground of being. The paradigmatic expression of this ground is not art as a whole, but the art of music in particular. Nietzsche's intention of emblemizing the expression of the Dionysian ground through what he calls Dionysian music also helps explain why his association of Dionysus and music is not jeopardized by his admission that Apollonian music exists, a problem that disturbs Silk and Stern (*Nietzsche on Tragedy*, pp. 244–245).

12. *TSZ*, p. 124; Schlechta, II, p. 279; *KGW*, VI/1, p.8.

13. *TSZ*, p. 124; Schlechta, II, p. 279; *KGW*, VI/1, pp. 7–8.

14. *TSZ*, p. 124; Schlechta, II, p. 279; *KGW*, VI/1, p.8.

15. See Alderman, p. 23.

16. *TSZ*, p. 126; Schlechta, II, p. 281; *KGW*, VI/1, p. 10.

17. *TSZ*, p. 125; Schlechta, II, p. 280; *KGW*, VI/1, p. 10.

18. *TSZ*, p. 125; Schlechta, II, p. 280; KGW, VI/1, p. 9.

19. *WP*, sec. 2, p. 9; Schlechta, III, p. 557; *KGW*, VII/2, p. 14.

20. *TSZ*, p. 125; Schlechta, II, p. 280; *KGW*, VI/1, p. 9.

21. *TSZ*, p. 125; Schlechta, II, p. 280; *KGW*, VI/1, p. 9.

22. *TSZ*, pp. 129–130; Schlechta, II, pp. 284–5/ *KGW*, VI/1, pp. 13–14.

23. *TSZ*, p. 124; Schlechta, II, p. 279; *KGW*, VI/1, p. 8.

24. Note that interpreters differ on whether the overman is an attainable goal. Compare Bernd Magnus, "The Deification of the Commonplace: *Twilight of the Idols*" (Paper delivered at "Reading Nietzsche," a symposium of American Nietzsche scholars, University of Texas at Austin, February 1985), pp. 32–34; and Nehamas, pp. 159–169.

25. *TSZ*, p. 124; Schlechta, II, p. 279; *KGW*, VI/1, p. 8.

26. *TSZ*, p. 126; Schlechta, II, p. 281; *KGW*, VI/1, p. 10.

27. See *TSZ*, p. 183; Schlechta, II, p. 333; *KGW*, VI/1, p. 88, where Zarathustra talks of love arousing thirst for the overman. See also *TSZ*, p. 168; Schlechta, II, p. 320; *KGW*, VI/1, p. 68.

28. *TSZ*, p. 168; Schlechta, II, p. 320; *KGW*, VI/1, p. 68.

29. *TSZ*, p. 156; Schlechta, II, p. 309; *KGW*, VI/1, p. 50.

30. See Kaufmann's commentary in *The Portable Nietzsche*, p. 115.

31. *TSZ*, p. 127–128; Schlechta, II, p. 282; *KGW*, VI/1, pp. 11–12.

32. *TSZ*, p. 130; Schlechta, II, p. 285; *KGW*, VI/1, p. 14.

33. See Alderman, pp. 28–31. Williams' analysis is more detailed if less easily accessible. See Robert J. Williams, "Recurrence, Parody and Politics in the Philosophy of Friedrich Nietzsche" (dissertation, Yale University, 1982), pp. 18–21.

34. *TSZ*, p. 131; Schlechta, II, p. 285; *KGW*, VI/1, p. 15.

35. The image of the lame-footed Oedipus recurs in the second section of Part III, "On the Vision and the Riddle." There a dwarf, in a gesture reminiscent of the Prologue's jumping jester, affixes himself to Zarathustra's back and berates him as someone who has thrown himself up high, where he has no business, and tells him that he is bound to fall. Zarathustra, in keeping with his gospel, attacks back. He contends that the dwarf and the tradition he represents are "lame, making lame" with the leaden thoughts they preach. (*TSZ*, p. 268; Schlechta, II, p. 407; *KGW*, VI/1, p. 194). The dwarf has the role of Oedipus in this section. Zarathustra calls him "lamefoot" and argues that it is the dwarf who cannot cope with the crossroads, the point on the way at which they meet. (*TSZ*, pp. 269–270; Schlechta, II, p. 408; *KGW*, VI/1, pp. 195–196). Zarathustra here establishes himself as one who has resisted the taunts of tradition and has established himself

as its enemy. For discussion of the implications of this section with respect to the doctrine of eternal recurrence, see Chapter 6.

36. This will become particularly evident in Chapter 6, where Zarathustra's ideal of the meaningful life is compared to the experience of music.

37. *TSZ*, p. 123; Schlechta, II, p. 278; *KGW*, VI/1, p. 6.

38. *TSZ*, p. 126; Schlechta, II, p. 281; *KGW*, VI/1, p. 10.

39. *TSZ*, p. 131; Schlechta, II, pp. 285–286; *KGW*, VI/1, p. 15.

40. *TSZ*, p. 132; Schlechta, II, p. 286; *KGW*, VI/1, p. 16.

41. *TSZ*, p. 132; Schlechta, II, p. 287; *KGW*, VI/1, p. 16.

42. *TSZ*, p. 132; Schlechta II, p. 287; *KGW*, VI/1, p. 17.

43. *TSZ*, pp. 132–133; Schlechta II, p. 287; *KGW*, VI/1, p. 17.

44. *TSZ*, p. 133; Schlechta, II, p. 287; *KGW*, VI/1, p. 17.

45. *TSZ*, p. 134; Schlechta II, p. 288; *KGW*, VI/1, pp. 18–19.

46. *TSZ*, p. 135; Schlechta, II, p. 289; *KGW*, VI/1, p. 19.

47. Martin Heidegger, "Who is Nietzsche's Zarathustra?" Trans. Bernd Magnus in *The New Nietzsche: Contemporary Styles of Interpretation*, ed. David B. Allison (New York: Dell Publishing, 1977), p. 64.

48. Alderman points out the importance of recognizing the fictional and dramatic character of the book throughout his *Nietzsche's Gift*, esp. pp. 11, 14, 17. Alderman also emphasizes that Zarathustra's speeches to himself perform an important function in Zarathustra's communication to the *reader*, if not obviously to any audience in the story (p. 39). He suggests as well that these speeches of Zarathustra to himself serve a crucial role in Zarathustra's communication *within* the story, but this point will be considered below. Anke Bennholdt-Thomsen similarly emphasizes Zarathustra's monologues and suggests that the speeches have been overvalued because of the tendency of interpreters to see Zarathustra as a mere mouthpiece for Nietzsche's ideas. Bennholdt-Thomsen, by contrast, concurs with us that much of the action of the book concerns Zarathustra's coming into contact with the "genius" of the doctrine. In her view, the statements of doctrine in Zarathustra's speeches amount to resting places along the way of Zarathustra's approaches to more immediate contact with insight. See Bennholdt-Thomsen, pp. 109, 198.

49. Alderman, p. 13.

50. For a sense of this, see *EH*, p. 312; Schlecta, II, p. 1143; *KGW*, VI/3, p. 350.

51. *TSZ*, p. 121; Schlechta, II, p. 277; *KGW*, VI/1, p.5.

52. Alderman, p. 14.

53. Some of Nietzsche's comments to this effect will be cited below. The book also shares many features with the type of ancient Roman novel that Bakhtin analyzes as an "adventure novel of everyday life." See M. M. Bakhtin, *The Dialogic Imagination: Four Essays*, ed. Michael Holquist, trans. Caryl Emerson and Michael Holquist (Austin: University of Texas Press, 1981), pp. 111–129. I shall however, defer discussion of this genre until Chapter 7, where I discuss Nietzsche's use of Apuleius' *Golden Ass* as a model for *Zarathustra*, Part IV. Bakhtin treats *The Golden Ass* as an everyday adventure novel, and while there is general kinship between this type of ancient novel and *Zarathustra* as a whole, the kinship is much greater between the everyday adventure novel and *Zarathustra*, Part IV.

54. A. K. Thorlby, "Bildungsroman," in *The Penguin Companion to European Literature*, ed. Anthony Thorlby (New York: McGraw-Hill 1969), p. 114.

55. See, e.g., Matt. 4:5–11, Luke 2:4–52, and John 2:1–12. See also Plato, *Symposium*, trans. Michael Joyce, in *Collected Dialogues*, ed. Hamilton and Cairns, line 201 c-d, p. 553.

56. W. A. Coupe, "Goethe, Johann Wolfgang von," in *Penguin Companion to European Literature*, p. 318, Nietzsche also ranks another *Bildungsroman*, Adalbert Stifter's *Nachsommer*, among the five instances of German prose literature "worth reading over and over again." (*HATH* II, "The Wanderer and His Shadow," Sec. 109, p. 250; Schlechta, I, p. 921–922; *KGW*, IV/3, p. 237.)

57. Heidegger, "Who Is Nietzsche's Zarathustra?" p. 68.

58. *GS*, Sec. 342, pp. 274–275; Schlechta, II, p. 203; *KGW*, V/2, p. 251.

59. *EH*, p. 299; Schlechta, II, p. 1131; *KGW*, VI/3, p. 337— quoting *GS*, Sec. 382, p. 347; Schlechta, II, p. 258–259; *KGW*, V/2, p. 319.

60. See, e.g., *TI*, p. 562; Schlechta, II, p. 1032; *KGW*, VI/3, p.

154. See also *WP*, Sec. 1029, p. 531; Schlechta, II, p. 432; *KGW*, VII/2, p. 29; and *WP*, Sec. 853, p. 453; Schlechta, III, p. 693; *KGW*, VIII/3, Sec. 17 (3), pp. 318–320.

61. Portions of the following section have been published in essay form as "Nietzsche's View of Philosophical Style," in *International Studies in Philosophy*, XVIII No. 2 (Summer 1986): 67–81.

62. *TSZ*, p. 148; Schlechta, II, p. 302; *KGW*, VI/1, p. 38.

63. Ludwig Wittgenstein, *Tractatus Logico-Philosphicus*, trans. C. K. Ogden (London: Routledge & Kegan Paul, 1922), p. 189.

64. *HATH* I, Sec. 374, pp. 191–192; Schlechta, I, p. 643; *KGW*, IV/2, pp. 267–268.

65. *TSZ*, pp. 253–254; Schlechta, II, p. 396; *KGW*, VI/1, p. 178.

66. *HATH* II, "The Wanderer and His Shadow," Sec. 88, p. 243; Schlechta, I, p. 916; *KGW*, IV/3, p. 231.

67. *EH*, p. 265; Schlechta, II, p. 1104; *KGW*, VI/3, p. 302.

68. *EH*, p. 261; Schlechta, II, p. 1100; *KGW*, VI/3, pp. 297–298.

69. *HATH* II, "Miscellaneous Maxims and Opinions," Sec. 58, p. 38; Schlechta, I, p. 491; *KGW*, IV/3, p. 40. Morgan observes that Nietzsche is convinced "that true communication, so far as it is possible at all, is so only between men of a kind." This does not disagree with the position defended here. But Morgan emphasizes Nietzsche's belief that many people will *never* be receptive to his message, which ultimately leads Nietzsche to give up the project of indiscriminately overflowing with his teaching, which he suggested in his first speech to the sun. See George Allen Morgan, Jr., *What Nietzsche Means* (Cambridge, Mass. Harvard University Press, 1941), p. 15.

70. This fact might serve as a basis for constructing a Nietzschean rebuttal to Socrates' suggestion, in the myth of Theuth and Thamus, that writing is inferior to verbal discourse. See Plato, *Phaedrus*, trans. R. Hackforth, in *The Collected Dialogues of Plato, Including the Letters*, lines 275a-b, p. 520.

71. *TSZ*, p. 368; Schlechta, II, p. 495; *KGW*, VI/1, p. 314.

72. Heidegger, "Who is Nietzsche's Zarathustra?" p. 68. Zarathustra's discourse with himself calls to mind the Christian tra-

dition along with the Platonic tradition. The Christian ideal of prayer is described by Evelyn Underhill as being "the deep and vital movement of the whole self, too utterly absorbed for self-consciousness, set over against its fussy surface energies" (Evelyn Underhill, *Mysticism: A Study in the Nature and Development of Man's Spiritual Consciousness* [Cleveland: World Publishing; 1960], p. 325). Zarathustra's meditations may be more self-conscious than this, but they seem to lack the Apollonian clarity of self-consciousness to a degree that makes it impossible for them to be represented.

73. Alderman makes this point in *Nietzsche's Gift*, pp. 20–21.

74. *GS*, sec. 355, pp. 300–301; Schlechta, II, pp. 222–223; *KGW*, V/2, pp. 275–277.

75. This position would seem to run counter to the "private language" argument that Wittgenstein presents in paragraphs 242 and 243 of *Philosophical Investigations*, 2nd ed., trans. G. E. M. Anscombe (New York: Macmillan, 1958), pp. 88–89. Wittgenstein denies the possibility of an essentially private language, through which the speaker could express inner experiences through a mode of communication that was exclusively for his on her own use in principle. Nietzsche, on the other hand, seems to suggest that the community's linguistic conventions pressure the individual to distort his or her understanding of the inner experience, which he or she could conceivably understand privately in greater detail. Even Wittgenstein, however, suggests that there is a private component to the experiences to which language refers. See the discussion of the private language argument in Robert J. Fogelin, *Wittgenstein*, Arguments of the Philosophers Series, ed. Ted Honderich (London: Routledge Kegan Paul, 1976), pp. 152–165, where Fogelin attributes to Wittgenstein only the relatively weak position that "an essentially private language as defined in Sec. 243 is not possible for human beings as we understand them" (p. 165).

Chapter 5

1. *TSZ*, p. 180; Schlechta, II, p. 331; *KGW*, VI/1, p. 84.

2. *TSZ*, p. 190; Schlechta, II, p. 339; *KGW*, VI/1, p. 97.

3. The sage who praises sleep is also, through this sermon's

style, satirically compared to Christ when he pronounces the Sermon on the Mount. Note the section's similarity with, for example, "Blessed are the meek, for they shall possess the earth" (Matt. 5:5). The section provides a good example of Nietzsche's pervasive tactic of simultaneously parodying more than one of his targets.

4. *EH*, p. 256; Schlechta, II, pp. 1096–1097; *KGW*, VI/3, pp. 293–294.

5. *TSZ*, p. 153; Schlechta, II, p. 306; *KGW*, VI/1, p. 45.

6. *TSZ*, p. 163; Schlechta, II, p. 315; *KGW*, VI/1, p. 60.

7. *TSZ*, p. 183; Schlechta, II, p. 333; *KGW*, VI/1, p. 88.

8. *TSZ*, pp. 173–174; Schlechta, II, p. 325; *KGW*, VI/1, p. 74.

9. This is particularly true in Part IV, as will be briefly discussed in Chapter 7. See Hayman, pp. 280–281.

10. There are several recent exceptions to this generalization. Williams argues in his dissertation that the doctrine of eternal recurrence undergoes revision throughout *Thus Spoke Zarathustra*, and that the three distinct formulations that are developed correspond to the perspectives of the camel, the lion, and the child that are imagistically described in the first of Zarathustra's speeches, "On the Three Metamorphoses" (Williams, pp. 6–175). Alderman, as we have noted, emphasizes that the book has a dramatic structure that has been largely ignored. While much of Alderman's own discussion in *Nietzsche's Gift* involves interpretation of what is overtly expressed in *Zarathustra*'s passages (a strategy that is consistent with his decision not to discuss Nietzsche's use of irony, as reported on p. 9), the larger concepts through which Alderman analyzes *Zarathustra* are concepts that inherently possess temporal structure (play, laughter, recurrent silences, and the structure of affirming life). Magnus' recent paper "Deification of the Commonplace: *Twilight of the Idols*," proposes an interpretation of *Zarathustra*, Part IV, that depends on a construal of the book as a temporal structure. He argues that the close of the book shows Zarathustra abandoning the doctrines by which he was earlier enraptured—the doctrines of the *Übermensch* and eternal recurrence—because he recognizes that he had been using them in a self-deceived fashion to assure himself that there is a kind of salvation that will redeem his life, despite

his public denials of such salvation. While I disagree with some of the details of Magnus' reading of the conclusion of *Zarathustra*, I am in sympathy with his position on the structural importance of Zarathustra's conclusion and with his view that this conclusion represents Zarathustra's recognition that he has been self-deceived in his adherence to his doctrines. My own analysis of Zarathustra's flash of insight will be presented in Chapter 7. See also Gadamer, pp. 346–363.

11. *TSZ*, p. 421; Schlechta II, p. 544; *KGW*, VI/1, p. 381. For an analysis of this strange section, see C. A. Miller, "Nietzsche's 'Daughters of the Desert': A Reconsideration," *Nietzsche-Studien*, II (1973): 157–195.

12. An example of an allusion to the New Testament that reinforces but is not crucial to recognizing the anti-Christian tenor of the text can be seen in the first paragraph of the section "On the Virtuous": "About you, the virtuous, my beauty laughed today. And thus its voice came to me: 'They still want to be paid' " (*TSZ*, p. 205; Schlechta II, p. 625; *KGW*, VI/1, p. 116). The allusion to the New Testament is not so striking as some of Nietzsche's allusions, but the passage certainly recalls Christ's parable of the employer who hires some workers in the morning, some workers at midday, and still others later in the afternoon, and then pays them all equally, with the consequence that all but the workers in the final group complain that they should be paid more (see Matt. 20:1–17). Nietzsche's allusion accords with Christ's gospel in criticizing the attitudes of those who view themselves as virtuous. It is anti-Christian in attacking Christians, not in attacking Christianity's founder. Nietzsche was evidently fond of this allusive attack on Christians, for he repeats it in his later work, *The Antichrist*: "The principle of 'Christian love': in the end it wants to be *paid* well" (*A*, p. 623; Schlechta II, p. 1209; *KGW*, VI/3, p. 220).

13. The doctrine of the Immaculate Conception holds that Mary, Jesus' mother, was conceived without sin. The consequence of this immaculate conception, according to the doctrine, is that Mary did not transmit original sin to Jesus. Nietzsche states his view of the doctrine succinctly in *The Antichrist*. After criticizing the usual Christian interpretation of the father-son symbolism

involved in the doctrine of the Trinity, he comments, "And a dogma of 'immaculate conception' on top of that? *But with that it has masculated conception*" (*A*, p. 608; Schlechta, II, p. 1196; *KGW*, VI/3, p. 205).

14. *TSZ*, pp. 234–235; Schlechta, II, pp. 377–378; *KGW*, VI/1, p. 153.

15. *TSZ*, pp. 235–236; Schlechta, II, p. 379; *KGW*, VI/1, p. 154.

16. *TSZ*, p. 235; Schlechta, II, p. 378; *KGW*, VI/1, p. 153.

17. *TSZ*, p. 234; Schlechta, II, p. 378; *KGW*, VI/1, p. 153.

18. Kaufmann, ed., *The Portable Nietzsche*, p. 193.

19. Nietzsche uses a similar image in *Beyond Good and Evil:* "Witness the ever madder howling of the anarchist dogs who are baring their fangs more and more obviously and roam through the alleys of European culture" (*BGE*, Sec. 202, p. 116; Schlechta, II, p. 660; *KGW* VI/2, p. 127). See also Bennholdt-Thomsen, pp. 70–73, where the relationship between the political theme and the more inward significance of the passage is discussed. It is significant that Bennholdt-Thomsen reads the section as a preliminary indication of Zarathustra's inner tension with respect to the not-yet-articulated doctrine of eternal recurrence (see p. 73). This reading—and Bennholdt-Thomsen's reading throughout—concurs in emphasis with my claim that Zarathustra's attitudinal dispositions toward his doctrines are crucial to the story being told in the book. *TSZ*, pp. 243–244; Schlechta, II, pp. 386–387; *KGW*, VI/1, pp. 165–166.

20. *TSZ*, p. 190; Schlechta, II, pp. 339–340; *KGW*, VI/1, pp. 97–98.

21. *TSZ*, p. 195; Schlechta, II, p. 341; *KGW*, VI/1, p. 101. Nietzsche did not write the parts consecutively. He claims to have written each of the parts in a ten-day spurt, but months elapsed between spurts (*EH*, p. 302; Schlechta, II, p. 1133; *KGW*, VI/3, p. 339). *Zarathustra*, Part I, was written in January 1883. *Zarathustra*, Part II, was completed in January 1884. *Zarathustra*, Part III, was a product of July 1884. And *Zarathustra*, Part IV, was completed in January 1885. See Hayman, pp. xxi, 278. See also Kaufmann's note in *EH*, p. 302.

22. *TSZ*, p. 195; Schlechta, II, p. 341; *KGW*, VI/1, pp. 101–102.

23. *TSZ*, p. 211; Schlechta, II, p. 357; *KGW*, VI/1, p. 124.

24. *TSZ*, p. 214; Schlechta, II, p. 359; *KGW*, VI/1, p. 127.

25. For a detailed analysis of this section, see Kathleen Higgins, "The Night Song's Answer," *International Studies in Philosophy*, XVII, No. 2 (Summer 1985):pp. 33–50.

26. *TSZ*, p. 253; Schlechta, II, pp. 395–396; *KGW*, VI/1, p. 177.

27. *TSZ*, pp. 253–254; Schlechta, II, p. 396; *KGW*, VI/1, p. 178.

28. *TSZ*, pp. 254–255; Schlechta, II, p. 397; *KGW*, VI/1, pp. 179–180.

29. *TSZ*, p. 257; Schlechta, II, p. 399; *KGW*, VI/1, pp. 183–184.

30. *TSZ*, pp. 257-259; Schlechta, II, pp. 399–401; *KGW*, VI/1, pp. 183–186.

31. *TSZ*, p. 259; Schlechta, II, p. 401; *KGW*, VI/1, p. 186.

32. Kaufmann, ed., *Portable Nietzsche*, p. 194.

33. *TSZ*, p. 257; Schlechta, II, p. 399; *KGW*, VI/1, p. 183.

34. See Underhill, pp. 380–412.

35. Underhill, pp. 381–382.

36. Underhill, p. 388.

37. Underhill, p. 395. Zarathustra's experience in this section resembles the Dark Night of the Soul in many respects, even in the sense that he, like the mystics that experience this state, is told that he must allow himself to break (see Underhill, pp. 399–400, on the surrender of self that the Dark Night functions to provoke). His mystical experience in "The Stillest Hour," and his Jeremiah-like unwillingness to go through with his vocation, establishes Zarathustra as a counterpart to the biblical prophets.

38. Alderman, p. 93, notes the similarity between Zarathustra and the religious saint in this passage, but he emphasizes the distance between Zarathustra and the saint.

39. This is essentially the Heraclitean point that one cannot step into the same river twice. It is clear that Nietzsche takes Heraclitus quite seriously. See, e.g., *EH*, pp. 273–274; Schlechta, II, p. 1111; *KGW*, VI/3, pp. 310–311, where Nietzsche claims that

many of the important themes in Heraclitus are "more closely related to me than anything else thought to date"; and suggests that his doctrine of eternal recurrence "might in the end have been taught already by Heraclitus."

40. *TSZ*, p. 220; Schlechta, II, p. 365; *KGW*, VI/1, p. 136.

41. *TSZ*, p. 221; Schlechta, II, p. 365; *KGW*, VI/1, p. 136.

42. *TSZ*, pp. 220–221; Schlechta, II, pp. 364–366; GW, VI/1, p. 137.

43. *TSZ*, p. 222; Schlechta, II, p. 366; *KGW*, VI/6, p. 137.

44. Plato, *Republic*, Book X, lines 599–601, 605, pp. 824–826, and 830–831.

45. Ibid., line 607b, p. 832.

46. *BT*, p. 89; Schlechta, I, p. 78 KGW, III, p. 87.

47. *TSZ*, pp. 238–239; Schlechta, II, p. 382; *KGW*, VI/1, pp. 159–160.

48. Plato, *Phaedrus*, line 247c, p. 494.

49. *TSZ*, p. 240; Schlechta, II, p. 383; *KGW*, VI/1, p. 160.

50. William Shakespeare, *Hamlet*, in *Complete Works*, ed. Alfred Harbage (New York: Viking Press, 1969), act 1, scene 5, lines 166–167, p. 942.

51. *TSZ*, p. 240; Schlechta, II, p. 383; *KGW*, VI/1, p. 161.

52. Johann Wolfgang von Goethe, *Faust: Part One and Sections from Part Two*, trans. Walter Kaufmann (Garden City, N.Y.: Doubleday, 1961), p. 503.

53. *TSZ*, p. 238; Schlechta, II, p. 382. Zarathustra also makes a disparaging allusion to the Eternal Feminine in *TSZ*, p. 239; Schlechta, II, p. 383; *KGW*, VI/1, pp. 159, 160.

54. *TSZ*, p. 240; Schlechta, II, p. 384; *KGW*, VI/1, p. 161.

55. *TSZ*, p. 246; Schlechta, II, pp. 389–390; *KGW*, VI/1, p. 169.

57. The dream, which focuses on the present moment as a link between the streams of past and future, is imagistically related to the doctrine of eternal recurrence. The function of this doctrine in *Zarathustra* is the topic of Chapter 6.

58. See *TSZ*, p. 122 ("Zarathustra's Prologue"), sec. 2; Schlechta, II, p. 278; *KGW*, VI/1, p. 12.

59. *TSZ*, p. 247; Schlechta, II, p. 390; *KGW*, VI/1, p. 170. Bennholdt-Thomsen, pp. 76–79, analyzes this dream in Freudian terms. Significantly for my purposes, she sees the dream as an

important development in Zarathustra's "becoming conscious" and an indication that he is not yet clear about his own role as the teacher of eternal recurrence, (pp. 79–81).

60. *TSZ*, p. 267; Schlechta, II, p. 406; *KGW*, VI/1, p. 192.

61. *TSZ*, p. 267; Schlechta, II, p. 406; *KGW*, VI/1, p. 192.

62. See, e.g., the section entitled "On Involuntary Bliss," *TSZ*, pp. 272–275; Schlechta, II, pp. 411–414; *KGW*, VI/1, pp. 199–202.

63. *TSZ*, p. 327; Schlechta, II, p. 461; *KGW*, VI/1, p. 266.

64. *TSZ*, p. 328; Schlechta, II, p. 462; *KGW*, VI/1, p. 267.

65. *TSZ*, pp. 328–329; Schlechta, II, p. 462; *KGW*, VI/1, p. 268.

66. *TSZ*, p. 329; Schlechta, II, p. 463; *KGW*, VI/1, p. 268.

67. *TSZ*, p. 329; Schlechta, II, p. 463; *KGW*, VI/1, p. 268.

68. *TSZ*, pp. 331–332; Schlechta, II, p. 465; *KGW*, VI/1, p. 271.

69. *TSZ*, p. 332; Schlechta, II, pp. 465–466; *KGW*, VI/1, p. 271.

70. *TSZ*, p. 332; Schlechta, II, p. 466; *KGW*, VI/1, pp. 271–272.

71. *TSZ*, p. 339; Schlechta, II, p. 472; *KGW*, VI/1, p. 28. Commentators have interpreted Zarathustra's whisper as a statement of the doctrine of eternal recurrence. See, e.g., Kaufmann, Portable Nietzsche, p. 263. Perhaps Zarathustra is so romantically inept that the doctrine of eternal recurrence is his idea of a sweet nothing. But this passage would seem to admit of any interpretation of the whisper that involved an assertion that he knows he will not betray life.

72. *TSZ*, p. 339; Schlechta, II, p. 472; *KGW*, VI/1, p. 281.

73. *TSZ*, pp. 339–340; Schlechta, II, pp. 472–473; *KGW*, VI/1, pp. 281–282.

74. *TSZ*, pp. 340–342; Schlechta, II, pp. 473–476; *KGW*, VI/1, pp. 284–287.

Chapter 6

1. *EH*, p. 295; Schlechta, II, p. 1129; *KGW*, VI/3, p. 333.

2. See, e.g., Bernd Magnus, "Nietzsche's Eternalistic Counter-Myth," *Review of Metaphysics*, XXVI (June 1973): 608. There Magnus notes that a literal interpretation of eternal recurrence as normative involves "severe internal inconsistencies." For a debate on the views expressed in Magnus' discussion here, the

reader might compare M. C. Sterling's criticism of these views ("Recent Discussions of Eternal Recurrence," *Nietzsche-Studien*, VI [1977]: 282–283, 284–288) and Magnus' response to Sterling ("Eternal Recurrence," *Nietzsche-Studien*, IX [1980]: 362–377).

3. Nehamas, p. 141. See also Martin Heidegger, *Nietzsche*, Vol. II: *The Eternal Recurrence of the Same*, trans. David Farrell Krell (New York: Harper & Row, 1984), p. 5.

4. *EH*, p. 295/ Schlechta, II, p. 1129; *KGW*, VI/3, p. 333.

5. Nietzsche makes this claim in *TI*, p. 563; Schlechta, II, p. 1032; *KGW*,VI/3, p. 154. Compare also *TI*, p. 556; Schlechta II, p. 1026; *KGW*, VI/3, p. 147, where Nietzsche claims that *Zarathustra* is "the most profound book" that mankind possesses, and the passage just cited, where he claims that eternal recurrence is the central thought of the book.

6. See Bernd Magnus, *Nietzsche's Existential Imperative* (Bloomington: Indiana University Press, 1978), pp. 140–142.

7. Readers interested in eternal recurrence as a cosmological theory should see: Danto, *Nietzsche as Philosopher*, pp. 203–209; Arnold Zuboff, "Nietzsche and Eternal Recurrence," in Robert Solomon, ed. *Nietzsche; A Collection of Critical Essays* (Garden City, N.Y.: Doubleday, 1973), pp. 348–357; Ivan Soll, "Reflections on Recurrence," in *Nietzsche*, ed. Solomon, pp. 326–335; Schacht, *Nietzsche*, pp. 254–258, 261–266; Sterling, "Recent Discussions of Eternal Recurrence," pp. 261–268, 275–281; Nehamas, *Nietzsche*, pp. 142–150; Magnus, *Nietzsche's Existential Imperative*, pp. 74–88, 90–110. Tracy B. Strong, *Friedrich Nietzsche and the Politics of Transfiguration* (Berkeley: University of California Press, 1975), pp. 265–266.

8. See, e.g., Strong, pp. 270–271, who argues that eternal recurrence provides a kind of selective principle to determine the value of our actions. See also Karl Jaspers, *Nietzsche: An Introduction to the Understanding of His Philosophical Activity*, trans. Charles F. Wallraff and Fredrick J. Schmitz (Chicago: Henry Regnery Co., 1965), pp. 353ff.

9. Immanuel Kant, *Fundamental Principles of the Metaphysics of Morals*, trans. Thomas K. Abbott (Indianapolis: Liberal Arts Press, 1949), p. 38. See Magnus' discussion of the normative interpretation in *Nietzsche's Existential Imperative*, pp. 104–141. See

also Kaufmann, *Nietzsche: Philosopher, Psychologist, Antichrist*, pp. 322–325.

10. Magnus, *Nietzsche's Existential Imperative*, p. 142. For a development of Magnus' view of eternal recurrence, see that entire work. See also Magnus, "Eternal Recurrence," pp. 362–377; and Magnus, "Nietzsche's Eternalistic Counter-Myth," pp. 604–616.

11. Nehamas sees the doctrine as emphasizing the essential interconnectedness of all that exists. The doctrine, as he formulates it, asserts, "If anything in the world recurred, including an individual life or even a single moment within it, then everything in the world would recur in exactly identical fashion" (*Nietzsche*, p. 156). He concludes from this that the insight of the doctrine is that the only life that could recur, if recurrence were to happen, would be *this* one (pp. 156–157). The attitude that eternal recurrence emblemizes is that of the fullest affirmation of this life, but it does not, as Magnus holds, represent an unattainable ideal, unattainable in part because our lives, unlike those of *Übermenschen*, are not lives in which every moment of our past could be willed to recur eternally (see Magnus, "The Deification of the Commonplace: *Twilight of the Idols*," pp. 26–27, 32–34). Nehamas argues that the attitude emblemized by the doctrine *is* instantiable. According to Nehamas, the doctrine draws attention to the potency of the present with respect to the past. By focusing on the interconnectedness of past, present, and future, the doctrine indicates that the significance of the past depends on the way it is interpreted in the present. The significance of the past is mutable because the interpretation given to it is mutable. In a moment of the sort that Nietzsche claims to have had when the thought of eternal recurrence first overtook him, the attitude emblemized in the doctrine is instantiated, because at such a moment one's joy in the present is so intense that one interprets the entirety of the past as affirmable, for it was all ingredient to the conditions which now constitute the present. See Nehamas, p. 159–165.

12. See Nehamas' discussion of the range of interpretations that Nietzsche's texts will support (*Nietzsche*, pp. 141–156).

13. Although the vast majority of passages that suggest the

cosmological interpretation occur, elsewhere, usually in Nietzsche's notes, they are not absent in *Zarathustra*. See ibid, pp. 146–149; see also, however, p. 145, where Nehamas observes, "It is very difficult to find any clear references to cosmology in Nietzsche's published discussions of the recurrence."

14. See Magnus, "Nietzsche's Eternalistic Counter-Myth," p. 608.

15. See Magnus, "Eternal Recurrence," p. 366.

16. Ivan Soll makes this point about recurrence in "Reflections on Recurrence," in *Nietzsche*, ed. Solomon, pp. 339–340. His conclusion is that eternal recurrence, if true, should be a matter of complete indifference to us (see Soll, pp. 339–342). See also Magnus' critical discussion of this view in Magnus, *Nietzsche's Existential Imperative*, pp. 107–110.

17. Wittgenstein, *Tractatus Logico-Philosophicus*, line 6.43, p. 185.

18. Heidegger makes the point that the time of our experience is attitudinally conditioned. See Martin Heidegger, *Being and Time*, trans. John Macquarrie and Edward Robinson (New York: Harper & Row, 1962), pp. 370–380 (H. 323–331).

19. *Ibid.*, p. 182 (H. 143), p. 188 (H. 148).

20. *TSZ*, p. 251; Schlechta, II, p. 394; *KGW*, VI/1, p. 176.

21. *TSZ*, p. 252; Schlechta, II, p. 394; *KGW*, VI/1, p. 176.

22. *TSZ*, pp. 252–253; Schlechta, II, p. 395; *KGW*, VI/1, pp. 176–177.

23. *A*, p. 595; Schlechta, II, p. 1186; *KGW*, VI/3, pp. 192–193.

24. I do not offer detailed commentary on this section, but others have done so. My view of the section, as it is in evidence here, was most strongly influenced by the commentary of Williams, pp. 46-54. I also recommend Magnus' commentary on the section, which appears in his *Nietzsche's Existential Imperative*, pp. 165–170.

25. *TSZ*, p. 270; Schlechta, II, p. 408; *KGW*, VI/1, p. 196.

26. Williams, p. 51.

27. Nietzsche does not make a radical distinction between mind and body. The mind and body are continuous, on his view, and he includes physiological urges among the unconscious mo-

tives. For a discussion of the arrangement between these and conscious will, see Schacht, pp. 309–312.

28. One might doubt the consistency of Nietzsche's position. Nietzsche does advocate self-assertion in one's actions, and this stance seems hard to square with his insistence that our desires, like other things, are caused. If our desires are triggered by other causes, it is hard to see how we can be said to have the option of asserting ourselves or not. But that option seems something that Nietzsche presupposes. This objection to Nietzsche's position takes the form of the standard objection to soft determinism. I will not rehearse the free will/determinism debate here; for a further discussion of Nietzsche's view in the context of that debate, see Schacht, pp. 304–312.

29. Victor Zuckerkandl, *Sound and Symbol: Music and the External World,* trans. Willard R. Trask, Bollingen Series XLIV (Princeton: Princeton University Press, 1956), pp. 35–37.

30. Ibid., p. 68.

31. Ibid., p. 168.

32. Ibid., p. 173.

33. Ibid., p. 231.

34. Ibid., p. 175.

35. Ibid., p. 233.

36. Cf. Heidegger's notion of resolute being-toward-death. See Heidegger, *Being and Time,* pp. 292–311 (H. 248–267), 341–348 (H. 295–301).

37. I am strongly influenced in these remarks by Leonard B. Meyer. See his "Some Remarks on Value and Greatness in Music," in *Aesthetics Today,* ed. Morris Philipson (New York: New American Library, 1961), pp. 169–187.

38. Deleuze emphasizes the playful character of the affirmation involved in accepting eternal recurrence in Gilles Deleuze, *Nietzsche and Philosophy,* trans. Hugh Tomlinson (London: Athlone Press, 1983), pp. 25–29. His interpretation of the necessity involved in eternal recurrence focuses on the present moment in that discussion to such an extent that the dynamic causal currents that flow into the moment are, in my view, somewhat underemphasized. But Deleuze's discussion is interesting for its con-

sideration of the relationship between eternal recurrence and chance, which Zarathustra frequently discusses and affirms for its role in human reality.

39. *EH*, p. 258; Schlechta, II, p. 1098; *KGW*, VI/3, p. 295.

40. Letter to Overbeck, August 28, 1883, Middleton, p. 219; Schlechta, III, p. 1214; *KGB*, III/1, p. 438.

41. *TSZ*, pp. 245-246; Schlechta, II, pp. 388–389; *KGW*, VI/1, p. 168.

42. Magnus, in *Nietzsche's Existential Imperative*, p. 154, indicates how much Nietzsche condenses in this formula.

43. *EH*, p. 335; Schlechta, II, p. 1159; *KGW*, VI/3, p. 372.

44. *WP*, Sec. 1052, pp. 542–543; Schlechta, III, p. 773; *KGW*, V111/3, Sec. 14(89), p. 58.

45. *GS*, Sec. 341, pp. 273–274; Schlechta, II, p. 200; *KGW*, V/2, p. 250.

46. Cf. Plato, *Phaedrus*, lines 274c–275d, pp. 520–521.

47. Heidegger, *Nietzsche*, Vol. II (trans. Krell), p. 57.

48. *TSZ*, p. 435; Schlechta, II, p. 557; *KGW*, VI/1, p. 398.

49. Although I agree with Magnus that the doctrine of eternal recurrence provides a kind of emblem of a certain attitude toward life, I disagree with his insistence that the affirmation of every moment of our lives recommended by Nietzsche through this doctrine would be impossible to any humane and balanced human being. Our disagreement on this matter stems, I think, from our different view of what Nietzsche means by "each and every moment." Magnus focuses, in his interpretation, on the total affirmation of *past* moments that would be involved in the adoption of the doctrine of eternal recurrence. I agree with him that there is something inhumane and therefore untenable about affirming the past wholesale, without grieving for the inhumanity that some moments of our past probably involved. I interpret Nietzsche's "each and every moment," however, to be a formulation that he uses to express the potency of *this* moment, whichever moment it might be. On this point my opinion resembles that of Nehamas, although I would express my interpretation of Nietzsche's view on the present's power over the past in more cautious terms than he does. The potency and challenge of the present moment, which draws threads from all of one's past together, is found (in my

interpretation of Nietzsche's view) in our present capacity to make that moment fully and affirmatively ours by using the material one receives from the past to do something that one can positively value. Although this effort cannot make all of the past beautiful ("the will cannot will backwards"), one can direct one's experiences of the past into a present integration of the self that is somehow beautiful—and thereby one can beautify or "redeem" the past to the extent that this *is* humanly possible. I am convinced that this is at least *an* important point that Nietzsche tries to make in the doctrine of eternal recurrence, even if he fails to articulate the doctrine consistently in a manner that accords with this reading.

50. See, in this connection, "On the Way of the Creator," *TSZ*, pp. 174–177; Schlechta, II, p. 325–328; *KGW*, VI/1, pp. 76–79. See also "The Night Song," *TSZ*, pp. 217–219; Schlechta, II, pp. 362–362; *KGW*, VI/1, pp. 132–134.

51. I am indebted to Roger Gathmann, of the Department of Philosophy at the University of Texas at Austin, for much of this analysis of eternal recurrence as a response to the loneliness that follows recognition of the death of God.

Chapter 7

1. *TSZ*, p. 175; Schlechta, II, p. 326; *KGW*, VI/1, p. 77.

2. Even Bennholdt-Thomsen, whose interpretation of *Zarathustra* emphasizes the developmental dramatic structure, contends that the action is, in a sense, closed with Part III and that Part IV reveals nothing materially new. She does, however, see a certain textual necessity in Part IV, which she analyzes as a satyr play. See Bennholdt-Thomsen, pp. 196, 205, 210–211.

3. R. J. Hollingdale, *Nietzsche: The Man and His Philosophy* (Baton Rouge: Louisiana State University Press, 1965), p. 190.

4. See, e.g., Henry David Aiken, "Introduction to *Zarathustra*," in *Nietzsche*, ed. Solomon, pp. 117–118; Hayman, p. 278; and Williams, p. 4.

5. Consider, e.g. the scene in which Zarathustra steps on a man and becomes so startled that he begins to beat him (*TSZ*, p. 360; Schlechta, II, p. 487; *KGW*, VI/1, p. 305).

6. See, e.g., *TSZ*, pp. 397–398; Schlechta, II, pp. 521–522; *KGW*, VI/1, p. 351, which introduces "that long-drawn-out meal which the chronicles call "the last supper.' " See also *TSZ*, p. 430; Schlechta, II, p. 552; *KGW*, VI/1, p. 392, where the narrator discusses the "strange wonders that occurred," such as the ass dancing.

7. Letter to Overbeck, end of May 1885, quoted in Hayman, p. 281; *KGB*, III/3, pp. 46–47.

8. Letter to Carl von Gersdorff, February 12, 1885, in Middleton, p. 235; Schlechta, III, pp. 1228–1229; *KGB*, III/3, p. 9.

9. Letter to Overbeck, March 31, 1885, in Middleton, p. 239; *KGB*, III/3, p. 33. See also letter to Carl Fuchs, July 29, 1888, in Middleton, p. 304; Schlechta, III, pp. 1306–1307; *KGB*, III/5, p. 374.

10. Letter to Gast, December 9, 1888, in Middleton, pp. 332–333; Schlechta, III, pp. 1339–1340/ *KGB*, III/5, pp. 514–515.

11. Hayman, p. 281.

12. See letter to Overbeck, March 31, 1885, in Middleton, p. 239; *KGB*, III/3, p. 33.

13. See also letter to Carl von Gersdorff, February 12, 1885, in Middleton, p. 35; Schlechta, III, p. 1228; *KGB*, III/3, p. 9. Also, *TI*, p. 556; Schlechta, II, p. 1026; *KGW*, VI/3, p. 147.

14. Letter to Overbeck, March 31, 1885, in Middleton, p. 239; *KGB*, III/3, p. 33.

15. See Hayman, p. 282.

16. I am using the expression "Menippean satire" in the sense that Northrup Frye uses it, and for the purposes of most of this discussion I simply assume that *The Golden Ass* is appropriately classified under this heading. I also take "Menippean satire" and "Varronian satire" to be equivalent expressions for my purposes. This does not follow the practice of contemporary classicists, who frequently distinguish between Menippean and Varronian satire. Menippean satire is taken to be a satirical form that employs both prose and verse, while the authorship of the genre that I consider below is often attributed to Varro, and hence is labeled "Varronian." *Zarathustra*, Part IV, might be classifiable as being in the Menippean tradition even on this account, since the prose of the satirical story is occasionally interrupted by poetry, but the generic features that I am concerned with in my discussion are

those that are common to *Zarathustra*, Part IV, and Apuleius' *Golden Ass*. While the question of whether or not Menippus had much to do with the satiric form that *The Golden Ass* exemplifies is controversial, some classical scholars are quite comfortable analyzing the work as a Menippean satire. See, e.g., Patrick Gerard Walsh, *The Roman Novel: The "Satyricon" of Petronius and the "Metamorphoses" of Apuleius* (Cambridge: Cambridge University Press, 1970), p. 4. It is evident even from Nietzsche's cited letter to Rodhe that he believes it is appropriate to speak of Menippus and Varronian satire in the same breath. Stronger evidence that Nietzsche associated the two appears in his own "Der Cyniker Menippus," a section of his "Beiträge zur Quellenkunde und Kritik des Laertius Diogenes," where he considers the relationship between Menippus and Varro, already a topic of heated debate. Nietzsche concludes that while the two figures were sufficiently distant in history that Varro could not be called Menippus' student, they shared a common worldview and cultivated the same literary genre. I am grateful to David Konstan of the Department of Classics at Wesleyan University for his advice regarding contemporary philological practice.

17. Letter to Erwin Rohde, November 9, 1868, in Middleton, pp. 36–37; Schlechta, III, pp. 996–997; *KGB*, I/2, p. 337. *Spoudegeloion* is the Menippean satire.

18. See letter to Rohde, in Middleton, p. 36 (Schlechta, III, p. 996; *KGB*, I/2, p. 337), where Nietzsche tells Rohde, in his account of his oratorical success, that he used only "notes on a slip of paper."

19. See *KGW*, II/1, pp. 233–241.

20. See Middleton, pp. 39–40n. Nietzsche's enthusiasm for Menippean satire is suggested also by his praise, much later, for Petronius, author of *Satyricon*, another work of this form. He calls Petronius "a master of *presto* in invention, ideas, and words," who had "the feet of a wind . . . , the rush, the breath, the liberating scorn of a wind that makes everything healthy by making everything *run*!" *BGE*, no. 28, p. 41; Schlechta, II, p. 594; *KGW*, VI/2, p. 42.

21. Northrup Frye, *Anatomy of Criticism: Four Essays* (Princeton: Princeton University Press, 1957), p. 309

22. Ibid., p. 309.

23. Ibid., pp. 309–310.

24. Ibid., p. 310.

25. Ibid., p. 311.

26. Ibid., p. 310.

27. *TSZ*, p. 390; Schlechta, II, p. 515 *KGW*, VI/1, p. 341.

28. *TSZ*, p. 413; Schlechta, II, p. 536; *KGW*, VI/1, p. 371.

29. *TSZ*, p. 356; Schlechta, II, p. 484; *KGW*, VI/1, p. 300.

30. *TSZ*, pp. 358–359; Schlechta, II, p. 486; *KGW*, VI/1, p. 302.

31. *TSZ*, pp. 397–398; Schlechta, II, p. 522; *KGW*, VI/1, p. 351.

32. *TSZ*, p. 422; Schlechta, II, pp. 544–545; *KGW*, VI/1, p. 382.

33. *TSZ*, pp. 424–425; Schlechta, II, p. 547; *KGW*, VI/1, pp. 384–385. In German the braying of the ass is noted as "I-A," which is phonetically equivalent to *ja*, the German word for "yes" (see Schlechta, II, p. 547). Strong points out that the higher men's acquiescence in a festival to an ass that brays *"ja-ja"* (like the English "yes-yes" or "yeah-yeah") indicates their status as yes-men who are incapable of making a positive act of life affirmation (Strong, p. 257). The association of the higher men with the *ja-ja* of the ass is also indicative of their inability to discriminate; Zarathustra himself suggests this: "But to chew and digest everything—that is truly the swine's manner. Always to bray *Yea-Yuh*—that only the ass has learned, and whoever is of his spirit" (*TSZ*, p. 306; Schlechta, II, p. 442; *KGW*, VI/1, p. 240). Accordingly, throughout the book the higher men remain unable to distinguish their projections from Zarathustra's teachings. They are similarly unable to distinguish Zarathustra's doctrine when it is conjoined with the spritual state it was formed to express from the same statement of doctrine when it is disconnected from its appropriate spiritual condition. Because of this inability the higher men are ultimately unable to share Zarathustra's insight at the end of the book—as my reading below will suggest, they, unlike Zarathustra, remain asses.

34. Lucian, *Lucius; or, The Ass*, in *Lucian*, trans. M.D. MacLeod, Vol. VIII (Cambridge, Mass.: Harvard University Press, 1967), pp. 47–145.

35. Apuleius, *The Transformations of Lucius, Otherwise*

Known as the Golden Ass, trans. Robert Graves (New York: Farrar, Straus ad Giroux, 1951), hereafter referred to as *Golden Ass.*

36. See Walsh, *Roman Novel,* pp. 145–146.

37. Nietzsche seems to have been consciously entertaining this image of a man in the skin of an ass while he worked on *Zarathustra.* In a letter to his sister Elisabeth in July 1883, he describes himself—and any person with a real goal—as one who has put "a veritable asshide around his essence" and who "goes on his way as the old ass, with his old Yea-Yuh." See *KGB*,II/1, p. 390.

38. See Walsh, p.6.

39. Until recently, the Nietzsche literature in English, had given remarkably little attention to *Zarathustra's* strange ending. When the contents of Part IV was treated directly at all, "The Drunken Song" has usually been the focus of more attention than "The Sign," with little concern shown for the potentially ironic implications of the former section's title (see, e.g., Kaufmann, *Nietzsche,* 4th ed., pp. 320–321; see also Aiken, "Introduction to *Zarathustra,*" p. 127). "The Sign" has become the focus of considerably more attention in the past ten years, however, and the range of recent comments demonstrates that the function of "The Sign" is far from a settled issue of interpretation. Hayman, p. 278, discusses the section briefly and facilely, suggesting that the animals that appear are forceful indications that Zarathustra's human companions are inadequate. Shapiro analyzes the section as simultaneously a turn to myth and an abdication of the text's narrative authority (Gary Shapiro, "Festival, Carnival and Parody in *Zarathustra IV,*" in *The Great Year of Zarathustra (1881–1981),* ed. Goicoechea, pp. 60–61). Williams argues that the section indicates a transformation of Zarathustra's understanding of time, which he conceives in a new version of the doctrine of eternal recurrence (pp. 100, 102–109, 133–139). Magnus has recently suggested a more radical interpretation of "The Sign," viewing it as a mocking statement about the project of pursuing salvation through the quest for the *Übermensch,* the quest that Zarathustra has been promoting throughout most of the book. On this reading, "The Sign" is centrally important to any inter-

pretation of *Zarathustra* as a whole; the final section deconstructs the implied context of Zarathustra's teachings in all sections that precede it (Magnus, "The Deification of the Commonplace," pp. 31–34).

40. Perry describes the authors of the two ancient ass stories in a way that makes Apuleius seem the more similar to Nietzsche in temperament. Lucian is more consistently a satirist who ridicules superstition evenly throughout his story and who seems quite content that his audience enjoy satire on its own account. Apuleius, by contrast, has a state of mind "more closely akin to that of the people whom Lucian ridicules." He was "not a satirist by temperament" but "fundamentally a serious-minded mystic and a seeker after hidden things." Thus, despite his skill in comedy and his letting "the bars of formility" down "farther than any other educated writer whose work has survived to us," he "has not dared to let his book stand forth before the world as nothing more than fiction for its own sake as entertainment, unredeemed by any show of serious purpose" (Ben Edwin Perry, *The Ancient Romances: A Literary-Historical Account of Their Origins* [Berkeley: University of California Press, 1967], pp. 232–233). One might compare the endings of *Zarathustra*, Part IV, and *The Golden Ass* strictly along the lines of their abrupt descent from wild comedy to religious seriousness, and I consider this matter below to some extent. Perry also describes the character of Apuleius' writing generally in a manner that invites comparison with *Zarathustra:* "Love of variety and the tendency to pass in rapid succession from the contemplation of one wonderful thing to another, with a minimum of logical connection, is profoundly characteristic of Apuleius in all his literary activity" (ibid., p. 243)

41. See *Golden Ass*, p. 204.

42. *TSZ*, p. 406; Schlechta, II, p. 530; *KGW*, VI/1, p. 362.

43. *TSZ*, pp. 407–408; Schlechta, II, p. 531; *KGW*, VI/1, p. 364.

44. *Golden Ass*, p. 265.

45. *TSZ*, p. 427; Schlechta, II, p. 549; *KGW*, VI/1, p. 388.

46. *TSZ*, p. 430; Schlechta, II, p. 552; *KGW*, VI/1, p. 392.

47. *TSZ*, p. 349; Schlechta, II, p. 477; *KGW*, VI/1, p. 291.

48. *Golden Ass*, p. 6.
49. See ibid., pp. 51–60.
50. See, e.g., ibid., pp. 158–159, where Lucius, like the bandits, is confused into thinking that the bridegroom of Charitë, the kidnapped girl, is a bandit.
51. Ibid., p. 147.
52. Ibid., p. 138.
53. Ibid., p. 93.
54. Ibid., p. 209.
55. Ibid., pp. 32–33.
56. Ibid., p. 207.
57. See ibid., p. 265.
58. *TSZ*, p. 425; Schlechta, II, p. 547; *KGW*, VI/1, p. 385.
59. *Golden Ass*, p. 152.
60. Ibid., p. 191.
61. Ibid., p.260.
62. Gary Shapiro similarly makes use of Bakhtin's analysis of literary form in his own interpretation of Part IV (Shapiro, "Festival, Carnival and Parody in Zarathustra IV," pp. 512). Although his account of Part IV resembles mine in certain respects—for example, in treating Part IV as a satire in Frye's sense (see *Anatomy of Criticism*, p. 48)—Shapiro focuses on Part IV's relationship to the popular carnival of the late Middle Ages.
63. Bakhtin, pp. 112–114.
64. Ibid., p. 112.
65. Ibid., p. 114.
66. Ibid., p. 116.
67. Ibid., p. 118.
68. Ibid., p. 119.
69. Ibid., pp. 119–120.
70. Ibid., p. 122.
71. Ibid., p. 123.
72. Ibid., p. 126.
73. Ibid., p. 128.
74. *TSZ*, p. 427; Schlechta, II, p. 549; *KGW*, VI/1, p. 388.
75. *TSZ*, p. 427; Schlechta, II, p. 550; *KGW*, VI/1, p. 388.
76. Magnus suggests that in the conclusion of *Zarathustra*, Nietzsche does indeed attempt to undercut the view—fortified

by the rest of the text—that Zarathustra's doctrines of eternal recurrence and the *Übermensch* are means to secular salvation in a godless era ("The Deification of the Commonplace," pp. 31–34).

77. See Walsh, pp. 176–177.

78. This is particularly so in Nietzsche's view. See *BT*, pp. 67–71; Schlechta I, pp. 55–59, *KGW*, III/1, pp. 60–65.

79. N.Y.: Cornell University Press, 1979), pp. 18, 35, 105.

80. Walsh, p. 223.

81. For a sense of the anti-Christian tenor of Apuleius' views, see Golden Ass, pp. 203–204. There he characterizes "the wickedest woman" he met in all his travels the single person identified as a Christian in *The Golden Ass:* "There was no single vice which she did not possess; her heart was a regular cesspool into which every sort of filthy sewer emptied. She was malicious, cruel, spiteful, lecherous, drunken, selfish, obstinate, as mean in her petty thefts as she was wasteful in her grand orgies, and an enemy of all that was honest and clean. She also professed perfect scorn for the Immortals and rejected all true religion in favor of a fantastic and blasphemous cult of an 'Only God.' In his honor she practiced various absurd ceremonies which gave her the excuse of getting drunk quite early in the day and playing whore at all hours."

82. Walsh, p. 183.

83. See Tatum, p. 75.

84. *TSZ*, pp. 428–429/; Schlechta, II, p. 551; *KGW*, VI/1, p. 390.

85. See Walsh, pp. 182–184.

86. The final book of *The Golden Ass*, as has often been said, is out of keeping with the rest of the work. The explanation of classical scholarship is that Apuleius tacked on a serious ending in order to justify his book—to make it appear something more than frivolous entertainment. See, e.g., Perry, pp. 233–234, 244.

87. Gary Shapiro also reads this implication in *Zarathustra*, Part IV. See Shapiro, p. 47: "An *ironic* movement... continues throughout Part Four. Every expectation that Zarathustra has reached a final, determinate conclusion of some sort is attacked in the text."

Conclusion

1. *BGE*, Sec. 94, p. 83; Schlechta, II, p. 629; *KGW*, VI/2, p. 90.

2. *TSZ*, p. 439; Schlechta, II, p. 561; *KGW*, VI/1, p. 404.

3. *TSZ*, pp. 438–439; Schlechta, II, pp. 560–561; *KGW*, IV/1, p. 403.

4. Cf. *Bhagavad Gita*, 2.47, 2.51, 18.6, 18.9. These passages praise work for the work's sake alone and condemn working for results as a route to misery.

5. *TSZ*, p. 439; Schlechta, II, p. 561; *KGW*, VI/1, p. 404.

6. *TSZ*, p. 439; Schlechta, II, p. 561; *KGW*, VI/1, p. 404.

7. *GS*, Sec. 334, p. 262; Schlechta, II, pp. 193–194; *KGW*, V/2, pp. 239–240.

8. *TSZ*, p. 388; Schlechta, II, p. 513; *KGW*, VI/1, p. 338.

Bibliography

Collections and Editions of Nietzsche's Works

Original Texts

Kritische Gesamtausgabe Briefwechsel. Edited by G. Colli and M. Montinari. 24 vols. in 4 parts. Berlin: Walter de Gruyter, 1975ff.

Kristische Gesamtausgabe Werke. Edited by G. Colli and M. Montinari. 30 vols. in 8 parts. Berlin: Walter de Gruyter, 1967ff.

Werke in Drei Baenden. Edited by Karl Schlechta. 3rd ed. Munich: Carl Hansers, 1965.

Translations

The Antichrist. (1895, written 1888) Translated by Walter Kaufmann. In *The Portable Nietzsche,* edited by Walter Kaufmann. New York: Viking Press, 1968.

Beyond Good and Evil: Prelude to a Philosophy of the Future (1886). Translated by Walter Kaufmann. New York: Random House, 1966.

The Birth of Tragedy (1872) (together with *The Case of Wagner*). Translated by Walter Kaufmann. New York: Random House, 1967.

The Case of Wagner (1888) (together with *The Birth of Tragedy*). Translated by Walter Kaufmann. New York: Random House, 1967.

Daybreak: Thoughts on the Prejudices of Morality (1881). Translated by R. J. Hollingdale. Cambridge, Eng.: Cambridge University Press, 1982.

Ecce Homo: How One Becomes What One Is (1908, written 1888) (together with *On the Genealogy of Morals*). Translated by Walter Kaufmann. New York: Random House, 1967.

The Gay Science, with a Prelude of Rhymes and an Appendix of Songs (1882, fifth book added 1887). Translated by Walter Kaufmann. New York. Random House, 1974).

Human, All Too Human: A Book For Free Spirits (1878). Translated by Marion Faber, with Stephen Lehmann. Lincoln: University of Nebraska Press, 1984.

Human, All Too Human, Vol. I (1878). Volume VI of *The Complete Works of Friedrich Nietzsche*. Edited by Oscar Levy. 18 vols. London: George Allen & Unwin, 1900.

Human, All Too Human, Vol. II (1880). Volume VII of *The Complete Works of Friedrich Nietzsche*. Edited by Oscar Levy. 18 vols. London: George Allen & Unwin, 1911.

Nietzsche: A Self-Portrait from His Letters. Edited and translated by Peter Fuss and Henry Shapiro. Cambridge, Mass.: Harvard University Press, 1971.

Nietzsche Contra Wagner (1895, written 1888).Translated by Walter Kaufmann. In *The Portable Nietzsche*, edited by Walter Kaufmann. New York: Viking Press, 1968.

"Nietzsche: Notes for 'We Philologists.' " Translated by William Arrowsmith. *Arion*, 1/2, new series (1973–1974): 279–380.

"Nietzsche on Classics and Classicists" Translated and selected by William Arrowsmith. *Arion* II (1963), Part I (issue no. 1, Spring): 5–18; Part II (no. 2, Summer): 5–27; Part III (no. 4, Winter): 5–31.

On the Advantage and Disadvantage of History for Life (1873). Translated by Peter Preuss. Indianapolis: Hackett Publishing, Co., 1980.

On the Genealogy of Morals (1887) (together with *Ecce Homo*). Translated by Walter Kaufmann and R.J. Hollingdale. New York: Random House, 1967.

Philosophy and Truth: Selections from Nietzsche's Notebooks of the Early 1870s. Translated and edited by Daniel Breazeale. Atlantic Highlands, N. J.: Humanities Press, 1979.

Philosophy in the Tragic Age of the Greeks. Translated by Mar-

Bibliography

ianne Cowan. Chicago: Henry Regnery, 1962.

Schopenhauer as Educator (1874). Translated by James W. Hillesheim and Malcolm R. Simpson. South Bend, Ind.: Gateway Editions, 1965.

Selected Letters of Friedrich Nietzsche. Edited and translated by Christopher Middleton. Chicago: University of Chicago Press, 1969.

Thus Spoke Zarathustra (Parts I-III, 1884; Parts I-IV, 1891). Translated by Walter Kaufmann. In *The Portable Nietzsche,* edited by Walter Kaufmann. New York: Viking Press, 1968.

Twilight of the Idols (1889, published 1876). Translated by Walter Kaufmann. In *The Portable Nietzsche* edited by Walter Kaufmann, New York: Viking Press, 1968.

Untimely Meditations (the last published 1876).Translated by R. J. Hollingdale. Cambridge, Eng.: Cambridge University Press, 1983.

The Use and Abuse of History (1873). Translated by Adrian Collins. Indianapolis: Bobbs-Merrill, 1957.

The Will to Power (first versions published 1904, 1910). Translated by Walter Kaufmann and R. J. Hollingdale, edited by Walter Kaufmann. New York: Random House, 1967.

Secondary Sources

Alderman, Harold. *Nietzsche's Gift.* Athens: Ohio University Press, 1977.

Allison, David B., ed. *The New Nietzsche: Contemporary Styles of Interpretation.* New York: Dell Publishing Co., 1977.

Andreas-Salomé, Lou. *Friedrich Nietzsche in seinen Werken.* Vienna: Carl Konegen, 1894.

Apuleius. *The Transformations of Lucius, Otherwise Known as the Golden Ass.* Translated by Robert Graves. New York: Farrar, Straus & Giroux, 1951.

Augustine. *The City of God,* in *Basic Writings of Saint Augustine.* 2 vols. Edited by Whitney J. Oates. Vol. II. New York: Random House, 1948.

Bakhtin, M. M. *The Dialogic Imagination: Four Essays.* Edited by Michael Holquist. Translated by Caryl Emerson and Michael Holquist. Austin: University of Texas Press, 1981.

Barrack, Charles M. "Nietzsche's Dionysus and Apollo: Gods in Transition." *Nietzsche-Studien,* III (1974): 115–129.

Bennholdt-Thomsen, Anke. *Nietzsches "Also Sprach Zarathustra" als literarisches Phaenomen. Eine Revision.* Frankfurt: Athenaeum, 1974.

Bergoffen, Debra B. "The Eternal Recurrence, Again." *International Studies in Philosophy,* XV/2 (Summer 1983): 35–46.

Bindschedler, Marie. *Nietzsche und die poetische Lüge.* Berlin: Walter de Gruyter, 1966.

Blanshard, Brand. *On Philosophical Style.* Manchester: Manchester University Press, 1954.

Blondel, Eric. *Nietzsche, le corps et la culture.* Paris: Presses Universitaires de France, 1986.

Boettner, Loraine. *The Reformed Doctrine of Predestination.* Grand Rapids, Mich.: William B. Eerdmans, 1932.

Brinton, Crane. *Nietzsche.* New York: Harper & Row, 1965.

Calder, W. M., III. "The Wilamowitz-Nietzsche Struggle: New Documents and a Reappraisal." *Nietzsche-Studien,* XII (1983): 214–254.

Carnap, Rudolf, "The Overcoming of Metaphysics Through Logical Analysis of Language." In *Heidegger and Modern Philosophy: Critical Essays,* edited by Michael Murray. New Haven: Yale University Press, 1978.

Conway, Daniel. "Nietzsche's Oblique Promotion of Moral Excellence: A Philosophical Interpretation of *Thus Spoke Zarathustra.*" Dissertation, University of California at San Diego, 1985.

Copleston, Frederick. *Friedrich Nietzsche: Philosopher of Culture.* London: Burns, Oates, & Washburn, 1942.

Dannhauser, Werner J. *Nietzsche's View of Socrates.* Ithaca, N.Y.: Cornell University Press, 1974.

Danto, Arthur C. *Nietzsche as Philosopher: An Original Study.* New York: Columbia University Press, 1965.

de Bleeckere, Sylvain, " 'Also Sprach Zarathustra': Die Neugestaltung der 'Geburt der Tragoedie.' " *Nietzsche-Studien,* VIII (1979): 279–290.

Bibliography

Del Caro, A. "Anti-Romantic Irony in the Poetry of Nietzsche," *Nietzsche-Studien*, XII (1983): 372–378.

―――."The Immolation of Zarathustra: A Look at 'The Fire Beacon.' " *Colloquia Germanica*, XVII, Nos. 3–4 (1984): 251–256.

Deleuze, Gilles. *Nietzsche and Philosophy*. Translated by Hugh Tomlinson. New York: Columbia University Press, 1983.

de Man, Paul. "Action and Identity in Nietzsche," *Yale French Studies*, LII (1975): 16–30.

―――. *Allegories of Reading: Figural Language in Rousseau, Nietzsche, Rilke, and Proust*. New Haven: Yale University Press, 1979.

―――. "Nietzsche's Theory of Rhetoric." *Symposium*, XXVIII (Spring 1974): 33–51.

Derrida, Jacques. *Spurs: Nietzsche's Styles/Éperons: Les Styles des Nietzsche*. Chicago: University of Chicago Press, 1978.

Else, Gerald F. *The Origin and Early Form of Greek Tragedy*. Cambridge, Mass.: Harvard University Press, 1965.

Faguet, Emile. *On Reading Nietzsche*. Translated by George Raffalovich. New York: Moffat, Yart, 1918.

Förster-Nietzsche, Elizabeth, ed. *The Nietzsche-Wagner Correspondence*. Translated by Caroline V. Kerr. New York: Liveright Publishing Co., 1921.

Fogelin, Robert J. *Wittgenstein*. Arguments of the Philosophers Series. Edited by Ted Honderich. London: Routledge & Kegan Paul, 1976.

Frizen, Werner. " 'Von der unbefleckten Erkenntnis': Zu einem Kapitel des *Zarathustra*." *Deutsche Vierteljahrsschrift für Literaturwissenschaft and Geistesgeschichte*, LVIII, No. 3 (1984): 428–453.

Frye, Northrup. *Anatomy of Criticism: Four Essays*. Princeton: Princeton University Press, 1957.

Gadamer, H. G. "Das Drama Zarathustras." *Nietzsche-Studien*, XV (1986): 1–15.

Gelvin, Michael. "Nietzsche and the Question of Being." *Nietzsche-Studien*, IX (1980): 209–223.

Gilman, Sander L. *Nietzschean Parody: An Introduction to Read-

ing Nietzsche. Bonn: Bouvier Verlag Herbert Grundmann, 1976.

Goethe, Johann Wolfgang von. *Faust: Part One and Sections from Part Two.* Translated by Walter Kaufmann. Garden City, N.Y.: Doubleday, 1961.

Goicoechea, David, ed. *The Great Year of Zarathustra (1881–1981).* New York: Lanham, 1983.

Guzzoni, Alfredo, ed. *90 Jahre philosophische Nietzsche-Rezeption.* Koenigstein/Ts.: Hain, 1974.

Haase, Marie-Luise. "Der Übermensch in *Also Sprach Zarathustra* and im Zarathustra-Nachlass, 1882–1885." *Nietzsche-Studien,* XIII (1984): 228–244.

Harper, Ralph. *The Seventh Solitude: Man's Isolation in Kierkegaard, Dostoevsky, and Nietzsche.* Baltimore: Johns Hopkins University Press, 1965.

Hayman, Ronald. *Nietzsche: A Critical Life.* New York: Oxford University Press, 1980.

Heidegger, Martin. *Being and Time.* Translated by John Macquarrie and Edward Robinson. New York: Harper & Row, 1962.

———. *Nietzsche,* 2 vols. Pfullingen: Neske, 1961.

———. *Nietzsche,* Vol. I: *The Will to Power as Art.* Translated by David Farrell Krell. New York: Harper & Row, 1979.

———. *Nietzsche,* Vol. II: *The Eternal Recurrence of the Same.* Translated by David Farrell Krell. San Francisco: Harper & Row, 1984.

———. *Nietzsche,* Vol. III: *Will to Power as Knowledge and as Metaphysics.* Translated by Joan Stambaugh and Frank A. Capuzzi. Edited by David Farrell Krell. San Francisco: Harper & Row, 1986.

———. *Nietzsche,* Vol. IV: *Nihilism.* Trans Frank A. Capuzzi. Edited by David Farrell Krell. San Francisco. Harper & Row, 1982.

———. "Nietzsche's Word: God Is Dead." In *The Question Concerning Technology and Other Essays.* Translated by William Lovitt. New York: Harper & Row, 1977.

———. "Who Is Nietzsche's Zarathustra?" Translated by Bernd

Magnus. In *The New Nietzsche,* edited by David B. Allison. New York: Dell 1977.

Heller, Erich. *The Artist's Journey into the Interior and Other Essays,* New York: Harcourt Brace Jovanovich, 1976.

———. *The Disinherited Mind: Essays in Modern German Literature and Thought.* 3rd ed. London: Bowes & Bowes, 1971.

———. *The Poet's Self and the Poem: Essays on Goethe, Nietzsche, Rilke, and Thomas Mann.* London: Athlone Press, 1976.

Heller, Peter. *Dialectics and Nihilism: Essays on Lessing, Nietzsche, Mann, and Kafka.* Amherst: University of Massachusetts Press, 1966.

Higgins, Kathleen. "Nietzsche on Music." *Journal of the History of Ideas* (October–December 1986): 663–672.

———. "Nietzsche's View of Philosophical Style," *International Studies in Philosophy,* XVIII (Summer 1986): 67–80

———. "The Night Song's Answer." *International Studies in Philosophy,* XVII, No. 2 (Summer 1985): 33–50.

Hollingdale, R. J. *Nietzsche.* Boston: Routledge & Kegan Paul, 1973.

———. *Nietzsche: The Man and His Philosophy.* Baton Rouge: Louisiana State Univerisity Press, 1965.

Hollinrake, Roger. *Nietzsche, Wagner, and the Philosophy of Pessimism.* London, George Allen & Unwin, 1982.

Howey, R. L. "Some Reflections on Irony in Nietzsche." *Nietzsche-Studien,* IV (1973): 36–51.

Jaspers, Karl. *Nietzsche: An Introduction to the Understanding of His Philosophical Activity.* Translated by Charles F. Wallraff and Frederick J. Schmitz. Chicago: Henry Regnery, 1965.

———. *Nietzsche and Christianity.* Chicago: Henry Regnery, 1961.

Kaufmann, Walter. *Nietzsche: Philosopher, Psychologist, Antichrist.* 4th ed. Princeton: Princeton University Press, 1974.

———, ed. The *Portable Nietzsche.* New York: Viking Press, 1968.

————. *Tragedy and Philosophy*. Princeton: Princeton University Press, 1968.

Kaulhausen, Marie Hed. *Nietzsches Sprachstil: Gedeutet aus seinem Lebensgefuehl and Weltverhaeltnis*. Munich: Oldenbourg, 1977.

Klages, Ludwig. *Die Psychologischen Errungenschaften Nietzsches*. Leipzig: Johann Amborsius Barth, 1926.

Lampert, Laurence. "Zarathustra and His Disciples." *Nietzsche-Studien*, VIII (1979): 309–333.

Lea, Frank A. *The Tragic Philosopher: A Study of Friedrich Nietzsche*, London: Methuen, 1957.

Löwith, Karl. *Nietzsches Philosophie der Ewigen Wiederkehr des Gleichen*, Stuttgart: W. Kohlhammer, 1956.

Lucian. *Lucius; or The Ass*, in *Lucian*. Vol. VIII. Translated by M. D. MacLeod. Cambridge, Mass.: Harvard University Press, 1967, pp. 47–145.

Luke, F. D. "Nietzsche and the Imagery of Height," in *Nietzsche's Imagery and Thought: A Collection-of Essays*. Edited by Malcolm Pasley. London: Methuen, 1978, pp. 104–122.

Luther, Martin. *Luther's Works*. Edited by Helmut Lehmann. Vol. XXXI: *Career of the Reformer: I*. Edited by Harold J. Grimm. Philadelphia: Fortress Press, 1957.

Magnus, Bernd. "The Deification of the Commonplace: *Twilight of the Idols*." To appear in *Reading Nietzsche*, edited by Robert C. Solomon and Kathleen Higgins, forthcoming.

————. "Eternal Recurrence." *Nietzsche-Studien*, VIII (1979): 362–377.

————. "Nietzsche's Eternalistic Counter-Myth." *Review of Metaphysics*, XXVI (June 1973): 604–616.

————. *Nietzsche's Existential Imperative*. Bloomington: Indiana University Press, 1978.

————. "Nietzsche's Philosophy in 1888: *The Will to Power* and the *Übermensch*," *Journal of the History of Philosophy*, XXIV, No. 1: 79–99.

————. "Perfectibility and Attitude in Nietzsche's Übermensch." Delivered in an earlier version under the title "Overman:

Attitude or Ideal?" at Brock University Conference on Nietzsche, Ontario, October 15–17, 1981.

Mansfeld, Jaap. "The Wilamowitz-Nietzsche Struggle: Another New Document and Some Further Comments." *Nietzsche-Studien*, XV (1986): 41–58.

Masini, Ferruccio. "Rythmisch-Metaphorische 'Bedeutungsfelde' in 'Also Spranch Zarathustra.' " *Nietzsche-Studien*, II (1973): 276–307.

Mayrhofer, M. "Zarathustra und Kein Ende?" *Acta Antiqua*, 25, Nos. 1-4 (1977): 85–90.

Meckel, Markus. "Der Weg Zarathustra also der Weg des Menschen: Zur Anthropolgie Nietzsches im Kontext der Rede von Gott im 'Zarathustra.' " *Nietzsche-Studien*, IX (1980): 174–208.

Mehregan, Hushang. "Zarathustra im Awesta und bein Nietzsche—Eine Vergleichende Gegenüberstellung." *Nietzsche-Studien*, VIII (1979): 291–308.

Meyer, Leonard B. "Some Remarks on Value and Greatness in Music," in *Aesthetics Today*. Edited by Morris Philipson. New York: New American Library, 1961, pp. 169–187.

Middleton, Christopher, ed. and trans. *Selected Letters of Friedrich Nietzsche*. Chicago: University of Chicago Press, 1969.

Miller, C. A. "Nietzsche's 'Daughters of the Desert': A Reconsideration." *Nietzsche-Studien*, II (1973): 157–195.

Miller, J. Hillis. "Ariadne's Thread: Repetition and the Narrative Line." *Critical Inquiry*, III (Autumn 1976): 57–77.

———. "*Gleichnis* in Nietzsche's *Also Sprach Zarathustra*." *International Studies in Philosophy*, XVII, No. 2 (Summer 1985): 3–15.

Montinari, Mazzino. *Nietzsche Lesen* Berlin: Walter de Gruyter, 1980.

Morgan, George Allen, Jr. *What Nietzsche Means*. Cambridge, Mass.: Harvard University Press, 1941.

Natoli, Charles M. *Nietzsche and Pascal on Christianity*. New York: Peter Lang, 1985.

Naumann, Barbara. "Nietzsches Sprache 'Aus der Natur': Ansätze zu einer Sprachtheorie in den frühen Schriften und ihre metaphorische Einlösung in 'Also Sprach Zarathustra.' " *Nietzsche-Studien*, XIV (1985): 126–163.

Nehamas, Alexander. *Nietzsche: Life as Literature*. Cambridge, Mass.: Harvard University Press, 1985.

O'Flaherty, James C. "The Intuitive Mode of Reasoning in 'Zarathustra.' " *International Studies in Philosophy*, XV, No. 2 (Summer 1983): 57–66.

O'Flaherty, James C., Timothy F. Sellner, and Robert M. Helen, eds. *Studies in Nietzsche and the Classical Tradition*. Chapel Hill: University of North Carolina Press, 1976.

————, eds. *Studies in Nietzsche and the Judaeo-Christian Tradition*. Chapel Hill: University of North Carolina Press, 1985.

O'Hara, Daniel, ed. *Why Nietzsche Now?* Bloomington: Indiana University Press, 1985.

Pangle, Thomas L. "The 'Warrior Spirit' as an Inlet to the Political Philosophy of Nietzsche's Zarathustra." *Nietzsche-Studien*, XV (1986): 140–179.

Paronis, Margot. *"Also Sprach Zarathustra": Die Ironie Nietzsches als Gestaltungsprinzip*. Bonn: Herbert Grundmann, 1976.

Pasley, Malcolm, ed. *Nietzsche, Imagery and Thought: A Collection of Essays*. London: Methuen, 1978.

Perkins, Richard. "The Genius and the Better Player: Superman and the Elements of Play." *International Studies in Philosophy*, XV, No. 2 (Summer 1983): 13–23.

Perry, Ben Edwin. *The Ancient Romances: A Literary-Historical Account of Their Origins*. Berkeley: University of Carolina Press, 1967.

Peters, H. P. *My Sister, My Spouse: A Biography of Lou Andreas-Salomé*. New York: Norton, 1962.

Pfeffer, Rose. *Nietzsche: Disciple of Dionysus*. Lewisburg, Pa.: Bucknell University Press, 1972).

Plato. *The Collected Dialogues, Including the Letters*. Edited by Edith Hamilton and Huntington Cairns. Bollingen Series LXXI. Princeton: Princeton University Press, 1961.

Reichert, Herbert William. *International Nietzsche Bibliography*. Compiled and edited by Herbert W. Reichert and Karl

Schlechta. Revised and expanded. Chapel Hill: University of North Carolina Press, 1968.

Rolleston, James. "Nietzsche, Expressionism, and Modern Poetics." *Nietzsche-Studien*, IX (1980); 285–301.

Rosen, Stanley. "Nietzsche's Image of Chaos." *International Philosophical Quarterly*, XX (March 1980); 3–23.

Rzepka, J. R., and W. Anuschewski *Index zu Friedrich Nietzsche, "Also Sprach Zarathustra."* Essen: W. Anuschewski, 1983.

Sasso, James. *The Role of Consciousness in the Thought of Nietzsche.* Washington, D.C.: University Press of America, 1977.

Schacht, Richard. *Nietzsche.* London: Routledge Kegan Paul, 1983.

Schlechta, Karl. *Nietzsches Grossen Mittag.* Frankfurt: Vittorio Klostermann, 1954.

Schopenhauer, Arthur. *The World as Will and Representation.* 2 vols. Translated by E. F. J. Payne. New York: Dover Publications, 1969 (Vol. I) and 1958 (Vol. II).

Schrift, Alan D. "Language, Metaphor, Rhetoric: Nietzsche's Deconstruction of Epistemology." *Journal of the History of Philosophy*, XXIII, No. 3 (July 1985): 371–395.

Schutte, Ofelia. *Beyond Nihilism: Nietzsche Without Masks.* Chicago: University of Chicago Press, 1984.

Shakespare, William. *Complete Works.* Edited by Alfred Harbage. New York: Viking Press, 1969.

Shapiro, Gary. "Festival, Carnival and Parody in Zarathustra IV," in *The Great Year of Zarathustra.* Edited by David Goicoechea. New York: Lanham, 1983.

———"The Rhetoric of Nietzsche's *Zarathustra.*" *Boundary Two*, 8, No. 2 (1980); 165–189.

Silk, M.S. and J. P. Stern. *Nietzsche on Tragedy* (Cambridge, Eng. Cambridge University Press, 1981.

Simmel, Georg. *Schopenhauer und Nietzsche: Ein Vortragszyklus.* Leipzig: Duncker and Humblot, 1907.

Soring, Jurgen. "Incipit Zarathustra—Von Abgrund der Zukunft." *Nietzsche-Studien*, VIII (1979): 334–361.

Solomon, Robert, ed. *Nietzsche: A Collection of Critical Essays.* Garden City, N.Y.: Doubleday, 1973.

Stambaugh, Joan. *Nietzsche's Thought of Eternal Return.* Baltimore: Johns Hopkins University Press, 1972.

Sterling, M.C. "Recent Discussions of Eternal Recurrence: Some Critical Comments." *Nietzsche-Studien,* VI (1977): 261–291.

Stern, J. P. *Friedrich Nietzsche.* New York: Penguin Books, 1978.

———*A Study of Nietzsche.* Cambridge: Cambridge University Press, 1979.

Strong, Tracy B. *Friedrich Nietzsche and the Politics of Transfiguration.* Berkeley: University of California Press, 1975.

Tatum, James. *Apuleius and The Golden Ass.* Ithaca, N. Y.: Cornell University Press, 1979.

Thatcher, David S. "Eagle and Serpent in *Zarathustra.*" *Nietzsche-Studien,* VI (1977): 240–260.

Thorlby, Anthony, ed. *The Penguin Companion to European Literature.* New York: McGraw-Hill, 1969.

Tillich, Paul. *Dynamics of Faith.* New York: Harper & Row, 1957.

Underhill, Evelyn. *Mysticism: A Study in the Nature and Development of Man's Spiritual Consciousness.* Cleveland: World Publishing, 1960.

Vaihinger, Hans. *Nietzsche als Philosoph.* Berlin: Reuther and Reichard, 1902.

———*The Philosophy of 'As-If': A System of Theoretical, Practical and Religious Fictions of Mankind.* New York: Harcourt, Brace, 1925.

Walsh, Patrick Gerard. *The Roman Novel: The "Satyricon" of Petronius and the "Metamorphoses" of Apuleius.* Cambridge: Cambridge University Press, 1970.

Weigand, Hermann J. "Nietzsche's Dionysus-Ariadne Fixation." *Germanic Review,* XLVIII (March 1973): 99–116.

Weiss, Allen S. "The Symbolism and Celebration of the Earth in Nietzsche's *Zarathustra.*" *Sub-Stance,* 22 (1979): 39–47.

Wilcox, John T. *Truth and Value in Nietzsche.* Ann Arbor: University of Michigan Press, 1974.

Williams, Robert J. "Recurrence, Parody, and Politics in the Philosophy of Friedrich Nietzsche." Dissertation, Yale University, 1982.

Wittgenstein, Ludwig. *Philosophical Investigations.* Second edition. Edited and translated by G. E. M. Anscombe. New York: Macmillan, 1958.

———*Tractatus Logico-Philosophicus.* Translated by C. K. Ogdon. London: Routledge & Kegan Paul, 1922.

Yovel, Yirmiyahu, ed. *Nietzsche as Affirmative Thinker: Papers Presented at the Fifth Jerusalem Philosophical Encounter, April 1983.* Martinus Nijhoff Philosophy Library, Vol. 13. Dordrecht: Martinus Nijhoff Publishers, 1986.

Zuckerkandl, Victor. *Sound and Symbol: Music and the External World.* Translated by Willard R. Trask. Bollingen Series. Princeton: Princeton University Press, 1956.

Zuckerman, Elliott, "Nietzsche and Music: *The Birth of Tragedy and Nietzsche Contra Wagner.*" *Symposium,* XXVIII (Spring 1984): 17–32.

Index

Abstraction, 123–126
Adventure story, 219–220
Aesthetic, the, 5, 8–9, 38, 128.
    See also Beauty; Images
Affirmation, 162, 184, 191, 197,
    198–201, 269, 271–273, 276.
    See also Amor fati; Eternal re-
    currence; Joy; Love, of life
Afterlife, 92, 129–130, 171, 173–
    174. *See also* Heaven; Hell;
    Immortality
Alderman, Harold, xiii, 71, 85, 96,
    97, 100, 258
Allusion, 126–131, 146, 214–219
Ambivalence, Zarathustra's, 119–
    57. *See also* Doctrine, ambiva-
    lence of
"Among Daughters of the Wilder-
    ness," 127
Amor fati, 184, 197. *See also* Af-
    firmation; Joy; Love, of life
Animals, Zarathustra's, 77, 93,
    153–155, 216
Antichrist, 5, 172, 174
Antichrist, The, xv, 43
Anti-Semitism, 7
Aphorism, xiii, 43–44, 46, 95
Apollo, 16, 22–23, 25, 75
Apollonian, 24–30, 32–39, 74–76,
    141, 142, 150, 153, 197
Apuleius, xvii, 126, 127, 206, 207,
    211–232, 277, 280
Art, 18, 24–26
Ass, 210, 211–219, 225, 226–230,

277; and festival, 211, 215, 217,
    218, 226–227, 230, 239; and
    story of, 207, 212, 213; Zara-
    thustra as, 226–230
Ass, Story of the, 212–213
Atheism, 41, 77, 78, 87, 92, 133
Attitude, 241; as component of
    any doctrine, 120; as compo-
    nent of doctrine of eternal re-
    currence, 160, 162, 165–166,
    179–184, 191–201; implicit in
    doctrine of sin, 166–174. *See
    also* Mood; Spiritual states
Audience, Zarathustra's, 76–78,
    109, 119, 235–38, 276. *See also*
    Companions
Augustine, St., 31

Bakhtin, M. M., 219–225
Balance, 86, 241–242
Beauty, 5, 13–14, 26. *See also*
    Aesthetic; Art; Images
Bennholdt-Thomsen, Anke, xiii,
    258, 264, 266–267, 273
Beyond Good and Evil, xiv, 3
Bible, xvi, xx, 10, 99, 100, 131.
    See also New Testament; Old
    Testament
Bildungsroman, 100, 101–102,
    104, 220–221. *See also* Educa-
    tion; Maturity
Biographical time, 220–221
Birth of Tragedy, The, xviii, 2, 3,

Index

Index

Index

Index